Learning Embedded Systems with MSP432 microcontrollers

MSP432P401R with Code Composer Studio

Fourth edition

January 2022

Byul Hur

Library of Congress Control Number: 2022900252

ISBN: 978-17365198-7-5

The eBook versions, ISBNs: 978-17365198-8-2 and 978-17365198-9-9, also contain the material appeared in this printed book.

Preface

This book is an outcome of compiling materials that I have been using in embedded system education over several years. This book was written to be used as a support material or textbook for an embedded system course. This book was written for undergraduate engineering students and the audience with similar prior knowledge and skills.

The first edition of this book was written in two volumes. The volume I was published in January 2022. The volume II was published in April 2020. The second edition in a single book was published in August 2020. These prior initial efforts made it possible to publish the third edition in August 2021. The contents of the book were revised further and expanded, and this fourth edition is published in January 2022.

This book covers basics including MSP432™, GPIO, timers, display, interrupt, and ADC. Moreover, this book covers topics of software architectures, PWM, motor control, serial communications, TI Driver library, TI RTOS, Power management, and embedded system security.

An MSP432 IC (Integrated circuit) is a microcontroller unit (MCU) introduced by Texas Instruments™ (TI). The CPU (Central Processing unit) of this MCU is a 32-bit Arm® Cortex®-M4F. There are several models of the MSP432 MCUs. These MSP432 devices include MSP432P4xxx devices and MSP432E4xxx devices. The MSP432P4xxx devices include MSP432P401R and MSP432P4111. These MSP432P4xxx MCUs are based on the 32-bit Arm® Cortex®-M4F and the peripherals that are similar to the MSP430. And, these MSP432P4xxx MCUs can be relatively easy to learn for those of who are already familiar with MSP430 MCUs. For MSP432E4xxx MCUs, the devices include MSP432E401Y and MSP432E411Y. The architectures of MSP432E4xxx devices are quite different from the MSP432P4xxx device architectures.

In this book, we will learn about an MSP432P401R MCU. This MSP432P401R MCU is one of the MSP432P4xxx devices, and it is a part of the TI SimpleLink™ microcontroller platform. After studying this platform, readers can continue to do study other TI SimpleLink microcontrollers. Moreover, in this book, an MSP-EXP432P401R Launchpad™ is used as a development tool. This MSP-EXP432P401R Launchpad is a low-cost development platform based on the MSP432P401R MCU.

The integrated development environment (IDE) that we primarily use in this book is Code Composer Studio™ from Texas Instruments. The Code Composer Studio supports TI MCUs including this MSP432P401R MCU. As of today, the latest version of the Code Composer Studio is 11. In this version, TI does not charge Code

Composer Studio license fees. Users/Developers can download the set-up file and install the IDE software on their PC, Mac®, or Linux machines.

This book can be adopted as an educational resource for an embedded system course. In order to be effective in teaching an embedded system course, it would be a good idea to have hands-on laboratory sessions. Laboratory sessions can help students to solidify their own learning. This hands-on learning approach can help students to understand the materials in this book.

If you have adopted this book as an educational resource, listed as a reference material, or used it as a part of education activities, please, feel free to contact the author to share your educational experience associated with this book. The contact information is posted on the website: www.rftestgroup.com/books

For the educators who need lecture resources such as lecture slides, they can contact the author by visiting the website. You can find book information as well as contact information on the website. If you have any comments or questions, please, do not hesitate to contact the author. I hope this book will be a good resource for you in learning about embedded systems.

Acknowledgement

I would like to express my appreciation to many people who have been supporting me in many ways in academia. I have been learning a lot of aspects as I work and teach in a higher educational environment. I am thankful for all those who have shown kindness through the journey in academia.

I am sincerely grateful to all of my family. Particularly, I would like to show my appreciation to Ms. Bongnou Jun, Mrs. Soohee Park, Mrs. Elisa Hur, and Ms. Erin Hur.

I would like to acknowledge current and former teaching assistants and graders. Moreover, I would like to thank my students who have given me insights into the engineering education.

Above all, I am deeply grateful to God the Father, God the Son, and God the Holy Spirit. I have dedicated my life to Him. I am thankful for the delicate guidance and care including this book publication journey.

Contents

Chapter 1. Introduction

Chapter 2. Development Tools

Chapter 3. MSP432 architecture

Chapter 4. Assembly Language

Chapter 5. General Purpose I/O

Chapter 6. Register level C/C++ programming

Chapter 7. Timer basics

Chapter 8. Interrupt

Chapter 9. Display

Chapter 10. Analog to Digital Converter

Chapter 11. ADC Applications

Chapter 12. Embedded Software Architectures

Chapter 13. Pulse Width Modulation

Chapter 14. DC Motor Control

Chapter 15. Servo Motor

Chapter 16. Basics of Serial Communications and UART

Chapter 17. RS-232, RS-485, and USB

Chapter 18. Serial Peripheral Interface (SPI)

Chapter 19. Inter-integrated Circuit (I²C)

Chapter 20. Time Measurement

Chapter 21. Wireless Modules

Chapter 22. Embedded System Integration

Chapter 23. Driver Library

Chapter 24. Introduction to TI RTOS

Chapter 25. Open Source Electronics Development Platform

Chapter 26. Power Management Considerations

Chapter 27. Embedded System Security

Chapter 28. Educational Embedded Linux System Platforms

Appendix A. Basic Digital Logic Circuits

Appendix B. Basic Verilog Hardware Description Language

Appendix C. Memory Mapped I/O

Appendix D. C/C++ Data Types

References

Chapter 1. Introduction

There are many embedded system applications for home or industrial uses. The core components in these embedded systems are microcontrollers and microprocessors. In this Chapter, we will learn about the differences between microcontrollers and microprocessors. Next, TI microcontrollers will be introduced. An Integrated Development Environment (IDE) is a useful tool in developing embedded systems. In this chapter, several IDEs for MSP432 microcontrollers will be introduced.

What is a Microcontroller?

A microcontroller unit (MCU) is typically a small sized integrated circuit (IC) that is used for specific operations in an embedded system. There are common components that are used in a microcontroller. Let us examine these components. Typically, a microcontroller has a center processing unit (CPU). This CPU can process digital arithmetic and logical calculations, and the CPU can access the data in registers and memory devices. The memory devices can be categorized into Read Only Memory (ROM) or Random Access Memory (RAM).

ROM typically contains permanent or semi-permeant data. For instance, a program such as a boot firmware can be stored in this ROM memory. RAM is a memory that can read and store the data. One of the examples is to use this RAM memory as a part of stack memory. The stack memory is a computer memory that which can store various temporary variables created by functions and programs.

One of the useful peripherals in microcontrollers is a General-Purpose Input and Output (GPIO). GPIO is a component that can generate a digital output signal to an external pin or read a digital signal from an external pin. This GPIO is a typical and useful peripheral in microcontrollers.

Another typical component is a timer. Timers are used for multiple purposes. A primary application of the timer is a digital counter that is capable of counting up or down. It is also common to find a special timer called watchdog timer. This timer can trigger a system reset process if a program is in a certain hardware or software failure condition.

In computing, it is typical to find the situation where the execution of the main program is paused, and the system needs to run a different program routine, if there is an internal or external request. These requests can be processed by an interrupt controller. This interrupt controller is a common component in microcontrollers.

For input signals, a type of the signals at the external pin of microcontrollers can be analog instead of digital. These analog signals can be converted to digital signals using an Analog to Digital Converter (ADC). Once the conversion is completed, the CPU can process the digital data, and store the data in registers and memory devices.

For output signals, a type of the signals through the external pin can be analog instead of digital. In this case, a Digital Analog Converter (DAC) can be used. A DAC can generate analog signals with various voltage levels.

The internal data stored in MCUs may need to be exchanged with an external devices or ICs. In order for this communication, serial communication peripherals can be used in microcontrollers. Serial communication peripherals allow to exchange digital data between microcontrollers and ICs with proper serial interfaces.

Clock signals in digital circuits are signals oscillating between high and low states. These signals can be used in synchronizing digital components. Clock signals can be provided by an oscillatory circuit component. For MCUs, it is typical to support multiple clock sources including internal and external oscillators.

In general, a typical microcontroller may have these common components mentioned previously. For some microcontroller models, they have specialized and additional components such as USB/ethernet/wireless communication modules, and precision ADCs.

For developers, they need to choose a proper microcontroller that meets the needs of their applications. They need to understand the available functions in their microcontroller model of choice. For an embedded system development, the choice of a microcontroller is an important process. In involves the understanding of the scope of the project and specification of the embedded system. The scope of the embedded systems may vary. For a simple embedded system, a decent microcontroller and a few external components could satisfy the needs of the desired project scope and the specification.

Microcontroller/Microprocessor

As it was described in the previous section, microcontrollers have been used in embedded systems. How about microprocessors? Can we implement an embedded system using a microprocessor? Yes, we can. The embedded system can be built using a microprocessor, and it can be considered as a microprocessor application and a microprocessor-based system. In order to understand the differences, simplified microprocessor-based system and microcontroller block diagrams are shown in Figure 1.1. At the top of Figure 1.1, it shows a microprocessor-based system. This is a system with ROM, RAM, I/O port, timer, and ADC, as introduced previously. A microprocess is used as shown on the left side. In order to make this system function properly, it would be typical to use additional external components. For instance, the system may need an external RAM memory IC and an external ADC IC. This microprocessor and the external components are connected using data bus and address bus lines. These components can be placed on the same PCB (Printed Circuit Board). For instance, a PCB module with a microprocessor and the external components such as memory ICs can be considered as a microprocessor-based system and it can be a part of an embedded system.

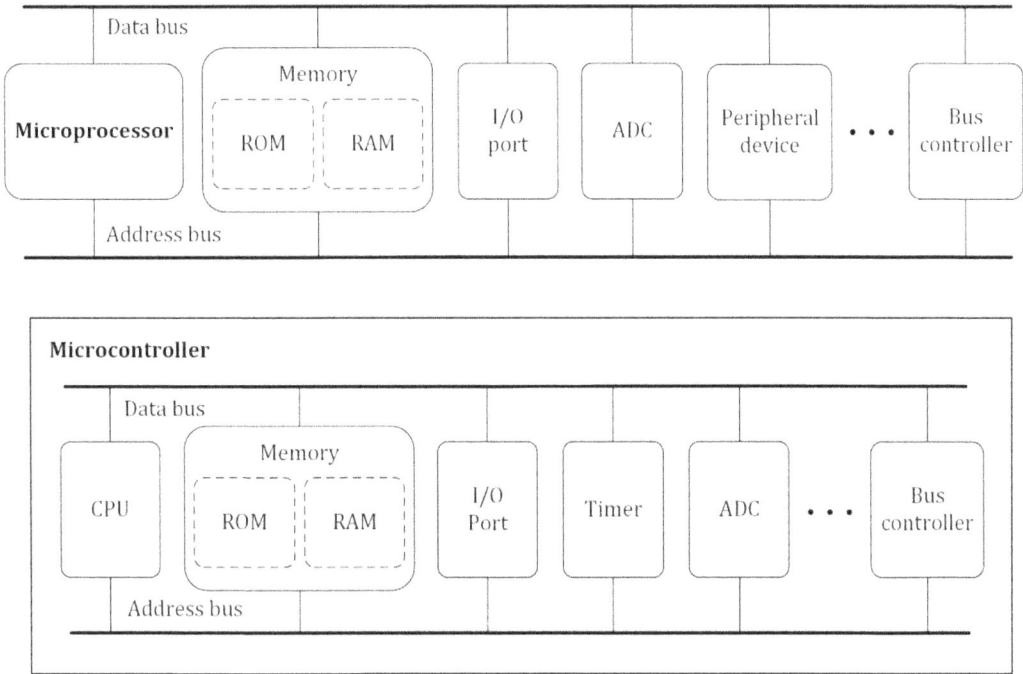

Figure 1.1. Microprocessor-based system and Microcontroller.

On the other hand, at the bottom of Figure 1.1, it shows a microcontroller with similar components to the ones we used in a microprocessor-based system. The difference is that all of the components shown in the grayed box are integrated on a single chip. Thus, this IC can provide multiple functions and it can be a part of an embedded system. This one chip already contained various components. A developer may need less effort and needs a smaller number of external components in creating an embedded system application. It can make the size of the embedded system compact. This is a great benefit of using a microcontroller instead. However, in general, microcontrollers may not be suitable for a system that requires fast and highly complex computations. This is partially because a microcontroller has a limited small memory space, and it might not be suitable to handle tasks that needs a large memory space and fast computation. If a developer needs to build a system that requires to process highly complex tasks, a microprocessor-based system might be a reasonable choice.

16-bit/32-bit Microcontrollers

There are 16-bit microcontrollers and 32-bit microcontrollers. The number of the bits is associated with the primary instruction length of a CPU. Typically, a 32-bit instruction may represent a bigger integer number than a 16-bit instruction.

Moreover, the number of the bits is also related to the widths of data bus, address bus, and registers. However, for some architectures, this number of the bits does not necessarily match with the widths of data bus, address bus, or registers. For instance, there can be an architecture that uses more bits for the address bus and/or registers. In general, a 32-bit microcontroller can process a bigger integer number per instruction cycle than a 16-bit microcontroller. And a 32-bit microcontroller has more widths of data bus, address bus, and registers than a 16-bit microcontroller. For a wide range of low-cost embedded systems, 16-bit microcontrollers are suitable. For a better performance and for complex systems, 32-bit microcontrollers can be used in embedded systems.

There are many IC manufactures providing various 16-bit and 32-bit microcontroller models. For instance, Microchip® (https://www.microchip.com) provides these 16-bit and 32-bit microcontroller units (MCUs). For 16-bit MCUs, they have 16-bit PIC® MCUs. For 32-bit MCUs, they have Arm® Cortex® and MIPS based MCUs. NXP® semiconductors (https://www.nxp.com) provides Arm processor based MCUs. And, Texas Instruments™ (TI) provides 16-bit and 32 MCUs. Some of the MCU models are shown in Table 1.1.

	Arm®-based MCUs	MSP430™ MCUs	Wireless connectivity MCUs	C2000™ MCUs
Features	Arm-based 32-bit MCUs	TI proprietary 16-bit MCUs Ultra-low power	Wireless Arm-based or TI proprietary MCUs	TI proprietary 32-bit MCUs or Arm-based 32-bit MCUs
Models	MSP432Pxxx MSP432Exxx TM4Cxxx	MSP430x2xxx MSP430x4xxx MSP430x5xxx MSP430x6xxx	CC1xxx CC2xxx CC3xxx RF430xxxxx	TMS320xxxx

Table 1.1. TI microcontrollers.

For 16-bit TI MCUs, there is a wide range of MSP430™ MCU models. These MSP430 MCUs are low power MCUs, and they are suitable for many embedded system applications. The CPU architecture is simple to understand, and these MCUs are based on a TI proprietary architecture. Although the CPU architecture is not fully disclosed, the manufacture provides documentations to help in understanding how it functions for developers.

For 32-bit MCUs , TI has MCUs that are based on Arm Cortex-M cores and TI peripherals. There are Tiva™ C and MSP432™ MCUs. For MSP432™ family MCUs, there are MSP432P4 devices. For an MSP432P4 MCU, it has an Arm® Cortex-M4F core with TI peripherals. The TI peripherals for an MSP432P4 MCU are similar to the ones for an MSP430™ MCUs. This 32-bit MCU can be useful in improving performance of a system that was developed using a 16-bit MSP430 MCU. Because the development effort in software is not necessarily complex, existing programs in C/C++ can be migrated easily from MSP430 to MSP432 without writing programs from scratch.

TI has introduced the SimpleLink™ family platform. Within the SimpleLink family devices, they can share the code without the much of the effort of code changes. For the code that follows the proper format and structure can be migrated to different device within the SimpleLink family devices easily. The technology behind this compatibility is based on a driver library and a real-time operating system. Later, in this book, an introductory level of these topics will be presented.

TI has 32-bit MCUs that are digital signal processors (DSPs) optimized for real-time control applications. They are C2000™ MUCs, and they can be used in a wide range of automotive and industrial applications including advanced motor control and digital power conversion applications.

For the wireless connectivity, there several low-power wireless microcontrollers. The available wireless technology includes Bluetooth®, WiFi®, Zigbee®, Near-field communication (NFC). The SimpleLink wireless MCU devices offers the portability of code and easy conversion to a different wireless MCU within SimpleLink wireless MCUs.

Low-power Microcontrollers

Some of the embedded systems are battery operated systems. The operating time of these systems is relevant to the use of the energy. In order to increase the operating time, there can be several efforts, and they include the choice of a low-power microcontroller and the use of low-power modes efficiently. Moreover, for some embedded systems that are not battery operated, they might need to purse in reducing the energy consumption.

MSP432 MCUs support low-power management techniques, and the MCUs offers Lower Power Mode. For an example, a specific model of each MSP432 and MP430 ICs has selected to compare the active and low power mode operations. For MSP432 MCUs, an MSP432P401R IC is selected, and for MSP430 MCUs, an MSP430F5529 IC is selected. The power consumption comparison between two MCUs is shown in Table 1.2.

	MSP432P401R (MSP432Pxxx)	MSP430F5529 (MSP430x5xxx)
Core	Arm Cortex-M4F (32-bit)	TI proprietary 16-bit core
Active Mode Current	[1]355 µA at 1 MHz (3.0 V) ([1]VCORE0, LDO-based)	[2]360 µA at 1 MHz (3.0 V) ([2]PMMCOREV0, Flash memory execution)
Low-power mode 4 (LPM4) Current	[3]0.5 µA (3.0 V) ([3]VCORE0, 25 °C)	[4]1.1 µA (3.0 V) ([4]PMMCOREV0, 25 °C)

Table 1.2. Power comparison between selected MSP432 and MSP430 MCUs [1][2].

In active mode, both MCUs have already shown relatively low current consumption. To further reduce the power consumption, these MCUs can be controlled to be in a low mode. The table shows the very current consumption when they are in low power mode 4. Both of these MSP432P4 MCU and MSP430 MCU support Low Power Mode. In this mode, they have shown that the power consumption is very low.

Users may need to understand and measure the power consumption of their embedded systems. If the system is a battery application, it is more important because it is related to the system life expectancy. Using the MSP432P4 Launchpad and the Code Composer Studio, users can measure the MCU current consumption easterly using EnergyTrace Technology. In Chapter 26, power management considerations and the low-power mode techniques for an MSP432P4 MCU will be presented.

Integrated Development Environment (IDE)

In order to test and debug a microcontroller, various development software packages need to be installed and used. The manual set up process and the use of the packages can be complicated. In this reason, an integrated development environment (IDE) can be used to make the development easy. An IDE may contain headers, library files, program templates, and plug-in files that are needed to build microcontroller and microprocessor applications. Moreover, an IDE typically provides a user-friendly GUI (Graphical User Interface).

There are several IDEs that can be used for the MSP432 application development. The summary of the IDEs is shown in Table 1.3. Texas Instruments provides an IDE called Code Composer Studio. This Code Composer Studio supports a wide range of TI's MCUs. It is optimized with C/C++ compilers. As of January 2022, the latest version is 11. The latest Code Composer Studio does not support Windows 32-bit system anymore. Developers need a 64-bit Windows operating system. Code Composer Studio provides large amounts of resources and libraries for free. However, if the users want to create a commercial product, it is encouraged to carefully check out the license agreement of Code Composer Studio and libraries that would be used in their program. In this book, we will choose to use this Code

Composer Studio, and the most of programs provided in this book have written and tested using Code Composer Studio IDE.

	Texas Instruments	IAR Systems	Arm Keil
Program	Code Composer Studio	IAR Embedded Workbench	MDK (Microcontroller Development Kit)
License	Full function No license fee	32 kB code size limit Upgradable	32 kB code size limit Upgradable
Compiler	TI C/C++	IAR C/C++	Arm C/C++ Compiler

Table 1.3. Software Development Packages for MSP432.

IAR systems® (https://www.iar.com) provides an IDE that supports TI MCUs and processors. This IDE is called IAR embedded workbench®. It also supports MSP432 and MSP430 MCUs. IAR systems provides a fully functional license for a 30-day time limited or a code size-limited kick start license without any time limit.

Arm® Keil® (https://www.keil.com) provides an IDE that also supports MSP432 and MSP430 MCUs. The IDE is called MDK® (Microcontroller Development Kit). MDK is a software development suite for Arm based microcontrollers. Arm Keil provides MDK Lite edition, and it is free, but the code size is limited.

For both IAR Embedded Workbench® and MDK IDEs, users can use the code size limited version of the IDEs at no cost. For educational or small size projects, code size limited IDEs may work fine for many educational programs. When the users would need to unlock the code size limit for complex projects, the license can be purchased later for the full functionally.

Chapter 2. Development Tools

To support a system development, MCU manufacturers often provide hardware kits for their MCUs, and users can build their functional prototypes using these kits. These hardware kits are typically called development boards (or dev. boards). The cost of these development kits is dependent on many factors and the cost may vary by the MCU models. In many cases, it is necessary to purchase an additional JTAG programming tool to load and debug the program.

Texas Instruments (TI) has introduced Launchpad™ boards, and they are affordable development kits for various TI MCUs. Launchpad boards have BoosterPack™ headers. There are various pre-assembled BoosterPack plug-in modules. Users can easily expand the functions of their systems by adding stackable BoosterPack plug-in modules to their Launchpad boards.

MSP432 ICs are microcontroller units (MCUs) introduced by Texas Instruments. There are several models of the MSP432 MCUs. The groups of the MSP432 MCUs include MSP432P4xxx devices and MSP432E4xxx devices. The MSP432P4xxx devices include MSP432P401R and MSP432P4111. For MSP432E4xxx MCUs, the devices of the MCUs include MSP432E401Y and MSP432E411Y.

There is an MSP432P401R Launchpad development kit. The part number of this Launchpad board is MSP-EXP432P401R. The color of the earlier version board (Rev. 1.0) was Black, and the color of the later version board (Rev. 2.0) is Red. In this book, we will learn about an MSP432P401R MCU using this MSP432P401R Launchpad (Red). In this book, this Launchpad board has been called an MSP432P401R Launchpad board or simply an MSP432P4 Launchpad. This is a low-cost development board. There is no need to purchase an extra JTAG programming tool. This development board has on-board XDS110 JTAG programmer. This low-cost Launchpad board makes it easy for users to begin with learning about the MSP432P4 MCU.

MSP432P401R Launchpad Overview

A picture of an MSP432P401R Launchpad is shown in Figure 2.1. This Launchpad board has 40-pin booster pack header pins. This header configuration is defined by Texas Instruments. There are various functional plug-in modules that are available and compatible with this header configuration.

This Launchpad board can be powered through the microUSB located at the top of Figure 2.1. There is a jumper block that has 10 shunt jumpers. They can be used to isolate the on-board JTAG block and the power lines.

There are two push buttons (S1 and S2) that are located at each side. Moreover, on this board, there is one Red LED (Light-emitting diode) (LED1) and one RGB LED (LED2). This RGB LED (LED2) has Red, Green, and Blue LEDs in a single IC package. A user can generate different colors by controlling each of three pins connected to these color LED components. For more details about this Launchpad board, you can obtain relevant resources visiting the TI's web page:

https://www.ti.com/tool/MSP-EXP432P401R

In this web page, you may be able to access a MS432P401R Launchpad Development Kit User's Guide file [1]. This document contains relevant information regarding the Launchpad board.

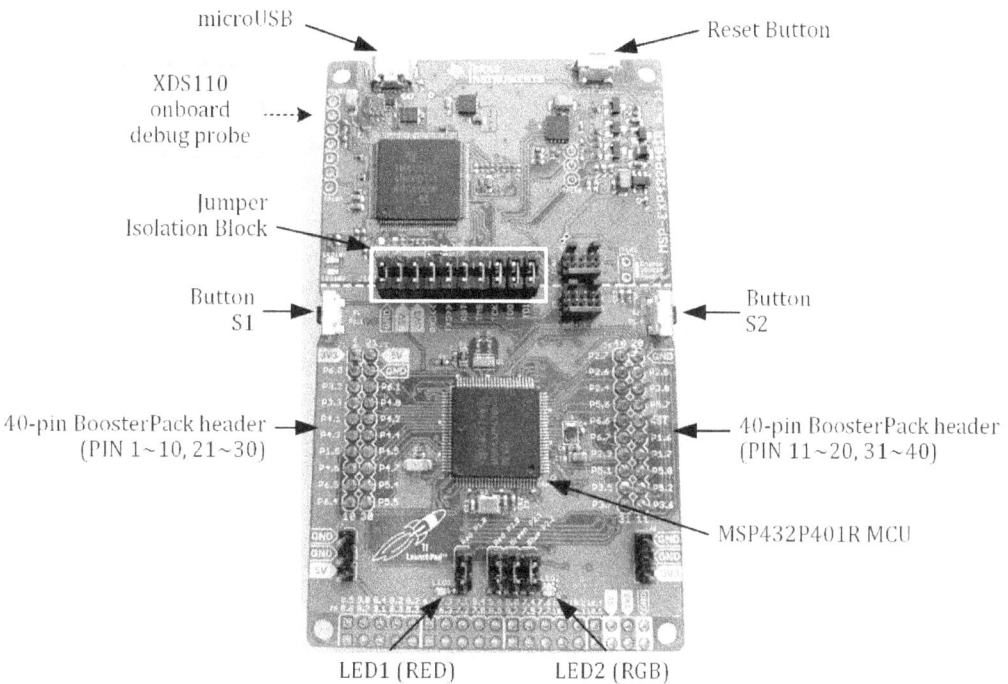

Figure 2.1. MSP432P401R Launchpad (MSP-EXP432P401R).

Let us examine some of other selected MSP432 Launchpad boards. One of them is an MSP432P4111 Launchpad. This board has an MSP432P4111 MCU, and it is one of the MSP432P4xxx devices. The brief introduction to this Launchpad will be followed in the next section.

MSP432P4111 Launchpad Overview

An MSP432P4111 Launchpad has an MSP432P4111 MCU. Specifically, the part number of this MCU is MSP432P4111IPZ. In comparison with an MSP432P401R MCU, memory sizes may be different. But, the major difference is related to the presence of an LCD (Liquid Crystal Display) controller peripheral. This MSP432P4111 MCU has an internal LCD controller module.

A picture of an MSP432P4111 Launchpad is shown in Figure 2.2. There are lots of similarities between MSP432P401R and MSP432P4111 Launchpad boards. For instance, there are two user buttons (S1 and S2) and two LEDs as well as the 40-pin BoosterPack headers. Moreover, the GPIO assignments for the 40 pin BoosterPack headers in these two Launchpad boards are equivalent to each other. In comparison with an MSP432P401R Launchpad, an MSP432P4111 Launchpad has a segment LCD and LMT70 analog temperature sensor on the MSP432P4111 Launchpad.

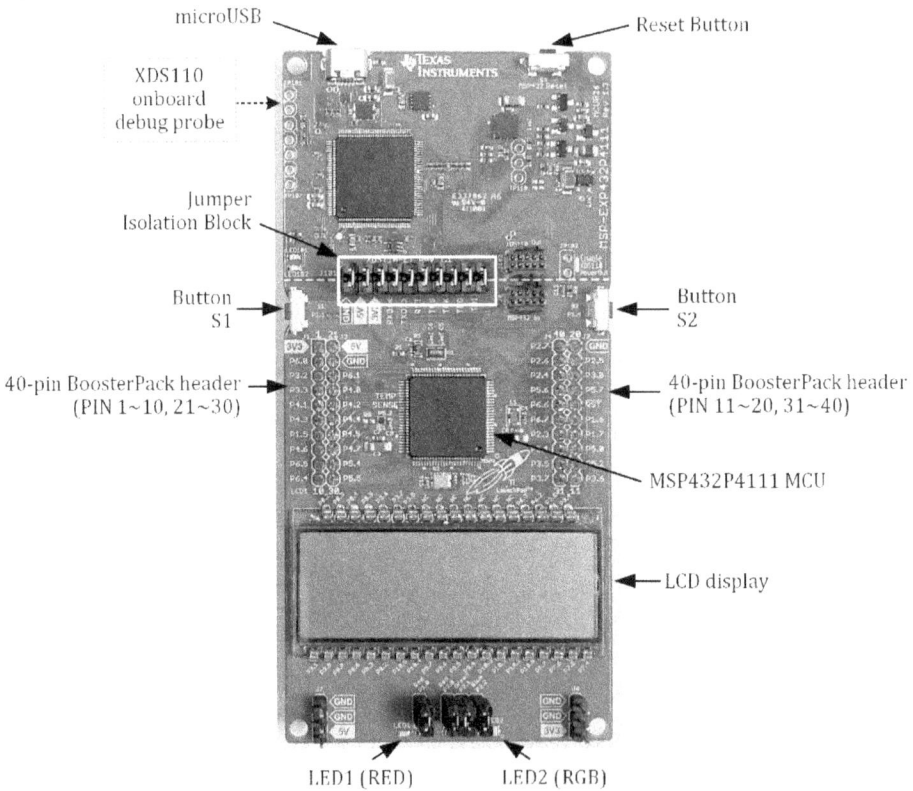

Figure 2.2. MSP432P4111 Launchpad (MSP-EXP432P4111).

There are MSP432 Launchpad boards based on MSP432E4xxx devices. As described, there are significant differences in the respect to the architecture and design between MSP432P4xxx devices and MSP432E4xxx devices. An MSP432E401Y Launchpad is one of MSP432E4 evaluation boards. The brief introduction to this MSP423E401Y Launchpad will be followed in the next section.

MSP432E401Y Launchpad Overview

An MSP432E401Y Launchpad has an MSP432E401Y MCU. The part number of this MCU is MSP432E401YTPDTR. This MCU has an Arm Cortex-M4F core. A picture of an MSP432E401Y Launchpad is shown in Figure 2.3. A noticeable feature is an Ethernet Port on the board. This MSP432E4 Launchpad can provide an Ethernet connectivity. There are four user LEDs and user buttons. There are two independent sets of 40-pin BoosterPack headers. This Launchpad board can be used in creating an IoT (Internet of Things) and Cloud application. SimpleLink platform includes MSP432E4xxx devices. Users can reuse their programs within SimpleLink family devices, and various network connectivity options are available within SimpleLink MCU devices.

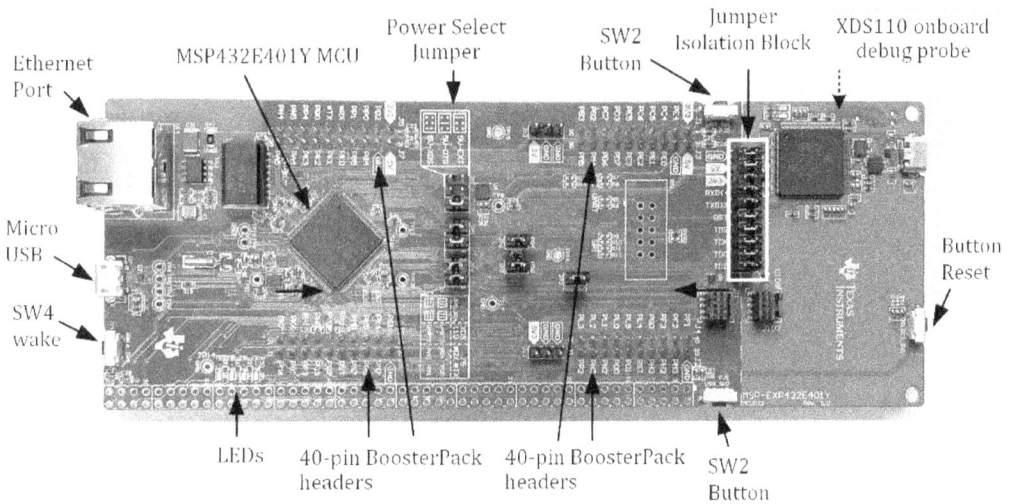

Figure 2.3. MSP432E401Y Launchpad (MSP-EXP432E401Y).

For an embedded system development in this book, we will use Code Composer Studio. Code Composer Studio supports TI MCUs including MSP432 MCUs. The following section will provide information about this development tool and the installation instructions.

Code Composer Studio (CCS)

Code Composer studio is an IDE for TI microcontrollers and microprocessors, which supports various TI MCU models. Code Composer Studio was built based on an Eclipse open-source software framework. Users can take advantage of the latest improvements of Eclipse, and TI provides useful resources, libraries, and examples for the users through Code Composer Studio IDE. This IDE can run under Windows, Mac®, and Linux machines.

CCS Download and Installation

The installation file of Code Compose Studio can be downloaded using the web link:

https://www.ti.com/tool/download/CCSTUDIO

There are off-line installer and web installer files. Users can choose either of them. During the installation process, you may be prompted to select components as shown in Figure 2.2. It is up to the users to choose any of these options. But, in order to support MSP432 MCUs, users need to select the MSP432 component as shown in the Figure 2.2. Additionally, users can select any other components in this list such as MSP430. You can review the list of the selected components. Then, you can click the next button to continue the installation process.

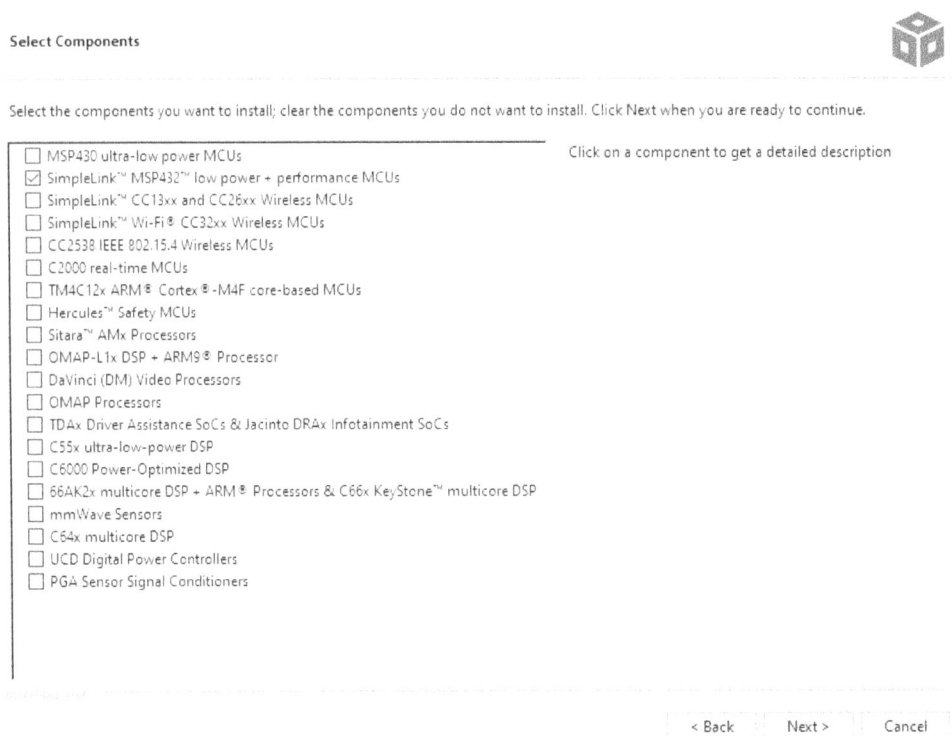

Select Components

Select the components you want to install; clear the components you do not want to install. Click Next when you are ready to continue.

Click on a component to get a detailed description

- [ ] MSP430 ultra-low power MCUs
- [x] SimpleLink™ MSP432™ low power + performance MCUs
- [ ] SimpleLink™ CC13xx and CC26xx Wireless MCUs
- [ ] SimpleLink™ Wi-Fi® CC32xx Wireless MCUs
- [ ] CC2538 IEEE 802.15.4 Wireless MCUs
- [ ] C2000 real-time MCUs
- [ ] TM4C12x ARM® Cortex®-M4F core-based MCUs
- [ ] Hercules™ Safety MCUs
- [ ] Sitara™ AMx Processors
- [ ] OMAP-L1x DSP + ARM9® Processor
- [ ] DaVinci (DM) Video Processors
- [ ] OMAP Processors
- [ ] TDAx Driver Assistance SoCs & Jacinto DRAx Infotainment SoCs
- [ ] C55x ultra-low-power DSP
- [ ] C6000 Power-Optimized DSP
- [ ] 66AK2x multicore DSP + ARM® Processors & C66x KeyStone™ multicore DSP
- [ ] mmWave Sensors
- [ ] C64x multicore DSP
- [ ] UCD Digital Power Controllers
- [ ] PGA Sensor Signal Conditioners

< Back   Next >   Cancel

Figure 2.2. Component selection for MSP432 MCUs.

Now, we will create a project and write a simple blink program for an MSP432P401R MCU. After successfully installed, you can run Code Composer Studio. As shown in Figure 2.3, you can create a new CCS project. Next, you can see the screen as shown in Figure 2.4. You need to select a proper microcontroller model. In this case, "blink" is typed in the project name filed. You can enter any other name instead.

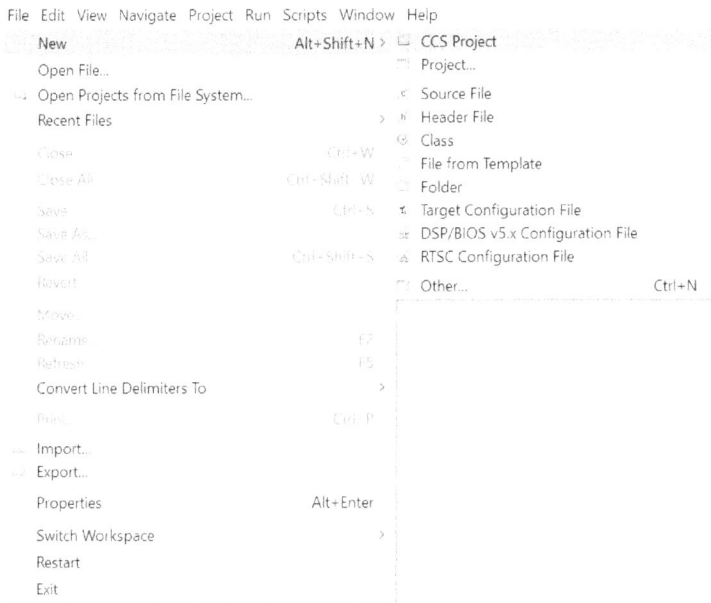

Figure 2.3. Creating a New Project.

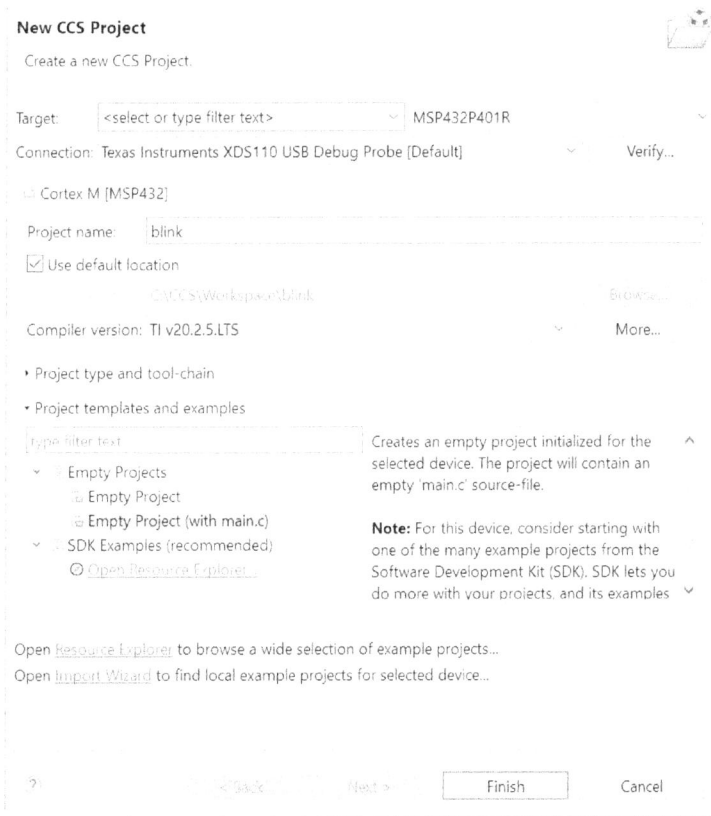

Figure 2.4. New CCS Project set up.

There are two project templates in *empty projects.* You can choose "the empty project (with main.c)." You can click "Finish" icon to create this project. You can see project files on the left side of the window of Code Composer Studio. You can double click "main.c," and you can edit this file to write your own code.

LED Blink Program in C/C++

You can write your program by modifying the *main.c* file. You can type the code as shown in Program 2.1. This program is a simple LED blink program. In this program, the first line inside of *main()* is associated with configuring a watchdog timer. The watchdog timer is configured to be on hold. This is simply for an education purpose to make it easier for students to write a program to avoid protection behaviors by the watchdog. However, it is desired and typical to enable this watchdog timer to manage certain fault conditions of hardware or software. In the following line, the GPIO direction was configured to be the output for P1.1. A Red LED (LED1) is internally connected to this P1.1. Next, the logical output of this port is configured to be high. In the following lines, it shows a loop using "while". In this while loop, the value of this P1.1 gets toggled. Also, the system gets delayed for a certain period of time. Thus, it will blink the Red LED (LED1) with a reasonable rate, and you can see the blinking LED.

```
#include "msp.h"
void main(void) {
    WDT_A->CTL = WDT_A_CTL_PW | WDT_A_CTL_HOLD;  // hold the watchdog timer
    P1->DIR |= 0x01;  // set the output direction
    P1->OUT |= 0x01;  // set the output value
    while (1) {
        P1->OUT ^= 0x01;  // toggle the output value
        __delay_cycles(500000);  // delay
    }
}
```

Program 2.1. LED Blink Test Program.

In case you are experiencing an issue with blinking the Red LED, you can check whether the shunt jumper for LED1 is placed properly. The shunt jumper for LED1 is located just next to the LED1. You will learn more details about GPIO in Chapter 5.

BH EDU Board Kit

In order to build and learn more about embedded systems, you would want to obtain additional parts and kits. In this book, you will learn about certain electronics parts and how to use them such as LCD module, Accelerometer, and motor driver.

For embedded system education, BH EDU boards have been developed. With several additional parts mentioned above, it is named BH EDU kit. This kit can be used in laboratory classes and users can conduct experimentations. A picture of a BH EDU board for an MSP43P4 Launchpad is shown in Figure 2.5. The details of this BH EDU board and TI BH EDU kit [4] can be found in the web link:

https://github.com/bh-projects/TI-BH-EDU-board-kit

TI BH EDU kits can assist students' experiential learning through laboratory sessions. Users can use these kits to build their own embedded systems.

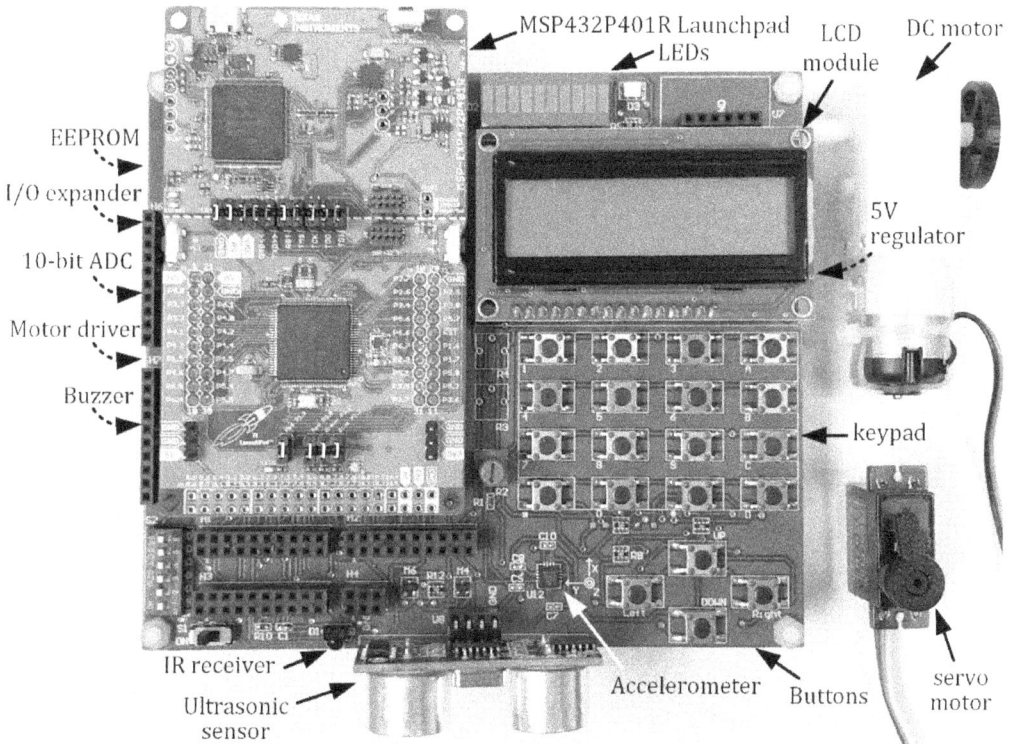

Figure 2.5. BH EDU board kit (Version 2.1.x) [4].

Readers can learn about MSP432 microcontrollers without this kit. It is not essential to obtain this kit to study the materials in this book. The circuit diagram and the generalized connections have been given in this book. Therefore, readers can obtain their own proper parts to perform their relevant experiments. However, readers may need to use the same model or the functionally equivalent components. For instance, a specific model of a LCD component is used, and it would be studied in this book. Some of knowledge can be common and generic. However, any of the hardware connections and software portion is not necessarily reusable in other LCD modules. If readers would choose to different hardware components or connections, they have chosen to conduct experiments at their own risk and description. They need to study and examine documentations from the manufacturer carefully, and they need to consult with the manufacturer for the further technical support.

While the author has prepared this book with his best effort, it makes no representation or warranty of any kind with regard to the contents of this book including hardware connection diagrams, schematics, and programs. It is worth of noting that the author shall not be liable in any event for incidental or consequential damage in connection with the use of the contents of this book.

Chapter 3. MSP432 architecture

MSP432 microcontrollers are based on 32-bit Arm Cortex-M4F cores. The peripherical of MSP432 MCUs are similar to the ones in MSP430 MCUs. As of today, you can find two groups of MSP432 MCUs. They are MSP432P4xxx devices and MSP432E4xxx devices.

MSP432P4xxx devices are suitable for embedded systems that need low-power operation and an integrated high-precision ADC (Analog-to-Digital Converter). For instance, they can be used as sensor nodes in a network. On the other hand, MSP432E4xxx devices are suitable for embedded systems that may need high performance with the built-in communication module support such as Ethernet and USB support. For instance, they can be used as a gateway in a network. Within each of the group, you can find several MCU models with different specifications.

Within the MSP432P4xxx device group, there are two Launchpad boards available from Texas Instruments as of today. They are MSP432P401R Launchpad and MSP432P4111 Launchpad boards. The MCUs on these Launchpad boards are MSP432P401R and MSP432P4111. There are some of the differences between an MSP432P401R MCU and MCP432P4111 MCU with the respect to the internal memory size and the cost. One of the major differences between an MSP432P401R MCU and an MSP432P4111 MCU would be the internal LCD controller support. An MSP432P4111 MCU has an internal LCD controller that can directly drive segment LCDs. As described previously, we will learn about the MSP432P401R MCU and we will use an MSP43232P401R Launchpad board in this book.

The MSP432P401R MCU is a 32-bit MCU with an Arm Cortex-M4F core. It has a floating-point unit and memory protection unit. The clock frequency can go up to 48 MHz. It has a 14-bit SAR ADC. The supply voltage range extends from 1.62 V to 3.7 V. In this book, we will use the 3.3-V supply voltage, and it is assumed that the supply volage for the MCU is 3.3 V. The supply voltage can be lowered if needed. Chapter 26 will present a power management consideration topic.

Pin Diagram of MSP432P401RIPZ

Several package options are available for MSP432P401R MCUs. One of the package options is a low-profile quad flat package (LQFP). The specific part number of this IC is MSP432P401RIPZ. This is the specific IC model that is mounted on the MSP432P401R Launchpad. The pin number of this IC is 100. The pin diagram of this IC is shown in Figure 3.1.

MSP432P401R MCUs use a similar port naming convention as they are used in MSP430 MCUs. This means that the ports are named Px.y. For instance, for the pin number of 56 in Figure 3.1, this pin is associated with P4.0. This is a general purpose input/output function, and this pin refers to the first bit (or bit 0) of Port 4. Moreover, this pin also can function as an analog input (A13) after a proper port configuration. This means the multiple functions are shared through this pin. This is the case for many other pins in this MSP432P401R MCU.

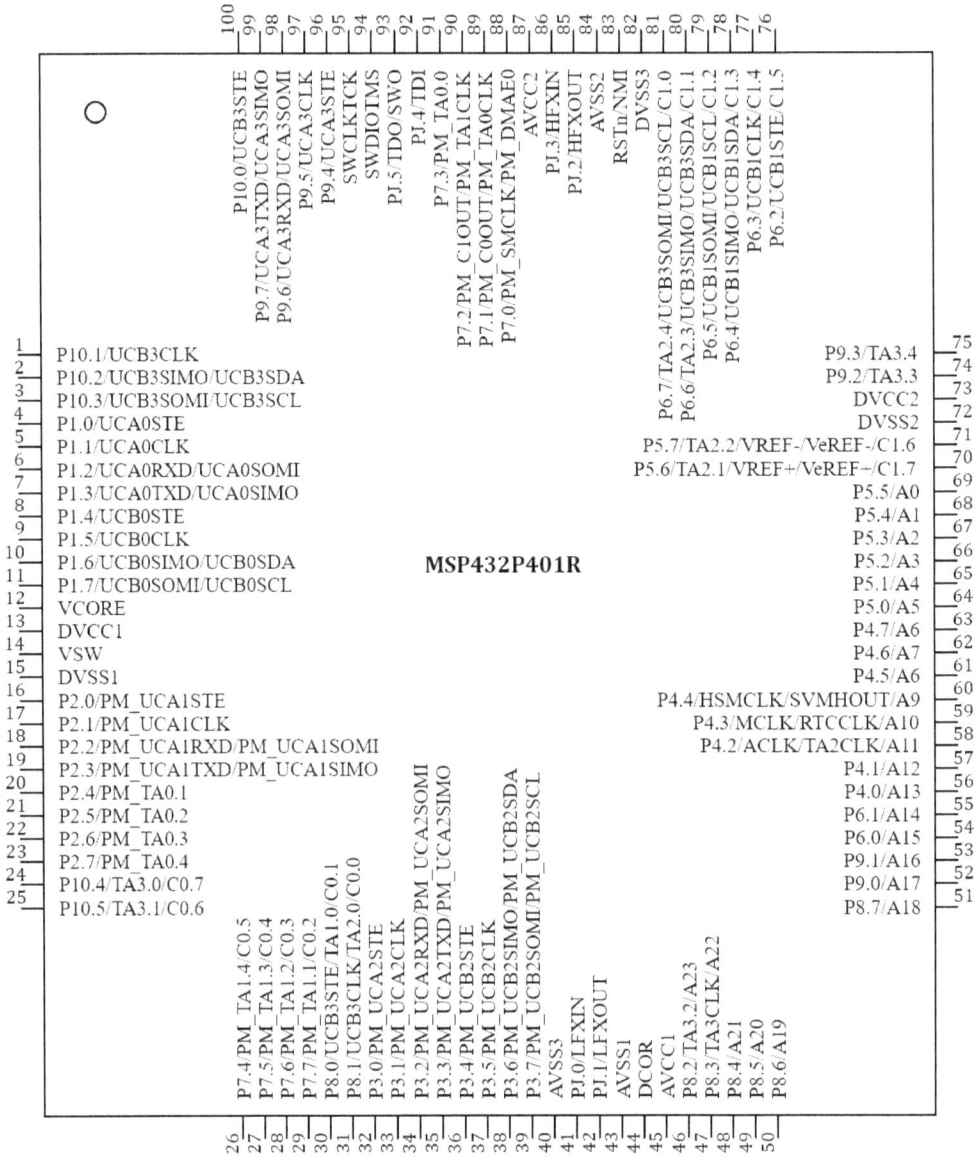

Figure 3.1. MSP432P401RIPZ Pin Diagram [1].

The details of this MCU have been provided by manufacturer. Readers can download and access the datasheet provided by Texas Instruments [1]. As of today, the latest revision of the datasheet was released in June 2019. The manufacturer may release new revision, if needed. The datasheet and technical documents can be found in the web link: https://www.ti.com/product/MSP432P401R

Functional Block Diagram

The MSP432P401R MCU has an internal 256 kB flash memory and 64 kB SRAM memory space. The functional block diagram is shown Figure 3.2. Flash and SRAM blocks are connected via address and data lines. Several peripheral module blocks are connected to these lines. A 14-bit SAR ADC block is shown, and it is connected to the address and data bus lines. There are eUSCI_Ax and e_USCI_Bx blocks. Moreover, there is a Timer_A general purpose timer block. Furthermore, there are more blocks connected to these address and bus lines, and they include clock system, watchdog timer, and voltage reference blocks. There is a bus control logic assuming that it can make the peripheral blocks and the CPU (Central Processing Unit) work together properly. For the CPU, this MSP432P4 MCU has an Arm Cortex-M4F core, and it is shown on the left side in Figure 3.2. Let us examine the Cortex-M4F core in the following sections.

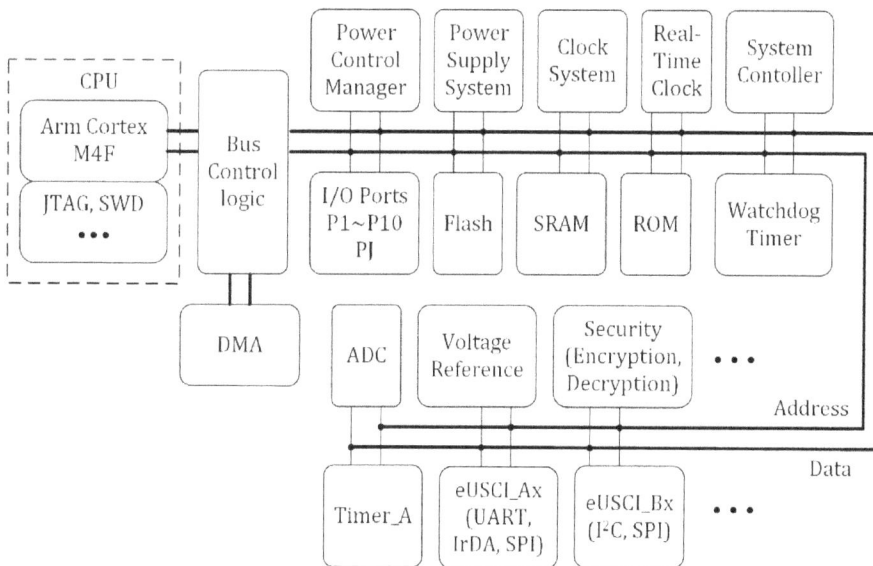

Figure 3.2. MSP432P401R Functional Block Diagram [1].

Arm Cortex-M4F Core

The instruction set architecture of an Arm Cortex-M4 core is based on Arm7 architecture. The architecture of the processor is based on a 3-stage pipeline Harvard architecture. The Arm Cortex-M4 core supports Thumb®-2 mixed 16-bit and 32-bit instruction sets. A simplified Arm Cortex-M4F core is shown in Figure 3.3. The Cortex-M4F core includes a floating-point unit (FPU), and the FPU unit is placed at the top of the Cortex-M4 core. This FPU unit can process 32-bit single precision floating point operations. Moreover, a Nested Vector Interrupt Controller (NVIC) unit is shown on the left side. This NVIC and the processor units are closely integrated to achieve low latency in processing interrupts. The memory protection unit (MPU) is shown below the Cortex-M4 core block. The MPU supports the Arm7 Protected Memory System Architecture model. There is a Data Watchpoint and Trace (DWT) unit that is located next to the MPU block. This unit is for watchpoints, data tracing, and the system profiling. And, there is a Flash Patch and Breakpoint (FPB) unit. This unit is for breakpoints and code patches. At the bottom of the figure, it shows a Bus Interfaces block. The Cortex-M4F core has three Advanced High-performance Bus-Lite (AHB-Lite) and one Advanced Peripheral Bus (APB) interfaces. For more details about the Cortex-M4F core, users can check out technical reference documentations and datasheets provided by the manufacturers.

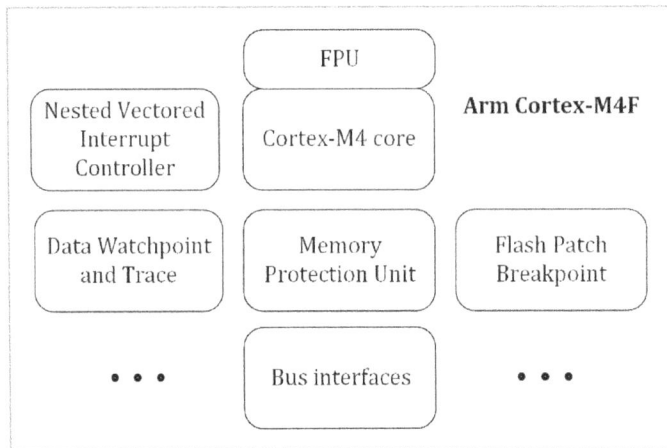

Figure 3.3. Simplified Cortex-M4F Block diagram [5][6].

Cortex-M4 Registers

Figure 3.4 shows Cortex-M4 registers. The registers from R0 to R12 are general-purpose registers. They can be accessed from either privilege or unprivileged mode. Low registers from R0 to R7 can be accessible by all instructions. However, high registers from R8 to R13 have some restrictions by types of instructions whether they are 16-bit or 32-bit instructions. Register R13 serves as a stack pointer (SP). Register R14 serves as a link register (LR). In addition, register R15 serves as a program counter (PC). It contains the address of the next instruction to be executed. On reset, the processor loads the PC with the value of reset vector. In addition, there are other special registers. They are Program Status Register (PSR), Priority Mask Register (PRIMASK), FaultMask Register (FAULTMASK), Base Priority Mask Register (BASEPRI), and Control Register (CONTROL). This figure showed Arm Cortex-M4 registers, Additionally, for a Cortex-M4F core, it has a floating-point unit. There are registers associated to the floating-point unit.

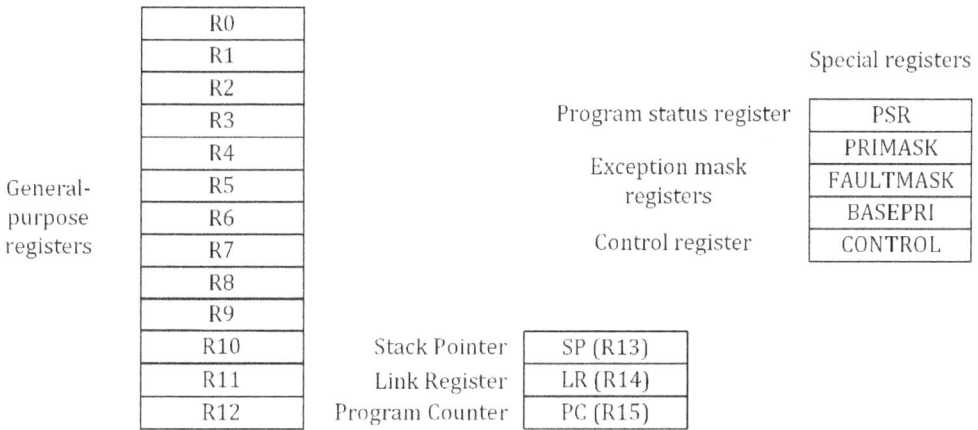

Figure 3.4. Cortex-M4 registers [5][6].

Program Status Register

Program Status Register (PSR) is also referred as xPSR. The PSR has three functions. They are Execution Program Status Register (EPSR), Application Program Status register (APSR), and Interrupt Program Status register (IPSR). In these three functions, the register bits are assigned differently as shown in Figure 3.5.

For EPSR, there are bits representing Interruptible-Continuable Instruction (ICI) and execution state fields and a Thumb state bit (T-bit). For ASPR, there are bits used for condition flags such as N, Z, C, V, and Q. For IPSR, there are bits for the exception type number of the Interrupt Service Routine (ISR). The value of the program status registers can be accessed using MSR or MRS instructions.

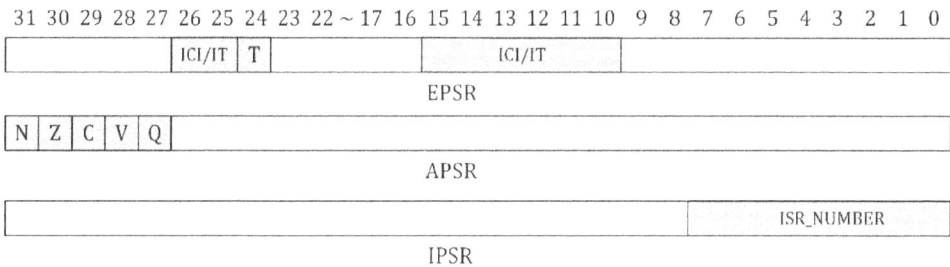

Figure 3.5. Program status register [5][7].

Memory Access Behavior

Table 3.1 shows the memory access behavior. From 0x0000 0000 to 0x1FFF FFFF, the program code or data can be stored. From 0x2000 0000 to 0x3FFF FFFF, this is the memory space for SRAM. For instance, the stack memory can use this memory area. From 0x4000 0000 to 0x5FFF FFFF, this is the address range for peripheral devices.

Address Range	Memory Region	Description
0x0000 0000 ~ 0x1FFF FFFF	Code	For program code and data
0x2000 0000 ~ 0x3FFF FFFF	SRAM	For data
0x4000 0000 ~ 0x5FFF FFFF	Peripheral	
0x6000 0000 ~ 0xDFFF FFFF	Reserved	
0xE000 0000 ~ 0xE00F FFFF	Private peripheral bus	NVIC, system timer, and system control block, and etc
0xE010 0000 ~ 0xFFFF FFFF	Reserved	

Table 3.1. Memory access behavior [6].

Exception Types

The Cortex-M4F core and NVIC can handle the exceptions. Exception types are shown in Figure 3.2. Reset can be called when the power is on, or the warm reset is triggered. There is a non-maskable interrupt (NMI). It is permanently enabled, and it cannot be masked or prevented.

Vector Address	Vector number	Exception Type	Priority
0x0000 0000	0	-	-
0x0000 0004	1	Reset	-3 (highest)
0x0000 0008	2	Non-Maskable Interrupt	-2
0x0000 000C	3	Hard Fault	-1
0x0000 0010	4	Memory management	Programmable
0x0000 0014	5	Bus Fault	Programmable
0x0000 0018	6	Usage Fault	Programmable
0x0000 002C	11	SVCall	Programmable
0x0000 0030	12	Debug Monitor	Programmable
0x0000 0038	14	PendSV	Programmable
0x0000 003C	15	SysTick	Programmable
0x0000 0040 and above	16 and above	Interrupts	Programmable

Table 3.2. Vector number and Exception types and Vector Address [6].

Hard Fault is an exception that occurs due to an error during exception processing. Usage Fault is an exception that occurs due to an error related to the execution of instructions. Debug Monitor is an exception caused by the debug monitor. SysTick is an exception generated by the system timer. Interrupt (IRQ) is an exception that occurred by peripheral and software requests.

Chapter 4. Assembly Language

For a Cortex-M4F core, Thumb-2 instructions can be used in writing an assembly program. The Thumb-2 instruction set is an enhanced version compared to a Thumb instruction set. The Thumb-2 instruction set has added 32-bit instructions from 16-bit Thumb instructions.

Unified assembly language (UAL) is the assembly syntax introduced by Arm. It may handle the ambiguities in the original Thumb-2 assembly syntax, and it can provide similar syntax for Arm Thumb and Thumb-2. The "*.thumb*" directive is used to specify Thumb or Thumb-2 UAL instructions. In this book, Arm assembly programs are shown and they were written for an MSP432P401R MCU based on the use of "*.thumb*" directive in Code Composer Studio.

There are several section definitions including ".text", ".data", and ".bss". For ".text" section, it contains the executable code. For ".data" section, it contains initialized data. For ".bss" section, it contains uninitialized variables. The executable instructions will be stored in the ".text" section.

An operation code (opcode) is an instruction such as **add**. An operand is a value or an argument. Let us continue to study a Thumb-2 instruction set. Two common instruction formats are listed as follows:

Instruction   destination, source1, source2

Assembly 4.1. **add** R0, R1, R2

Instruction   destination, source

Assembly 4.2. **add** R0, R1

Simple **add** instruction examples are described in Assembly 4-1 and Assembly 4.2. For Assembly 4-1, this is a three-operand instruction. The result of adding R1 and R2 is to be written to the register R0. For Assembly 4-2, this is a two-operand instruction. The result of adding R0 and R1 is to be written to the register R0.

Selected arithmetic Thumb-2 instructions are shown in Table 4.1. The table includes add, subtract, multiply, and divide operations. For these add, subtract, and divide cases, three operand instruction examples are shown. For multiply operations, **mul** instruction can be used. The least significant 32-bit result of the multiplication can be obtained. Moreover, four operand multiply instructions such as **umull** or **smulls** can be used for the multiplication. In these cases, two 32-bit registers are used to write the result of the multiply operation.

For add or subtract operations, the calculations can be extended for higher bits than 32 bits using multiple add or subtract instructions that are used sequentially. In this case, carry bits need to be processed properly. Table 4.1 includes the instructions related to add or subtract with carry bit. The subtraction operation subtracts the value in the second operand from the value in the first operand. There is a reverse subtraction operation that is to subtracts the value in the first operand from the value in the second operand. This can be performed using a **rsb** reverse subtract instruction.

Instruction	Execution	Description
add R0, R1, R2	R0 ← R1 + R2	Add
adc R0, R1, R2	R0 ← R1 + R2 + Carry bit	Add with carry bit
sub R0, R1, R2	R0 ← R1 – R2	Subtract
sbc R0, R1, R2	R0 ← R1 – R2 – ((NOT) Carry bit)	Subtract with carry bit (CB)
rsb R0, R1, R2	R0 ← R2 – R1	Reverse subtract
rsc R0, R1, R2	R0 ← R2 – R1 – ((NOT) Carry bit)	Reverse subtract with CB
mul R0, R1, R2	R0 ← (R1 × R2)[32bit]	Multiply
umull R0, R1, R2, R3	[R1, R0] ← (unsigned)(R2 × R3)	Unsigned multiply long
smull R0, R1, R2, R3	[R1, R] ← (signed)(R2 × R3)	Signed multiply long
sdiv R0, R1, R2	R0 ← (signed)(R1 ÷ R2)	Signed divide
udiv R0, R1, R2	R0 ← (unsigned)(R1 ÷ R2)	Unsigned divide

Table 4.1. Selected arithmetic Thumb-2 instructions [8][9].

Selected logical and move instructions are shown in Table 4.2. Bitwise logical AND, OR, and XOR operations can be performed using **and**, **orr**, **eor** instructions, respectively. Moreover, clearing a bit is a useful operation. There are several methods to active this operation. One of them is to use a **bic** instruction that can selectively clear bits.

Instruction	Execution	Description
and R0, R1, R2	R0 ← R1 (AND) R2	Bitwise AND
orr R0, R1, R2	R0 ← R1 (OR) R2	Bitwise OR
eor R0, R1, R2	R0 ← R1 (XOR) R2	Bitwise XOR
bic R0, R1, R2	R0 ← R1 (AND) ((NOT) R2)	Clear bits
mov R0, R1	R0 ← R1	Move, registers
mvn R0, R1	R0 ← (NOT) R1	Move, bitwise NOT
movw R0, #(16-bit data)	R0[31~16] ← 0, R0[15~0] ← (16-bit data)	Move, wide
movt R0, #(16-bit data)	R0[31~16] ← (16-bit data), R0[15~0]: unaffected	Move, top

Table 4.2. Selected logical/move Thumb-2 instructions [8][9].

Furthermore, move instructions are shown in Table 4.2. The value of one register can be moved to another register using a **mov** instruction. And, 16-bit immediate data can be written to a register using a **movw** instruction. For the immediate data, a number sign "#" is used in front of the number. For instance, the value of the R0 is to be 12 after the execution of the "*movw R0, #12*" instruction. And, the value of the R0 is to be 0xFFFF after the execution of the "*movw R0, #0xFFFF*" instruction.

Next, there is a **mvn** instruction, and it may result in the operation that is similar to a bitwise NOT operation. If the value of R1 is 0xFFFF, the value of the R0 is to be 0xFFFF 0000 after the execution of the "*mvn R0, R1*" instruction.

Moreover, 16-bit immediate data can be written to the top half word of a register using a **movt** instruction. For instance, if the value of R0 was 0xFFFF, the value of the register R0 will become 0x1234 FFFF after the execution of the "***movt R0, #0x1234***" instruction.

To write an immediate 32-bit value into a register, two instructions of **movw** and **movt** can be used. For instance, if the desired value is 0x1234 5678. Two instructions of "***movw R0, #0x5678***" and "***movt R0, #0x1234***" can be executed in sequence. These **movw** and **movw** instruction examples are shown in the test program example later in this chapter.

Selected compare and branch instructions are shown in Table 4.3. There are several methods available for compare operations. A **cmp** instruction can be used to compare the values of two registers. The condition flags are to be updated on the result of the subtract operation of two values. There is a **cmn** instruction that can be used for the compare operation. This is similar to the **cmp** instruction. However, the difference is that the condition flags are to be updated on the result of the add operation of the two values.

Instruction	Execution	Description
cmp R0, R1	Update condition flags, (R0 – R1)	Compare
cmn R0, R1	Update condition flags, (R0 + R1)	Compare negative
tst R0, R1	Update condition flags, (R0 (AND) R1)	Test
teq R0, R1	Update condition flags, (R0 (XOR) R1)	Test equivalence
it(pattern) (cond) (ex) ittee eq	(pattern): up to three more conditional letters (t or e), (cond): Condition Field	If-Then
b _label	PC ← address of _label	Branch
bl _label	LR ← address of next instruction, PC ← address of _label	Branch with link
bx LR	PC ← LR	Branch and exchange

Table 4.3. Selected compare/branch Thumb-2 instructions [8][9].

A **tst** instruction can be used to compare the bitwise logical values of two registers. The values of the condition flags are to be updated on the result of the bitwise AND operation of two values. There is a **teq** instruction that can be used for a bitwise logical compare operation. The values of the condition flags are to be updated on the result of the bitwise XOR operation of the values.

A *If-Then* operation can be used for a conditional execution. This instruction begins with "**it**" and three more conditional letters can be added. The conditional letter is either **t** or **e**. Next, a condition field is used as an operand. This *If-Then* operation allows up to four following instructions with proper suffixes to be executed conditionally.

A simple unconditional branch operation can be performed using the instruction with the letter "**b**" followed by the label of the destination as an operand. Conditional branch instructions can be formed by adding proper suffixes. Selected conditional branch instructions are shown in Table 4.4. Thumb-2 supports various combinations of condition fields.

Instruction	Description	Condition Field
beq _label	Jump to _label if Equal	eq
bne _label	Jump to _label if Not equal	ne
bge _label	Jump to _label if greater than or equal (signed)	ge
blt _label	Jump to _label if less than (signed)	lt
bgt _label	Jump to _label if greater than (signed)	gt
ble _label	Jump to _label if less than or equal (signed)	le
bhi _label	Jump to _label if higher (unsigned)	hi
bls _label	Jump to _label if lower (unsigned)	ls
bcs _label	Jump to _label if Carry Set	cs
bcc _label	Jump to _label if Carry Clear	cc
bvs _label	Jump to _label if Overflow	vs
bvc _label	Jump to _label if No overflow	vc

Table 4.4. Selected conditional branch Thumb-2 instructions [8][9].

To call a function, a **bl** instruction can be used. When the brank with link (**bl**) instruction is executed, the address of the next instruction is to be saved to the link register (LR) for the use as a return address.

The **bx** instruction can be used to exit the subroutine and return. The value of PC (Program Counter) can be be updated using the address stored in the link register. This task can be performed by the execution of the "***bx** LR*" instruction.

Selected several instructions such as address, program status register, and push/pop instructions are shown in Table 4.5. The register-relative address for a label can be obtained using an **adr.w** instruction. The **adr** instruction with **.w** enforces the generation of a 32-bit instruction. For the access of the program status register, the value of the program status register can be written to a register using a **mrs** instruction.

Instruction	Execution	Description
adr.w R0, _label	R0 ← address of _label	PC relative address to R0
mrs R0, APSR	R0 ← APSR	PSR in any mode to R0
push {R0, R1}	STMDB SP!, {R0, R1}	Push registers to the stack
pop {R0, R1}	LD M SP!, {R0, R1}	Pop registers from the stack

Table 4.5. Selected address/program status registers/push/pop Thumb-2 instructions [8][9].

For some operations, the values of registers may need to be stored in stack memory. This operation can be performed using a **push** instruction. Moreover, for other operations, the data in stack memory can be loaded to restore the value of the registers. This operation can be performed using a **pop** instruction. These push/pop instructions support processing multiple registers.

Selected load and store memory instructions are listed in Table 4.6. The load instruction is **ldr**, and the store instruction is **str**. These load/store instructions are memory operations. However, a certain memory area can be associated with physical I/O devices. Performing load/store instructions using this memory area may result in accessing physical I/O devices. This is related to the topic of a memory mapped I/O. This topic has been introduced in Appendix C.

Instruction	Execution	Description
ldr R0, [R1]	R0 ← [address] (Word)	Load, word
ldrb R0, [R1, #2]	R0 ← [address+2] (Byte)	Load, register offset
str R0, [R1]	[address] ← R0 (Word)	Store, word
strb R0, [R1, #2]	[address+2] ← R0 (Byte)	Store, register offset

Table 4.6. Selected load/store word Thumb-2 instructions [8][9].

In this chapter, we have seen some of the selected assembly instructions and the brief introduction to these selected instructions. For readers who wish to learn more about Arm assembly language programming, more information and documentations are available through the manufacturers [7-9].

Assembly Language Test Environment

Texas Instruments provides an Arm TI compiler that is integrated with Code Composer Studio. In order to write an assembly program, a user needs to follow the TI assembler convention. For the detail of the TI assembler convention, readers can study an Arm Assembly Language Tools documentation [7].

In general, Assembly language programming can be power and effective, if it is well codded by an experienced programmer. Moreover, it is important to study Assembly language programming to deepen the knowledge about the instruction set architecture. However, for a fairly complicated system, it may not be practical to write an entire code in Assembly language. However, a portion of code such as several subroutines can be written in Assembly language. Therefore, both C/C++ and Assembly language implementations can be used in the same embedded system. This method can be understood as Mixing C and Assembly programming.

To test a portion of code in Assembly language, we will use an approach that is similar to mixing C and assembly programming. We will use C program for a main routine, and assembly program for a subroutine. The detail of this set-up process will be followed.

Assembly Test Program Setup Process

As it was described in Chapter 2, you can create a sample project. Once the project is successfully created, you can see "*main.c*" in the project folder. The main program in C language is shown in Program 4.1. In this program, an extern subroutine named *_main()* is defined and called in the main routine. This is a minimal and simple main program written in C language. In this main program, a subroutine that is written in Assembly language is called.

```
#include "msp.h"
extern void _main(void);  // extern assembly subroutine
void main(void) {
    WDT_A->CTL = WDT_A_CTL_PW | WDT_A_CTL_HOLD;  // hold the watchdog timer
    _main();  // call an assembly subroutine
}
```

Program 4.1. Test main program in C language.

The filename that contains the assembly code is *_main.asm*. You can create a file with this name as shown in Figure 4.1. This is a text file with the file extension name of *asm*. You can click "File -> New -> File From Template." Then, you can enter source file name as "_main.asm" and uncheck "User Template". Then, you can see an empty text file with the filename of "_main.asm". Now, you can enter your assembly code. A sample test program in Assembly language will be presented in the following section.

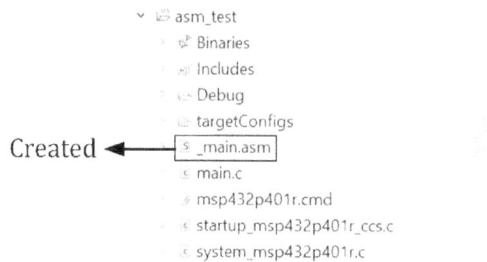

Figure 4.1. Creation of an Assembly test program file

You can open the "*_main.asm*" file and enter the assembly code as shown in Program 4.2. This is a simple assembly program that can execute several simple instructions. This program has move, add, and subtract instructions. When you type and enter this code, it would be helpful to know that proper indentations or tabs need to be kept. Once you can make this test code work, you can modify this test program to create your own assembly program that can perform a complicated task.

```
            .global  _main
            .thumb
            .data
            .text
_main:
            movw R0, #12   ; R0: 12
            movw R1, #10   ; R1: 10
            add R2, R0, R1   ; R2: R0+R1
            sub R3, R0, R1   ; R3: R0-R1
            rsb R4, R0, R1   ; R4: R1-R0
_loop:
            b _loop
            bx LR
            .end
```

Program 4.2. Assembly test program (_main.asm).

For debugging purposes, you can use "step into" or "step over" to step through the program. These "step into" and "step over" icons are shown in Figure 4.2. They are useful in debugging a program in C/C++ language. You can use "assembly step into" or "assembly step over" instead. At the code line of "_main()", you can use "assembly step into". Then, it will open the assembly code. Or, you can set a breakpoint in the assembly code. Breakpoints are also very useful in debugging a program. In this case, you can set a breakpoint at the first line in the "_main" block in the assembly code as shown in Figure 4.2. Then, once the program gets started in debug mode, the program will suspend at the line where you have set the breakpoint. You can step through the assembly code.

Using this test assembly program, users can try to find their own suitable assembly programing and debugging environment. Now, let us examine a functional Assembly program. A simple LED blink example in Assembly language will be presented in the following section,

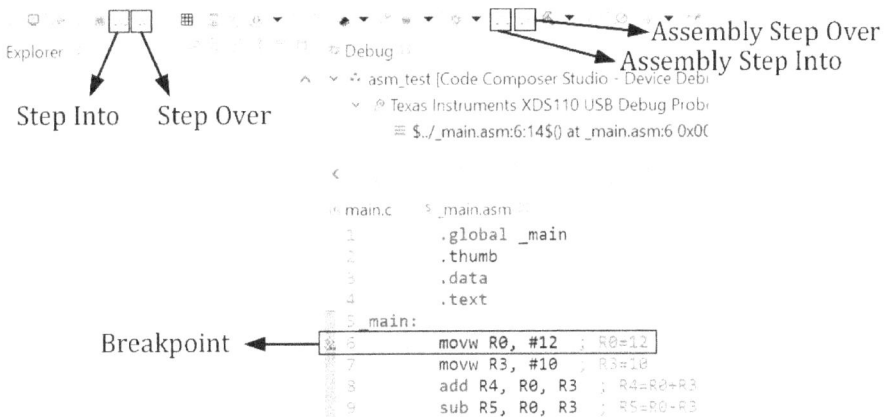

Figure 4.2. Debugging environment for Assembly language.

LED Blink Program in Assembly Language

A simple test program that can blink an LED in C language was presented previously in Chapter 2. In this section, an Assembly program is presented. This Assembly LED blink program is shown in Program 4.3.

movw instructions are used to write the immediate data to the register R0, R1 and R2. For the register R3, **movw** and **movt** instructions are used to write 32-bit data that is 0x4000 4C04. This is the address of the Port 1 direction register. The byte data of R2 will be stored in the Port 1 direction register using a **strb** instruction. Next, in this similar fashion, 32-bit data can be processed using **movw** and **movt** instructions. The data is 0x4000 4C02, and this is the address of the Port 1 output register. The byte data of R2 will be stored in the Port 1 output registers using a **strb** instruction. The details of Port 1 direction and output registers will be studied in the following chapter.

```
            .global  _main
            .thumb
            .data
            .text
_main:
            movw R0, #0x00    ; R0: 0
            movw R1, #0x01    ; R1: 1
            movw R2, #0x01    ; R2: 1
            movw R3, #0x4C04  ; R3: 0x4C04
            movt R3, #0x4000  ; R3: 0x4000 4C04
            strb R2, [R3]     ; store
            movw R3, #0x4C02  ; R3: 0x4C02
            movt R3, #0x4000  ; R3: 0x4000 4C02
            strb R2, [R3]     ; store
_loop:
            eor R2, R1        ; R2: R2 XOR R1
            strb R2, [R3]     ; store
            movw R4, #0x8C00  ; R4: 0x8C00
            movt R4, #0x0002  ; R4: 0x0002 8C00
_lp1:
            sub R4, R1        ; R4: R4-R1
            cmp R4, R0        ; compare
            bne _lp1
            b _loop
            bx LR
            .end
```

Program 4.3. Assembly LED blink program (_main.asm).

In the main assembly loop (_loop), a bitwise XOR operation using an **eor** instruction will be performed. After a few more instructions, this assembly program executes the code block that is defined as "_lp1". This is a code block that is for a delay function. In this _lp1 block, the value of the register R4 gets decreased. Using a **cmp** compare instruction, the values of the program status flags can be updated. Depending on the results, the *bne _lp1* can be executed. When the R4 becomes zero, it will execute an unconditional jump. It will go to the stat of the main assembly loop (_loop). Although, this program has an instruction with the line of "*bx LR*". The execution of this instruction means that the program exits this subroutine and return. However, since this program keeps repeating the loop (_loop), in a normal condition, this program does not reach at the line of "*bx LR*". When the program is running successfully, you can see that a Red LED (LED1) is blinking.

We have briefly mentioned about P1 direction register and P1 output register, which are related to a general purpose I/O topic. In the following chapter, we will study General Purpose I/Os.

Chapter 5. General Purpose I/O

A general purpose input/output (GPIO) is a part of circuits that makes it possible to read digital input signals or generate digital output signals through I/O pins. A peripheral in microcontroller is typically a device, module, or a part of circuits other than a CPU and a memory device that can be used for interfacing with systems outside of the microcontroller. In this aspect, a GPIO is a peripheral, and it can be used for interfacing to external circuits and devices.

GPIOs are useful for various applications. An MSP432P401RIPZ IC model has 84 I/O pins. GPIO circuits for each pin have similarities but, they are slightly different each other because each pin can may provide different alternative functions.

The MSP432P401R IC has 11 digital I/O ports such as P1~P10 and PJ. There are internal GPIO registers associated these names. While some of them has less, most of ports have eight I/O pins. For instance, P1.0 means that it is related to Port 1. There are several registers using this port name of P1. In these registers, the first least significant bit (LSB) is the relevant bit. And this bit is associated with the physical pin number 4. In some cases, this pin or the extended node in a circuit diagram simply is referred as P1.0. In this chapter, Port 1 (P1) is selected as an example. However, readers can extend this setting to other ports such as P2 or P3.

Functional GPIO Block Diagram

Port 1 (P1) is associated with eight I/O pins. These eight pins are related to P1.0~P1.7. To simplify the explanations, let us choose P1.0 as an example. Figure 5.1 shows a simplified functional block diagram of a GPIO block for P1.0.

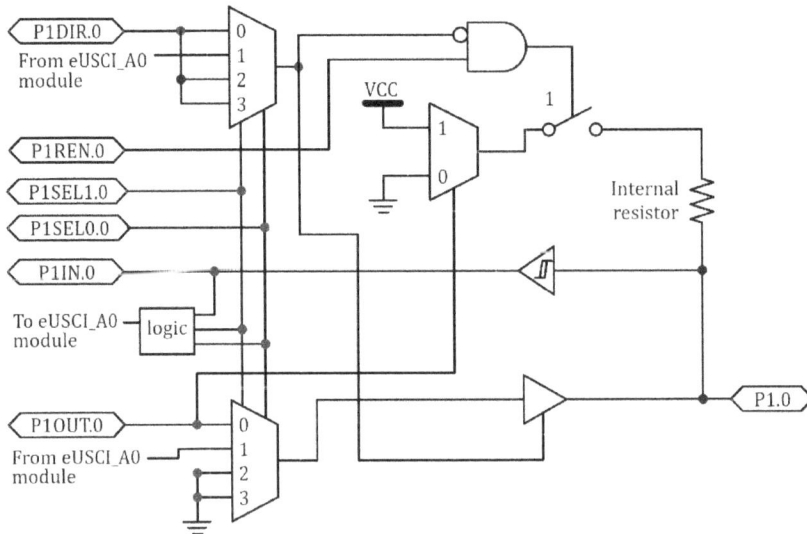

Figure 5.1. Simplified functional block diagram for P1.0 [1].

This functional block diagram shown in the figure does not necessarily represent the physical circuit implementation on a chip; however, it can be used to help readers understand the functional behavior. There are various registers related to Port 1. Let us examine the functional behavior based on each of these registers.

Direction Register (P1DIR)

A direction register of P1 is named P1DIR. Each bit in P1DIR register can select the direction of the associated I/O pin. If the first least significant bit (LSB) of the P1DIR is 0, the direction of P1.0 is input. If the first LSB of the P1DIR is 1, the direction of P1.0 is output. For instance, if the P1DIR is 1, the direction of P1.0 is output.

If the direction of a pin is supposed to be input, however, if it would be accidently configured as output instead, in the unfortunate case, it might cause a hardware problem. Users need to be cautious in configuring output directions if they are debugging a system with a potential hardware issue.

Output Register (P1OUT)

When the direction is configured as output, each bit in P1OUT register can determine the logical output signal of the corresponding I/O pin. First, the direction of the pin needs to be configured as output. Then, the logical output value is to be 0, if the associated bit of the P1OUT register is cleared. Or, the logical output value is to be 1, if the associated bit of the P1OUT register is set.

For instance, the direction of the pin can be configured as output by setting the first LSB of the P1DIR. Then, if P1OUT is 0, the logical output value of P1.0 is to be 0. Or, if P1OUT is 1, the logical output value of P1.0 is to be 1.

Pull-up or Pull-down Resister Enable Register (P1REN)

A GPIO has internal resistors as shown in Figure 5.1. Internal resistors can be enabled by setting P1REN register. Next, the corresponding pins need to be properly configured as input in order to enable these internal resistors. Then, they can be configured either pull-up or pull-down depending on the values of P1OUT as shown in Table 5.1.

P1REN.y	P1DIR.y	P1OUT.y	I/O configuration
0	0	0	Input
0	0	1	Input
0	1	0	Output
0	1	1	Output
1	0	0	Input / internal pull-down resistor
1	0	1	Input / internal pull-up resistor
1	1	0	Output
1	1	1	Output

Table 5.1. I/O port configuration [6].

According to the datasheet [1], this internal resistor value is 30 kΩ. This is not a high precision resistor, and the resistor value may vary for each IC, and the range of the resistor is 20 kΩ to 40 kΩ according to the datasheet.

Users can configure GPIO registers in order to use this internal resistor as a pull-up or pull-down resistor without the need of placing an external resistor. This technique can be useful and effective in some cases depending on applications.

Output Drive Strength Selection Registers (P1DS)

A GPIO pin can be used to drive an external circuit component or device such as an LED. In this case, it is recommended to understand the specification of the output drive strength. There are two options. They are regular drive strength and high drive strength. This option can be selected by the configuration of P1DS register. Setting bits of P1DS can activate the high drive strength functions; however, this high drive strength function may not be available or not implemented in some pins. You can refer to the device datasheet for the details. For instance, on an MSP432P401R Launchpad, P2.0 ~ P2.2 are connected to an LED. These pins can be configured to be in high drive strength mode.

Input Registers (P1IN)

When the direction is configured as input by clearing bits in P1DIR, the associated pins would function as input. In this state, the logical value of each bit of P1IN register will follow the same logical level of the corresponding I/O pin. For instance, the direction can be configured as input by P1DIR=0. Then, the value of the first LSB of P1IN gets updated to be the same as the logical input signal of P1.0.

Interestingly, as it was shown in Figure 5.1, the first LSB of input register P1IN is to be the same as the logical value of P1.0 regardless of the direction. This is because, as you can sese, the P1IN.0 and P1.0 are directly connected through a Schmitt trigger. This means the values of P1IN will get updated even the direction is configured as output. Readers can check this behavior by generating logical signals for a pin and monitor the values of input registers.

Moreover, regarding P1N registers, they are read only registers. Writing to these registers may result in increased current consumptions while attempting to write.

Function Select Registers (P1SEL1, P1SEL0)

Most of pins in an MSP432P401R MCU are internally multiplexed with other relevant peripheral modules. This means that they can provide alternative functions. P1SEL1 and P1SEL0 registers are used to select these alternative functions.

There are four combinations based on PSEL1 and PSEL0 registers as shown in Table 5.2. When both bits of P1SEL1 and P1SEL0 are cleared, the function of the associated pin is a GPIO. Other than this case of the configuration, there are three alternative functions. The alternative function assignments may vary by pin. For more information, users can refer to the datasheet [1].

For instance, a physical pin number 4 can function as a typical GPIO for P1.0. Or, it is possible to make it function as UCA0STE instead depending on the value of P1SEL1 and P1SEL0 registers. This UCA0STE is an *eUSCI_A0 SPI slave transmit enable* associated with eUSCI_A0. In Chapter 16 and Chapter 18, we will learn about eUSCI and SPI. By selecting this alternative function, this pin may not function simply as a GPIO.

P1SEL1.y	P1SEL0.y	I/O function
0	0	GPIO
0	1	Alternate function / Primary module
1	0	Alternate function / Secondary module
1	1	Alternate function / Tertiary module

Table 5.2. I/O function selection [6].

Moreover, when an alternative function is selected, P1DIR register may not necessarily control the pin direction. It may vary by pin. Developers may refer to the datasheet [1] to gain the understanding of the behavior of the relevant alternative function.

Port Interrupts
Port 1 Interrupt Enable Register (P1IE) enables P1 interrupt flag (P1IFG). P1IFG interrupt flag can be set when the selected signal edge occurs at the pin. Interrupt Edge Select Registers (P1IES) makes pins responsive to either low-to-high or high-to-low transitions.

LEDs and Buttons on MSP432P401R Launchpad
The MSP432P401R Launchpad has two LEDs (LED1 and LED2) and push buttons as shown in Figure 5.2. LED1 is connected to P1.0, and it is a Red color LED. Shunt jumper JP8 can free up P1.0 because it disconnects from the LED1. LED2 is an RGB LED. Each color portion can be turned on or off by controlling P2.0, P2.1 and P2.2. It is worth of mentioning that these pins can be freed up by opening the shunt jumpers of JP9, JP10, and JP11.

Two push buttons (S1 and S2) are on the board. P1.1 and P1.4 are related to S1 and S2, respectively. For S1, if the push button is pressed, P1.1 can be 0. However, if the push button is not pressed, P1.1 could be at a high impedance state, and the value of P1IN may not be relevant to the physical push button state. Therefore, in this case, it may need a pull-up resistor. An external resistor can be connected to the P1. If the performance of the switch is not a primary concern, the internal pull-up resistor can be used as we have studied previously.

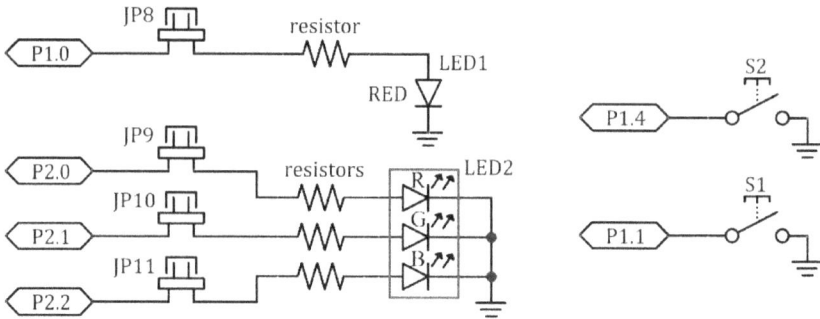

Figure 5.2. LEDs and push buttons on MSP432P401R Launchpad [1].

Now, since the pull-up resistor is configured, we need to revisit the behavior of this switch. If the push button is left as is (not pressed), P1.1 can read 1 through the pull-up resistor connection. If the push button is pressed, P1.1 can read 0. In order to understand this behavior, we can write a simple code to test this button and the Red color LED.

Button Test Program

The button test program is shown in Program 5.1. LED1 and S1 will be used. In this code, a pull-up resistor is configured for P1.1. In the while loop, it checks whether P1.1 is set or not. In the parentheses, it performs a masking operation. This technique is to obtain relevant bits only in P1IN. Or, you can understand it as filtering out unwanted data.

```c
#include "msp.h"
void main(void) {
    WDT_A->CTL = WDT_A_CTL_PW | WDT_A_CTL_HOLD;  // hold the watchdog timer
    P1->DIR |= 0x01;  // output pins
    P1->OUT &= ~0x01;  // clear the output value
    P1->DIR &= ~0x02;  // input pins
    P1->REN |= 0x02;  // enable internal resistor
    P1->OUT |= 0x02;  // pull-up resistor
    while (1) {
        if ((P1->IN & 0x02)==0)  // read P1 and perform masking
            P1->OUT |= 0x01;  // set the output value
        else
            P1->OUT &= ~0x01;  // clear the output value
    }
}
```

Program 5.1. Button test program in C/C++.

Debouncing Switches

Previously, we have tested a simple push button switch. We will study more about the switch behavior and switch applications. Push buttons are common electrical components in electronics. The input signals from push buttons can be asynchronous, and, practically, the signals may not be electronically clean. This means that the transition is not clean between 0 and 1 when the button is pressed or released.

This behavior is described in Figure 5.3. This figure shows the signals from a switch as the button is pressed or released. The data changes 1 to 0 and it also changes 0 to 1. Between these signals. You can see many noise signals fluctuating 0 and 1 during the transitions. This random behavior may could an unexpected status for an embedded system. This behavior is related to switch bounce. This non-ideal behavior needs to be dealt with debouncing switches. We can put an effort in resolving this issue by hardware and/or software approaches.

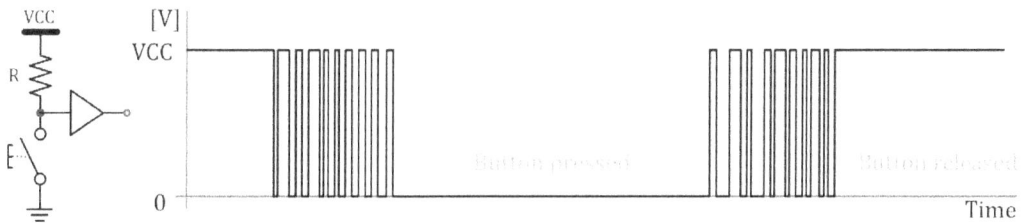

Figure 5.3. Switch bounce.

Hardware for debouncing switches

Figure 5.4 shows simple hardware switch debouncers. The circuit on the left has one RC filter and one inverter. This is a simple circuit; but this is effective if the parameters of the RC filter are designed properly. In this configuration, the charging time may not be balanced. In order to control the charge time, a diode can be used as shown on the right.

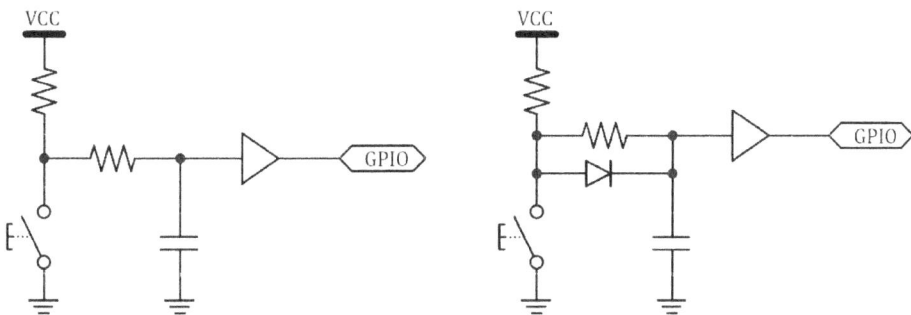

Figure 5.4. A simple switch debouncer.

A better hardware solution is to use two cross-coupled NAND gates to form a simple Set-Reset (SR) latch, and it also needs to use a double-throw switch as shown in Figure 5.5. Two pull-up resistors connections may pass a logical high level, while the switch may a logical low level.

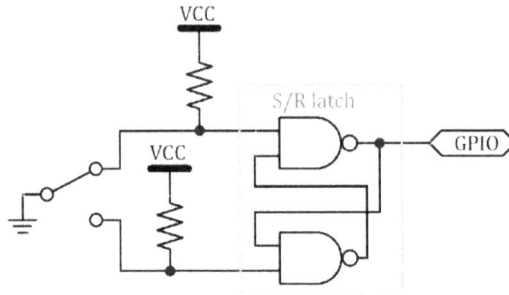

Figure 5.5. Switch debouncer using SR Latch.

Software for debouncing switches

Software debounce routines ranges simple to complex algorithms in order to handle multiple switches. Developers may resolve it without completely understanding of the problem of noise signals. However, it is a good idea to estimate or measure this noise by testing.

In this respect, one of the solutions is to delay processing the input signals using the delay obtained from measurements. Generally, the slow read rate can ignore some of the noise and may seem to resolve problems. However, one downside is a slow response. The developer may need to determine an optimum delay for their specific embedded system.

Keypad Matrix

It is common to find electronics that have many switches. For a computer keyboard, it may have more than 100 push button switches. Instead of using each GPIO pin per switch, the connection of the switches can be formed as an array or matrix. Therefore, the input status of many switches can be read using a smaller number of GPIOs. Figure 5.6 shows a 16-key keypad, and each key has one switch. 16 keys are connected in array or matrix.

The keypad component is drawn as an abstract block diagram, and it is shown Figure 5.7. The pin arrangement is also shown in the figure.

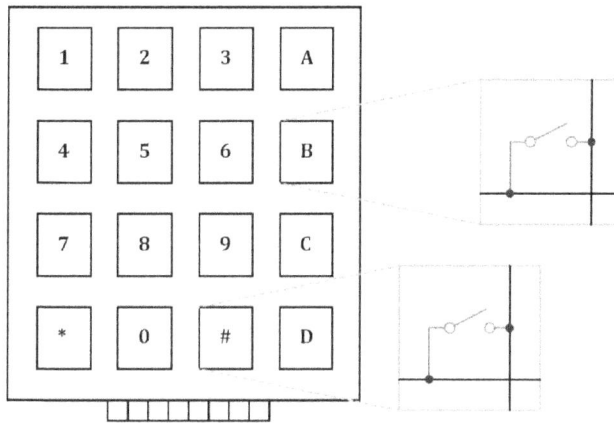

Figure 5.6. Keypad matrix.

There are many 16 keypad modules For instance, one of the 16-keypad module from Vellman® [10]. For a 16-keypad module, there can be 4 rows and 4 columns. None of the lines has been connected each other until one of the switches is pressed. For instance, if the key 5 is pressed, ROW2 and COL2 lines are getting connected.

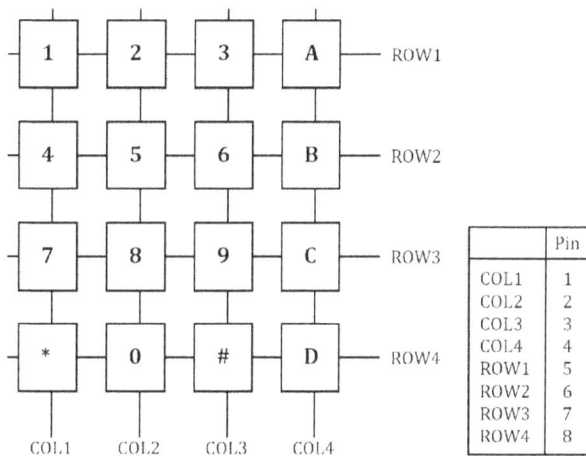

Figure 5.7. Keypad matrix connection [10].

Now, this keypad is configured to make a connection to an MSP432P401R Launchpad as shown in Figure 5.8. Eight pins are connected to P2.0 ~ P2.7. External pull-up resistors at P2.0 ~ P2.3 are placed. Four resistors in series were connected at P2.4, P2.5, P2.6, and P2.7. These resistors in series are added for protection. The port directions for P2.0 ~ P2.3 need to be configured as input, and the port directions for P2.4 ~ P2.7 need to be configured as output.

The push button status can be determined by scanning process. First, let us control P2.4 is to be a logical low level, and the rest pins of P2.5, P2.6, and P2.7 are to be logical high levels. In this state, the button state of ROW1 can be read through P2.0 ~ P2.3. For instance, in this state, one button on the far right is pressed. Then, P2.0 can read a logical low level and the rest of them can read logical high levels.

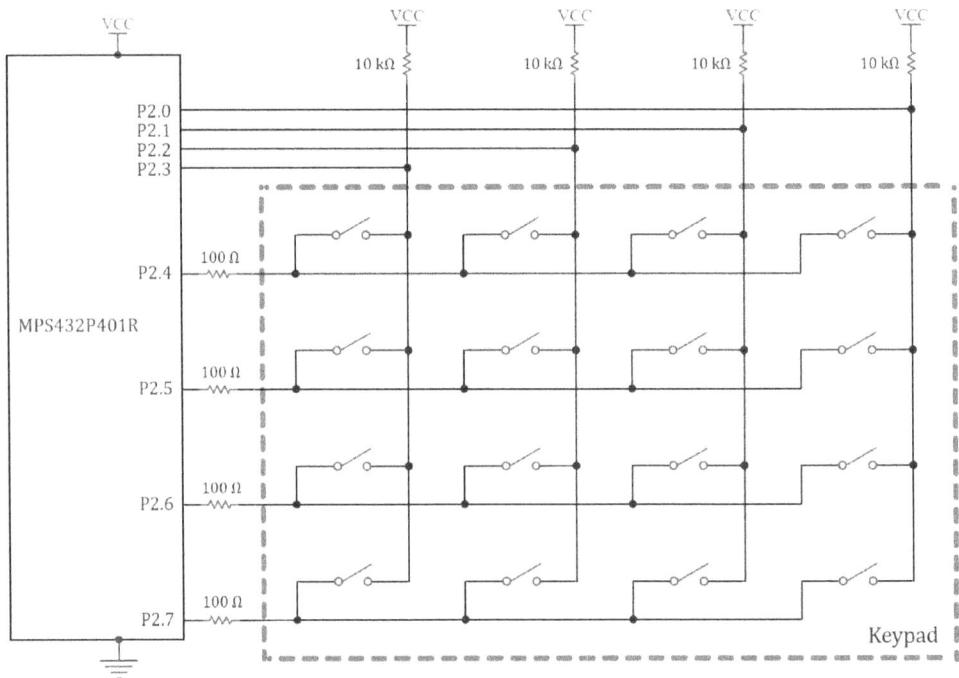

Figure 5.8. Keypad matrix example.

The push button status can be determined by scanning process. First, let us control P2.4 is to be a logical low level, and the rest pins of P2.5, P2.6, and P2.7 are to be logical high levels. In this state, the button state of ROW1 can be read through P2.0 ~ P2.3. For instance, in this state, one button on the far right is pressed. Then, P2.0 can read a logical low level and the rest of them can read logical high levels.

For the next cycle, P2.5 is controlled to be a logical low level and the rest ports of P2.4, P2.6, and P2.7 are controlled to be logical high levels. In this state, the button state of ROW2 can be read. After taking two more similar steps for the rest of ROW3 and ROW4, it will complete a scanning cycle, and the position of the button that was pressed can be determined.

This scanning process can detect not only one button press response but also multiple keypad responses. However, the detection of multiple keypad presses in the same column may cause shorting power to the ground.

Some keypad models have internal resistance. For these keypad models, it may not result in a critical issue. However, if the matrix keypad connections are made using individual switches and there is no protection resistor, it may cause a critical condition that cause shorting power to ground. For this reason, extra resistors were added in series to avoid excessive current conditions as shown in Figure 5.8. On the BH EDU board, this protection scheme was already applied, and the external pull up resistors were placed. A user can use the keypad by simply connecting jumpers to the proper header positions.

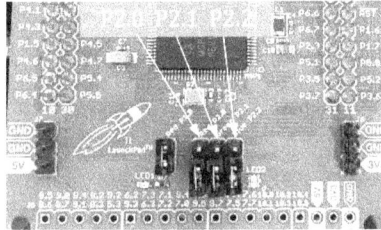

Figure 5.8. Jumper removal for P2.0, P2.1 and P2.2.

In this example, P2.0, P2.1, and P2.2 have been used. These pins are connected to an RGB LED. However, these pins can be accessible if the jumpers (JP9, JP10, and JP11) are removed. After removing these jumpers, you can see the two pins per jumper. The exposed pins that are close to the MCU are the breakout pins for P2.0, P2.1, and P2.2. The jumpers that were removed can be kept safe separately, or they can be still left on board but with the jumper connection open as shown in Figure 5.8.

Chapter 6. Register level C/C++ programming

MCUs can execute a machine code that may be consisted of a binary number code written for the machine. For low level programming, users can write a program in Assembly language. An assembler that is a program can convert the assembly code to the machine code. Assembly language is more human friendly as it is a higher-level abstraction compared to the machine code. It can effectively describe the low-level behavior of the MCU. However, if users choose to use only Assembly language for a complex system, it could take a high level of effort in describing this system. Therefore, a higher-level abstraction can help in writing a program. C or C++ can be a reasonable choice for users in describing some of embedded systems. This C/C++ language is a higher level of abstraction than Assembly language.

There are several styles of the C/C++ programming in embedded system development. One of low-level approaches is a register level C programming. This is one of typical implementation methods. In this approach, the level of abstraction is not very high. This method is related to controlling registers directly to gain the access of the MCU. This method helps a developer to understand low-level hardware and software aspects of an embedded system. So, it could help in learning fundamental concepts of a microcontroller. In this book, we will learn about how to operate the MSP432P401R MCU based on this register level C/C++ programming style. Later in this book, we will learn about even higher-level abstraction styles in C/C++ programming based on a TI driver library and real-time operating system.

Conventions

Let us consider some of the typical conventions of programing in C/C++ for an MSP432P401R MCU. If a user wants to generate a logical output for P1.0, we can write a line as follows:

        P1OUT = 1;

As we have studied before, the direction needs to be configured to be output. Let us assume you already have configured P1DIR properly. Now, we can use a hexadecimal number instead. The following code lines are equivalent.

        P1OUT = 0x01;

        P1OUT = 01h;

There are predefined names such as for common numbers in the MSP432 header. They are BIT0 ~ BIT7. BIT0 is the same as 0x01, BIT1 is the same as 0x02, and so forth. This is a convenient way in describing the one bit of a register. Therefore, the following line is equivalent.

```
P1OUT = BIT0;
```

It is common to find in expressing a number using a left shift. For instance, 1 << 1 means 0x02 because it performs one left bit shift using 1. This is the same as BIT1. For instance, 1 << 2 means 0x04, and it is the same as BIT2. Therefore, the following line is equivalent.

```
P1OUT = 1<<0;
```

Each developer may prefer different styles. That means you may find these variations in different programs. So, it would be useful for a developer to understand these common conventions.

Bit Access

Let us revisit the code of P1OUT=0x01. This code can set the first least significant bit (LSB). That is the desired behavior. However, this code clears other bits. If there is another device that is connected at P1.1, this code will clear the value of P1.1. However, this means there is a chance that the other bits that were cleared were not supported to happened. In fact, that is why it is important to access and update the relevant bits only. Let us consider the following code line.

```
P1OUT |= 0x01;
```

This is one of the ways to set the first bit only while it leaves other bits unchanged. To understand the behavior, let us expand it, and it is P1OUT=P1OUT | 0x01. The behavior can be understood better in this expanded form. However, it is not common to write a code line in this expanded form because this might not generate an efficient code for the complier.

Now, let us consider a method that can clear the first LSB only and leaves other bits unchanged, we can write the code line as follows.

```
P1OUT &= ~0x01;
```

To understand the behavior, let us expand it. It is P1OUT=P1OUT & ~0x01. The behavior can be understood better in this way. For the same reason, it is not common to write a code line in this expanded form.

It is worth of mentioning that an MSP432P401R MCU is capable of accessing each bit using bit-banding. This is an advanced and a hardware method of changing individual bits. The details of this techniques are not covered in this book. This is available in Arm Cortex M3/M4 processors.

MS432 Port Convention

In the MSP432P401R header, each port is defined as a **struct** type. Each member needs to be accessed using an arrow operator. In this configuration, the equivalent bit access code line are as follows:

P1->OUT |= 0x01;

P1->OUT &= ~0x01;

This expression using struct types has been used in the programs in TI MSP432P401R example projects. This expression has been used in the example programs in this book.

ISR example

Interrupts will be covered in following chapters. But, now, let us consider one code line that is related to an interrupt configuration.

NVIC->ISER[1] = 1 << ((PORT1_IRQn) & 31)

NVIC has ISER1 and ISER0 registers. ISER1 can process IRQ 32 to 63. PORT1_IRQn means Port 1 interrupt, which is defined simply number 35 in the header. Therefore, bitwise AND operation of PORT1_IRQn and & 31 will result in 3.

In short, this is NVIC->ISER[1] = 1 << 3. Because "1<< 3" is the same as 0x08, this can be also considered to be NVIC->ISER[1] = 0x08. This expression above has been used as a part of setting up an ISR in Chapter 8.

Chapter 7. Timer basics

Timers are versatile and useful peripherals for embedded system applications. An MSP432P401R MCU has a watchdog timer as well as general-purpose 16-bit timers and 32-bit timers. In this book, you will learn about Timer_A, which is a 16-bit timer, and you will learn how to use it in various applications. One of key parameters in a timer is the selection of a clock source. Let us study an MSP432P4 clock system first. There are several clock resources and system clock signals.

Clock Resources

External oscillators can be used in providing clock signals for the MCU. A low-frequency oscillator (LFXT) such as a 32.769 kHz crystal or a high frequency oscillator (HFXT) such as a 48 MHz crystal can be connected to the MCU to provide the clock signals.

An MSP432P401R MCU can be operated without any external oscillators. It has an internal digitally controlled oscillator (DCO) with programmable frequencies. There are several calibrated DCO frequency settings. In Chapter 2, you have selected a new CCS project, and you have created "empty project (with main)". You have entered your code in main.c file to blink an LED. In this project setting of "empty project (with main)", a master clock (MCLK) is configured to use a 3 MHz DCO clock. In this book, we will provide program examples using this clock source setting. It is worth of mentioning that users can change the setting to generate a different frequency for the master clock (MCLK).

There is an internal low-power low-frequency oscillator (REFO) with selectable 32.768-kHz or 128-kHz typical frequencies, Moreover, there is a Very-low-power Low-frequency Oscillator (VLO). Furthermore, there is MODCLK that is an internal low-power oscillator with 25-MHz typical frequency, Also, there is a SYSOSC that is an internal oscillator with 5-MHz typical frequency.

Clock Signals

There are many clock resources, and there are several clock signals available in the clock module. Some of the relevant clock signals are Auxiliary clock (ACLK), Master clock (MCLK), and Subsystem master clock (HSMCLK)

Auxiliary clock (ACLK) is selectable as LFXTCLK, VLOCLK, or REFOCLK. ACLK. It can be divided by up to 128. The maximum frequency is limited to 128 kHz. This ACLK can be used by peripheral modules.

Master clock (MCLK) is selectable as LFXTCLK, VLOCLK, REFOCLK, DCOCLK, MODCLK, or HFXTCLK. This MCLK can be divided by up to 128. The MCLK is used by the CPU, and it can be used by peripheral modules.

Subsystem master clock (HSMCLK) is selectable as LFXTCLK, VLOCLK, REFOCLK, DCOCLK, MODCLK, HFXTCLK. This HSMCLK can be divided by up to 128. The HSMCLK can be used by peripheral modules.

Low-speed subsystem master clock (SMCLK) uses the HSMCLK clock resource, and it can be divided further by up to 128. This SMCLK can be used by peripheral modules. For a timer clock source, it is common to select ACLK or SMCLK. ACLK is a low frequency clock and SMCLK is a frequency clock.

SMCLK can be used to provide clock signals for peripherals. In this book, SMCLK will be used in many programing examples. As it described, when you have created "empty project (with main)", your project contains the clock signal system configuration. The master clock (MCLK) is configured to use a 3 MHz DCO clock. Also, SMCLK is also configured to use the 3 MHz DCO clock. Using this configuration, the waveform of SMCLK at 3 MHz is shown in Figure 7.1.

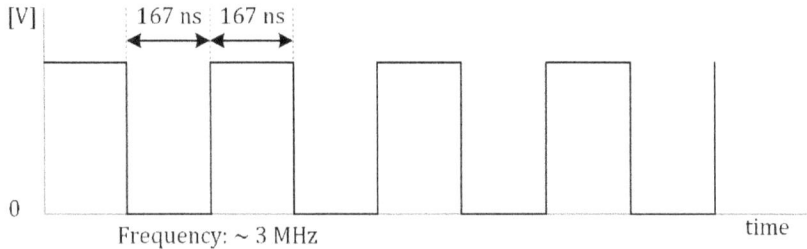

Figure 7.1. SMCLK waveform at 3 MHz.

Timer_A

An MPS432P401R MCU has 16-bit general purpose timers. Timer_A is a 16-bit timer and counter. Each Timer_A may have up to seven capture and compare registers. This timer module supports multiple capture and compare components. It can generate PWM outputs. A simplified functional block diagram of Timer_A0 is shown in Figure 7.2. There are multiple Timer_A modules available such as Timer_A0, Timer_A1, Timer_A2, and Timer_A3 in an MSP432P401R MCU. To simplify explanations, only Timer_A0 will be described in this chapter. For Timer A0, a clock source is selectable. TASSEL bits are associated with the clock source selection. This clock source can be divided by two divider blocks. The divider settings can be configured by ID and TAIDEX bits. Then, at the rising edge of this clock signals, the timer TA0R value will be increased or decreased. There are 7 capture and compare blocks of TA0CCR0 ~ TA0CCR6. The Timer_A0 can be used to generate PWM signals, or it can be used a capture function of digital signals. These functions are in the dotted boxes named OUTPUT MODE and CAPTURE MODE, respectively. In this chapter, we will focus on the timer and compare functions. Later, in this book we will revisit this timer block to cover the rest of these OUTPUT MODE and CAPTURE MODE functions.

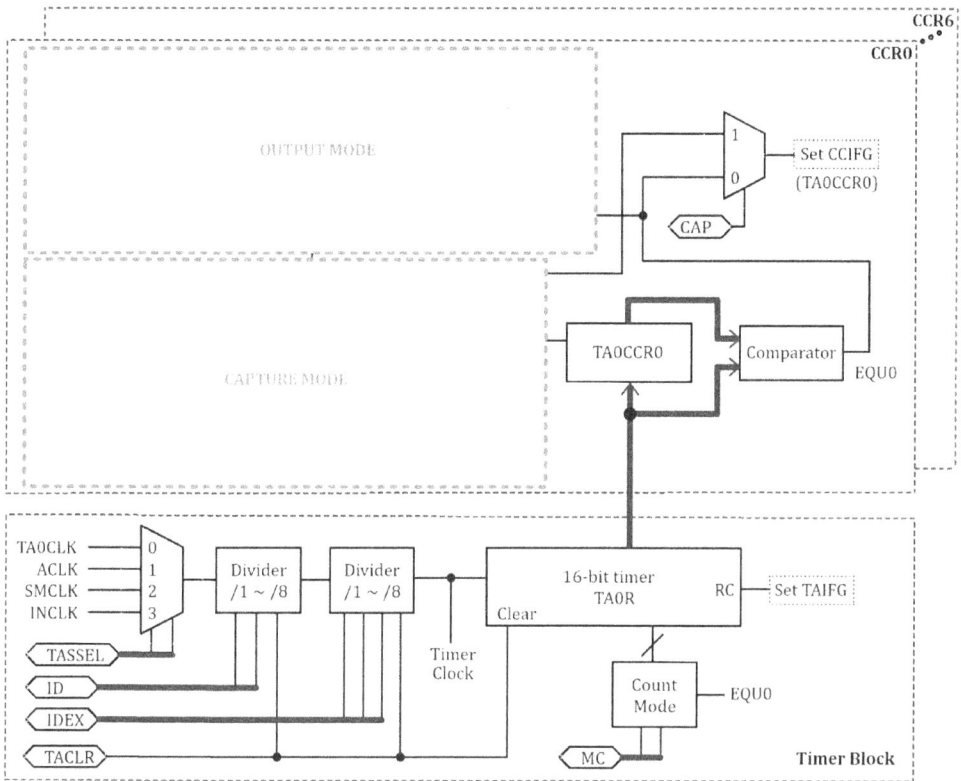

Figure 7.2. Simplified functional block diagram of Timer_A0 [6].

16-Bit Timer Counter

The timer register TA0R holds the value, and it can be counted up or down. MC bits control this timer mode behavior. TA0TACLR bit can clear the value of the counter. There is a TAIFG, which is an interrupt flag. It can be set, when the counter overflows and it rolls off to zero.

As described, the clock source for Timer_A is selectable. The choice depends on the functional requirements. In general, you can choose ACLK, if it is preferred to use a counter that is running slow for your application. If you need a counter that is running fast, you can choose SMCLK. The clock speed of the SMLCK is programmable. As it was mentioned, the SMCLK clock frequency is 3 MHz as it was described for the "Empty Project (with main)" setting. This SMCLK clock can be slowed down for the counter through the two dividers in series, if needed. ID bits can configure the divider up to 8, and the further division can be done up to 8 by setting TAIDEX bits. Timer can be halted when MC bits are cleared. There is a

TA0CCR0 register. This is an important register because this may set the upper bound of the counter in certain timer modes.

Timer Modes

Timer modes are listed in Table 7.1. As it was described, if MC bits are cleared, the timer can be halted. Other than this state, the timer keeps counting up or down. If the MC bits are configured to 1, this timer is in up mode.

Mode	MC bits	Description
Stop	0	Timer is halted.
Up	1	Timer counts up to TA0CCR0 value, then, rolls off to zero (Repeatedly)
Continuous	2	Timer counts up to 0xFFFF, then, rolls off to zero (Repeatedly)
Up/Down	3	The timer counts up to the TA0CCR0 value and counts down to zero (Repeatedly)

Table 7.1. Timer Modes [6].

The timer counts up to the value of TA0CCR0, then it rolls off to zero. This is a pattern of operation, and it will keep repeating. This count pattern for up mode is shown in Figure7.3.

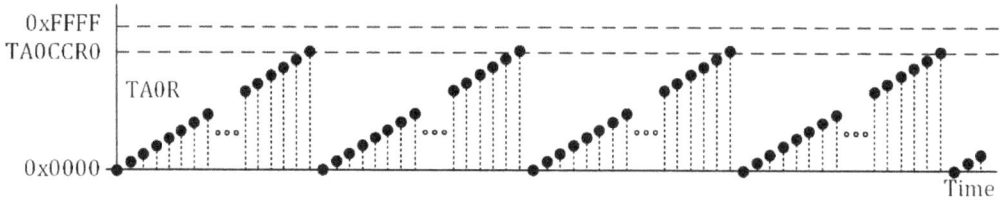

Figure 7.3. Count pattern for up mode [6].

The value of TA0R keeps increasing but it reset the counter when it reaches at TA0CCR0. Let us examine the interrupt flag behaviors in up mode. The flag setting in up mode is shown in Figure 7.4.

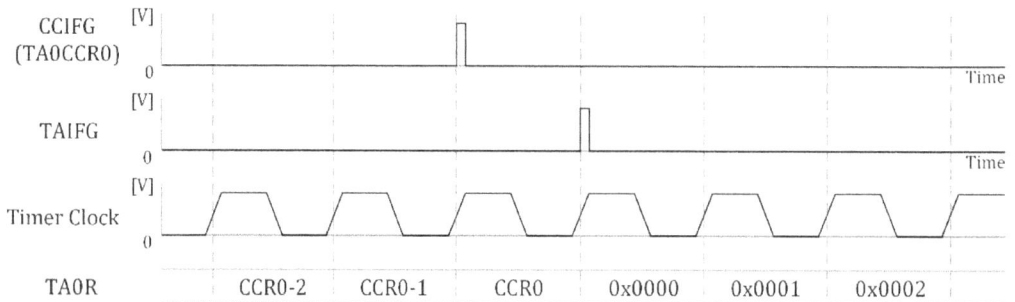

Figure 7.4. Up mode Flag setting [6].

There are two important interrupt flags associated with the Timer_A0. They are CCIFG and TAIFG. The CCIFG is a part of TA0CCR0, and the TAIFG is a part of TA0CTL. There is one TAIFG in TA0. However, there are multiple CCIFGs in TA0. For instance, a CCIFG bit is in TA0CCR0. And, there is another CCIFG bit in TA0CCR1.

In this up mode, the counter behavior is dependent on CCIFG in TA0CCR0. As the counter reaches at the TA0CCR0, a CCIFG interrupt flag is to be triggered. Then, as the counter is rolled off to zero, a TAIFG interrupt flag is to be triggered.

Next, if the MC bits are configured to 2, this timer is in continuous mode. In this mode, timer can count up to 0xFFFF. Then it rolls off to zero. This is the count pattern, and it will keep repeating. The count pattern in continuous mode is shown in Figure7.5. This figure shows that the value of TA0R keeps increasing, and it rolls off to zero.

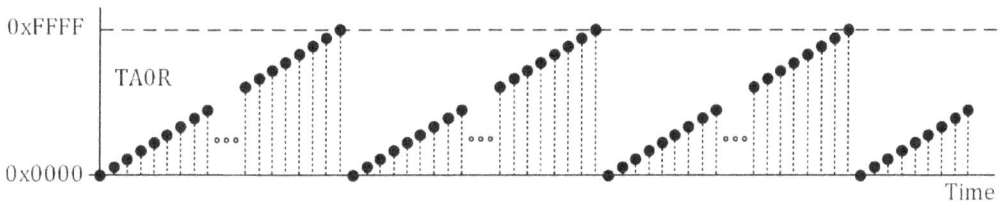

Figure 7.5. Count pattern for Continuous mode [6].

Let us examine an interrupt flag behavior as shown in Figure 7.6. Since this is in continuous mode, a CCIFG is not necessarily relevant. However, as the value of TA0R rolls off to zero, a TAIFG interrupt flag is to be triggered.

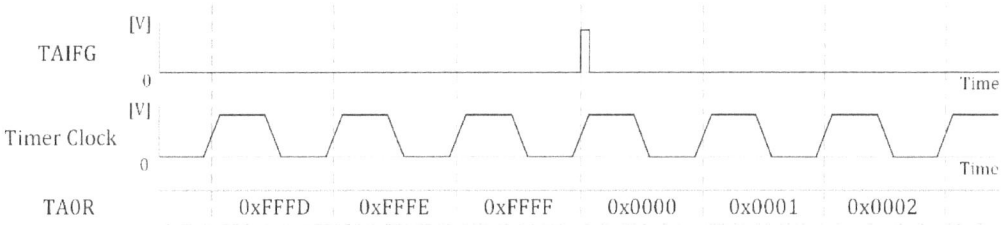

Figure 7.6. Continuous mode Flag setting [6].

A pulse generation program is shown in Program 7.1. This code is based on the use of a CCIFG flag, and it is also based on a polling method. In this example, P3.0 is chosen to generate an output signal. TA0CCR0 is initialized as 5000. TA0CTL is configured to use SMCLK as the clock source, and it is configured in up mode. In the while loop, it keeps checking whether the CCIFG flag is set or not. If it is set, it toggles an output value of P3.0, and clear the CCIFG flag. This code generates digital signals at P3.0. It is recommended to use an oscilloscope to check this waveform. You can see that it is the square wave clock, and the frequency is about 300 Hz.

```c
#include "msp.h"
void main(void) {
    WDT_A->CTL = WDT_A_CTL_PW | WDT_A_CTL_HOLD;  // hold the watchdog timer
    P3->DIR |= BIT0;  // output direction
    TIMER_A0->CCR[0] = 5000;  // set the value of TA0CCR0
    TIMER_A0->CTL = TIMER_A_CTL_TASSEL_2 | TIMER_A_CTL_MC_1 |
TIMER_A_CTL_CLR;  // TA0CTL setup, up mode
    while(1) {
        if ((TIMER_A0->CCTL[0] & TIMER_A_CCTLN_CCIFG)!=0) {  // check CCIFG flag
            P3->OUT ^= BIT0;  // toggle P3.0
            TIMER_A0->CCTL[0] &= ~TIMER_A_CCTLN_CCIFG;  // clear CCIFG flag
        }
    }
}
```

Program 7.1. Pulse generation program using CCIFG flag (Polling).

Another pulse generation program is shown in Program 7.2. This code is based on the use of a TAIFG flag, and it is also based on a polling method. In the next chapter, we will examine ISR based programs instead.

Similar to the previous Program 7.1. P3.0 is an output port in Program 7.2. TA0CCR0 is initialized as 5000. The TA0CTL configuration in Program 7.2 is the same as the one in Program 7.1. In the while loop, it keeps checking whether the TAIFG is set or not. If it is set, it will toggle an output value of P3.0, and it will clear the TAIFG flag. Using an oscilloscope, you can see whether it can generate about the square wave clock with the frequency of about 300 Hz at P3.0.

```c
#include "msp.h"
void main(void) {
    WDT_A->CTL = WDT_A_CTL_PW | WDT_A_CTL_HOLD;  // hold the watchdog timer
    P3->DIR |= BIT0;  // output direction
    TIMER_A0->CCR[0] = 5000;  // set the value of TA0CCR0
    TIMER_A0->CTL = TIMER_A_CTL_TASSEL_2 | TIMER_A_CTL_MC_1 |
TIMER_A_CTL_CLR;  // TA0CTL setup, up mode
    while(1) {
        if ((TIMER_A0->CTL & TIMER_A_CTL_IFG)!=0) {  // check TAIFG flag
            P3->OUT ^= BIT0;  // toggle P3.0
            TIMER_A0->CTL &= ~TIMER_A_CTL_IFG;  // clear TAIFG flag
        }
    }
}
```

Program 7.2. Pulse generation program using TAIFG flag (Polling).

Piezo buzzer

We have generated square wave clock signals, and the clock frequency was within an audible frequency range. This means it can be used to generate an audible sound, if we can use a component such as a piezo buzzer.

A piezo buzzer has a piezoelectric disk element as shown in Figure 7.7. Piezo is from the Greek root, peizein, which means "to press." This is a transducer component. A transducer can convert energy from one form to another form, and in this case, piezoelectric disk element can covert the electrical energy to mechanical energy and vice versa. A piezo buzzer is a component with the piezoelectric disk element in a plastic package, which can be used as a small low-quality speaker.

piezoelectric
disk element

piezo buzzer

Figure 7.7. Piezoelectric disk element and piezo buzzer.

A connection diagram for a piezo buzzer application is shown in Figure 7.8. It shows a piezo buzzer component, and it can be a small size generic piezo buzzer. On a BH EDU board, TDK piezo buzzer model, PS1740P02E, is mounted [11].

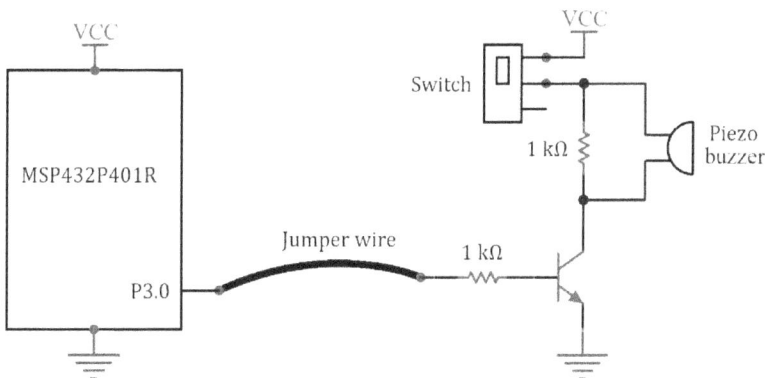

Figure 7.8. Piezo buzzer application.

A transistor and two resistors are used in this his buzzer application circuit. In addition, there is a switch (SW). This switch is not essential; however, it would be useful because it can cut off the sound immediately by isolating the power. The reason of adding this cut-off switch is to provide a method of turning off the buzzer while students, while users are developing an application. Otherwise, it could become uncomfortable as they have to hear the buzzer sound for a while. This switch can be replaced with a jumper.

If a developer needs to pursue a simpler circuit configuration, there is an alternative connection scheme. A piezo buzzer can be connected directly to P3.0. But, users need to add a resistor such as a 1kΩ resistor in series between the piezo buzzer and P3.0. The other node of the piezo buzzer pins needs to be connected to ground.

In case, users want to generate a musical tone. As a reference, selected frequencies of musical notes are shown in Table 7.2. C4 is the middle C in a piano keyboard. The frequency is 261.626 Hz. They can hear the buzzer sound when they can execute either of Program 7.1 or Program 7.2. The frequency that users have generated is about 300 Hz. It is in between D4 and D#4. For an experiment, users can generate different frequencies to play a music scale. It will help to play the basic musical notes. Different frequencies can be generated by changing the value of TA0CCR0. Next, users can create their own simple buzzer music song using these basic musical notes.

Note	Freq. (Hz)	Note	Freq. (Hz)	Note	Freq. (Hz)
C4	261.626	C5	523.251	C6	1046.502
C#4	277.183	C#5	554.365	C#6	1108.731
D4	293.665	D5	587.330	D6	1174.659
D#4	311.127	D#5	622.254	D#6	1244.508
E4	329.628	E5	659.255	E6	1318.510
F4	349.228	F5	698.457	F6	1396.913
F#4	369.994	F#5	739.989	F#6	1479.978
G4	391.995	G5	783.991	G6	1567.982
G#4	415.305	G#5	830.609	G#6	1661.219
A4	440.000	A5	880.000	A6	1760.000
A#4	466.164	A#5	932.328	A#6	1864.656
B4	493.883	B5	987.767	B6	1975.533

Table 7.2. Selected frequencies of musical notes.

Chapter 8. Interrupt

Typical microcontrollers/microprocessors can suspend what they are doing and process an interrupt service routine (ISR) if an interrupt service is requested. This interrupt can solve a response problem, and it is important in providing a capability to process and run many tasks concurrently. However, there could be some problems if they are not properly handled.

When the interrupt is requested, its full context including registers, processor status, and some of the relevant data may need to be saved properly. When returned, the context may need to be restored properly. If there is shared data that was not managed properly, the system may suffer from a shared data problem between concurrent tasks.

Moreover, there are non-maskable interrupts. They cannot be disabled by a program or a user. Interrupt priority was already defined in a hardware level. Low priority interrupts may suffer from latency. We will study how to resolve these matters through various software architectures in Chapter 12.

An Arm Cortex-M4F core provides a Nested Vectored Interrupt Controller (NVIC). It supports handling various interrupts and exceptions. This NVIC was customized to be operated properly with a specific hardware configuration. An MSP432P401R has an Arm Cortex-M4F core as well as the NVIC for handling exceptions and interrupts. Although there can be some similarities across Arm Cortex-M3/M4 core model, their NVIC configuration might vary by MCU model.

NVIC in an MSP432P401R MCU

The NVIC in an MSP432P401R MCU prioritizes and handles all exceptions, and it has 64 external interrupt lines and 8 levels of priority. When an exception occurs, it is processed in Handler mode. The context gets stored in stack memory and restored at the end of ISR. The relevant ISR vector is fetched and processed. Each exception would be in one of the states, and they are *Inactive*, *Pending*, *Active*, or *Active and Pending*. If it is in *Pending state*, this means the exception is not serviced yet; but it is waiting to be serviced. An exception in *Active state* means it is being serviced but it is not completed. An exception in *Active and Pending* means it is being serviced, but, there is a pending exception from the same source.

Exception types were briefly covered in Chapter 3 as shown in Table 3.2. There are various exception types. For the vector numbers higher than 16, they are for peripheral interrupts. These peripheral interrupts can be implemented differently by MCU. For an MSP432P401R MCU, exception numbers for ISER1 and ISE0 registers are listed in Table 8.1. As it was briefly discussed in Chapter 6, the ISER0 can process IRQ from 0 to 31 and the ISER1 can process IRQ from 32 to 63. For P1

I/O port interrupt, the exception number is 35 from the table. This means the BIT3 in ISER1 register. PORT1_IRQn header was predefined, and it is simply 35.

Exception number	Source		Exception number	Source
0	PSS		21	eUSCI_B1
1	CS		22	eUSCI_B2
2	PCM		23	eUSCI_B3
3	WDT_A		24	Precision ADC
4	FPU_INT		25	Timer32_INT1
5	FLCTL		26	Timer32_INT2
6	COMP_E0		27	Timer32_INTC
7	COMP_E1		28	AES256
8	Timer_A0		29	RTC_C
9	Timer_A0		30	DMA_ERR
10	Timer_A1		31	DMA_INT3
11	Timer_A1		32	DMA_INT2
12	Timer_A2		33	DMA_INT1
13	Timer_A2		34	DMA_INT0
14	Timer_A3		35	P1 I/O Port
15	Timer_A3		36	P2 I/O Port
16	eUSCI_A0		37	P3 I/O Port
17	eUSCI_A1		38	P4 I/O Port
18	eUSCI_A2		39	P5 I/O Port
19	eUSCI_A3		40	P6 I/O Port
20	eUSCI_B0		41 - 63	Reserved

Table 8.1. Exception numbers for ISER1 and ISE0 registers (MSP432P401R) [1].

I/O Port ISR

Program 8.1 shows an ISR based button and LED example. The function of this program is similar to the one shown in Program 5.1. In this code, there is P1IE register, it enables the interrupt for P1.1. P1ES register is configured to be responsive to high-to-low transition. A global interrupt needs to be enabled to take an effect on processing interrupts. Also, NVIC is configured properly for Port 1 in this code.

You can find the "Port1_IRQHandler" subroutine. This ISR gets to be executed, as the interrupt is request. First, it checks whether the interrupt flag for BIT1 is set or not. If the flag is set, it will toggle the value of the output of P1.0. It will toggle the Red LED. The program has a line adding a time delay. This is for the switch debounce. Then, it clears the interrupt flag.

In the while loop, it can blink a Red color of an RGB LED. Let us say this is a main task. Users can add their own task in this main loop as needed. Then, it can process this task in the main loop and the button process task concurrently. This program is "functional." However, this program contains a bad practice that is not typically recommended in an ISR code. A good practice is to write a short ISR code as possible. This means it is a good idea to spend a short amount of time on an ISR routine and manage the program to spend most of CPU time on a main routine. In this ISR routine, an extra time delay was intentionally added. This was needed for the switch debounce. For this reason, this code may need to be revised. One of the possible solutions is to use a shared variable and process this variable in the main loop for the short delay and suspending another ISR process. Making ISR short is very important and a recommended practice. This topic is related to software architectures that we will study in Chapter 12.

```
#include "msp.h"
void main(void) {
    WDT_A->CTL = WDT_A_CTL_PW | WDT_A_CTL_HOLD;  // hold the watchdog timer
    P1->DIR |= BIT0;  // output direction for P1.0
    P2->DIR |= BIT0;  // output direction for P2.0
    P1->DIR &= ~BIT1;  // input direction for P1.1
    P1->REN |= BIT1;  // enable internal resistor
    P1->OUT |= BIT1;  // pull-up resistor
    P1->IES |= BIT1;  // interrupt on high-to-low transition
    P1->IFG &= ~BIT1;  // clear interrupt flag
    P1->IE |= BIT1;  // enable interrupt for P1.1
    _enable_irq();  // enable global interrupt
    NVIC->ISER[1] = 1 << ((PORT1_IRQn) & 31);  // NVIC setup
    while(1) {
        // main task
        P2->OUT ^= BIT0;  // toggle an LED
        _delay_cycles(500000);  // delay
    }
}

void PORT1_IRQHandler(void) {
    if(P1->IFG & BIT1) {
        P1->OUT ^= BIT0;  // toggle an LED
    }
    _delay_cycles(1000);  // switch debounce
    P1->IFG &= ~BIT1;  // clear interrupt flag
}
```

Program 8.1. ISR based button and LED program.

Timer_A0 ISR

In the previous chapter, we have studied the timer_A0 and the two cases of example programs. They were based on polling methods. In this section, ISR based programs will be presented. Program 8.2 shows the ISR based pulse generation program using CCIFG. In this code, TA0CCIFG interrupt is enabled. This was achieved by the code line as follows:

TIMER_A0->CCTL[0] = TIMER_A_CCTLN_CCIE

As it was described previously, a global interrupt needs to be enabled. NVIC is configured for Timer_A0 as follows:

NVIC->ISER[0] = 1 << ((TA0_0_IRQn) & 31);

TA0_0_IRQn is pre-defined, and it is simply 8. Since it is less than 31, it needs to be stored in ISER[0]. Previously, it was stored in ISER[1] for Port 1. In the while loop, it blinks the LED. The name of the ISR subroutine is "TA0_0_IRQHandler." It can toggle P3.0. The piezo buzzer is assumed to be connected to this pin. After toggling P3.0, it clears the CCIFG flag.

This code can blink the Red LED and it can generate digital clock signals concurrently. In the previous Chapter, it was suggested to write a simple piezo buzzer music as an experiment. Using this interrupt-based code, the simple piezo buzzer music program can be written easier and more efficiently.

It is worth mentioning that this is a flexible clock generation method, and it can generate the clock signals at any of the GPIO pins. There is a hardware-based method of generating the clock signals. In this method, the signals can be generated through a specific pin. In Chapter 13, we will study a hardware method that can be used in generating variable frequencies.

```
#include "msp.h"
void main(void) {
    WDT_A->CTL = WDT_A_CTL_PW | WDT_A_CTL_HOLD;  // hold the watchdog timer
    P1->DIR |= BIT0;  // output direction for an LED
    P3->DIR |= BIT0;  // output direction
    TIMER_A0->CCR[0] = 5000;  // set the value of TA0CCR0
    TIMER_A0->CTL = TIMER_A_CTL_TASSEL_2 | TIMER_A_CTL_MC_1 |
TIMER_A_CTL_CLR;  // TA0CTL setup, up mode
    TIMER_A0->CCTL[0] = TIMER_A_CCTLN_CCIE;  // enable CCIE interrupt
    _enable_irq();  // enable global interrupt
    NVIC->ISER[0] = 1 << ((TA0_0_IRQn) & 31);  // NVIC setup
    while(1) {
        P1->OUT ^= BIT0;  // toggle an LED
        _delay_cycles(500000);  // delay
    }
}

void TA0_0_IRQHandler(void) {
    if((TIMER_A0->CCTL[0] & TIMER_A_CCTLN_CCIFG)!=0) {  // check CCIFG flag
        P3->OUT ^= BIT0;  // toggle P3.0
        TIMER_A0->CCTL[0] &= ~TIMER_A_CCTLN_CCIFG;  // clear CCIFG flag
    }
}
```

Program 8.2. Pulse generation program using CCIFG flag (ISR based).

Now, pulse generation code using TAIFG flag is shown in program 8.3. In comparison with the code using CCIFG flag, this code using TAIFG flag has a different interrupt configuration. For instance, in order to configure a TAIFG interrupt flag, TAIE needs to be enabled as follows:

TIMER_A0->CTL |= TIMER_A_CTL_IE;

The name of the ISR subroutine is "TA0_N_IRQHandler." This is a different one from the one used previously in the previous CCIFG case. In this ISR, it checks whether TAIFG is set or not. If it is set, it can toggle a P3.0 bit. Then, it clears the TAIFG flag. Similar to the previous case, this code also can blink the LED, it can generate the clock signals concurrently. Both of Program 8.2 and Program 8.3 can perform the similar tasks as we have seen in Chapter 7. However, the internal operations such as the method of processing and generating the clock signals are different.

```
#include "msp.h"
void main(void) {
   WDT_A->CTL = WDT_A_CTL_PW | WDT_A_CTL_HOLD;  // hold the watchdog timer
   P1->DIR |= BIT0;  // output direction for an LED
   P3->DIR |= BIT0;  // output direction
   TIMER_A0->CCR[0] = 5000;  // set the value of TA0CCR0
   TIMER_A0->CTL = TIMER_A_CTL_TASSEL_2 | TIMER_A_CTL_MC_1 |
TIMER_A_CTL_CLR;  // TA0CTL setup, up mode
   TIMER_A0->CTL |= TIMER_A_CTL_IE;  // enable TAIE interrupt
   _enable_irq();  // enable global interrupt
   NVIC->ISER[0] = 1 << ((TA0_N_IRQn) & 31);  // NVIC setup
   while(1) {
      P1->OUT ^= BIT0;  // toggle an LED
      _delay_cycles(500000);  // delay
   }
}

void TA0_N_IRQHandler(void)
{
   if((TIMER_A0->CTL & TIMER_A_CTL_IFG)!=0) {  // check TAIFG flag
      P3->OUT ^= BIT0;  // toggle P3.0
      TIMER_A0->CTL &= ~TIMER_A_CTL_IFG;  // clear TAIFG flag
   }
}
```

Program 8.3. Pulse generation program using TAIFG flag (ISR based).

Chapter 9. Display

In many embedded systems, it is common to use a small or large display module. The requirement for a product may vary, and there is a wide selection of the display modules. The display modules can be categorized in several ways. First, we can categorize it whether it is a monochrome or color display. It is common to see color displays in embedded systems. If the product does not require a color display, the implementation would become easier as the system can use a monochrome display instead. Next, we can categorize it whether it is a graphic or character display. A graphic display is common because it is flexible in displaying data on a screen, and it is typically user friendly. One of the problems is that the development may take longer. If the requirement of the product is simply to display the numeric or character data, a character display may be a reasonable choice as it can reduce the developmental effort. In this chapter, we will study a monochrome character LCD module and we will learn how to control it.

Liquid Crystal Display (LCD)

A liquid-crystal display (LCD) is an electronically modulated optical device. It uses the light modulating properties and polarizers. LCD does not emit light directly. It is used with a backlight display or a reflect.

LCDs can be either positive or negative. This is dependent on the polarizer arrangement. For instance, a character on a positive LCD has Black letter on a backlight color background. On the other hand, a character on a negative LCD has a backlight color letter on a Black background.

A typical LCD module includes an LCD controller and an LCD glass. There are many small units of two polarizers between two electrodes on an LCD glass. An LCD controller can generate alternating voltages across the two electrodes. LCD segments glow when both of their back and front planes are enabled.

For an MSP432P401R MCU, in this book, we use the supply voltage of 3.3 V, and we will use a 3.3-V LCD module in order to minimize the extra design effort. However, it would be easier find 5-V LCD modules, and some of 5-V LCD module models can be used instead with careful and proper specification considerations.

LCD module

As described, a 3.3-V LCD module is selected to make it work with an MSP432P401R MCU. The part number is NHD-0216HZ-FSW-FBW-33V3C. There are many generic LCD modules with a similar programming method. This LCD is the one used in a BH EDU board. For the reader who owns a generic LCD module, the theory and the programming method in this chapter can be applied since there are similarities. But, they may need to refer to the datasheet from the LCD manufacturer carefully.

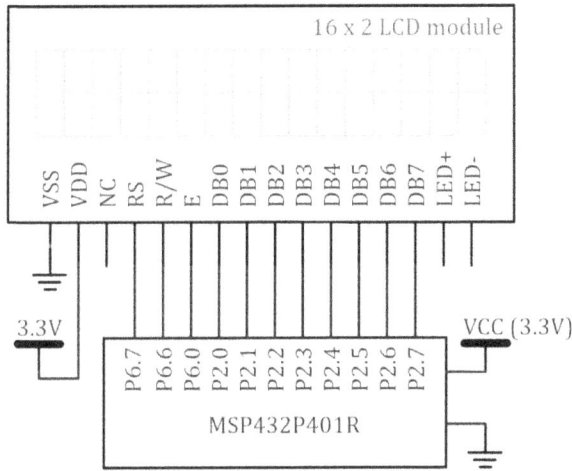

Figure 9.1. Connection diagram for the LCD module (NHD-0216HZ-FSW-FBW-33V3C).

The connection diagram using this specific 3.3-V LCD module (NHD-0216HZ-FSW-FBW-33V3C) is shown in Figure 9.1. The third pin from the right is N/C (no connect) for this module. This is different from a generic LCD module. This pin is, typically, "contrast adjust" in a generic LCD module. It can change the contrast of the LCD screen by applying a different voltage level to this pin. This voltage level provided through this pin is important to display the characters correctly. In this 3.3-V LCD module, this pin is not used.

Symbol	Pin	Description
VSS	1	Ground
VDD	2	Supply Voltage (+3.3V)
NC	3	No Connect
RS	4	Register Select signal. RS=0: Command, RS=1: Data
R/W	5	Read/Write select signal. R/W=1: Read, R/W=0: Write
E	6	Enable signal (Falling edge triggered)
DB0 ~ DB7	7~14	Data bus lines.
LED+	15	Backlight LED Anode (+3.0V)
LED-	16	Backlight LED Cathode (Ground)

Table 9.1. Pin description [12].

The pin descriptions are shown in Table 9.1. In this chapter, an 8-bit operation will be used, which means we use DB0 ~DB7. However, it is possible to use it in a 4-bit operation instead. In that case, users can use only DB4 ~ DB7 from the data bus lines. On a BH EDU board, the connections to the backlight LED (pin 15 and pin 16) were intentionally removed. If needed, users can enable the backlight LED. However, the normal voltage for this backlight LED is 3.0 V and the max voltage is 3.2 V.

Instruction

There are two control pins of *RS* and *R/W*. Moreover, in order for communication, the edge signal of *E* with a proper time delay needs to be generated manually. It is worth of mentioning that the input through the *E* is a falling edge sensitive. The operations according to *RS* and *R/W* bits are shown in Table 9.2. If *RS* pin is low, this means that it is related to "command". If *RS* pin is high, this means it is related to "data" operations. *R/W* pin is simply for the choice between *read* or *write* operations. In some of open hardware designs, it can be found that this pin is connected to ground. In that case, data can be written to the LCD module; but, the data cannot be read from the LCD module. These open hardware designs are functional but, this is not an efficient method. For an optimal control of an LCD, a programmer can check the busy flag before sending the data. In that case, we may need to read data from the LCD module.

RS	R/W	Operation
0	0	Write command
0	1	Read Busy flag (DB7) and address counter (DB0 ~ DB6)
1	0	Write data
1	1	Read data

Table 9.2. Operations according to RS and R/W bits [12].

Busy Flag (BF)

As mentioned, a busy flag can be checked before sending the data. If *RS* is low and *R/W* is high, busy flag can be read through DB7. If *BF* is high, it indicates that the internal operation is still in processing.

Address Counter (AC)

Address Counter (AC) can be used for the Display Data RAM (DDRAM) address or Character Generator ROM (CGROM) address.

Display Data RAM (DDRAM)

Display data RAM (DDRAM) can be used for display data in an 8-bit character code. The 8-bit character code contains a part of an ASCII code set; but, it is not the same as an ASCII code. You can refer to datasheet for the character set [12]. The DDRAM address for the 2 x 16 character display case is shown in Figure 9.2. The first line address starts from 0x00 and it ends at 0x0F. However, the second line address starts from 0x40 and it ends at 0x4F. There is a noticeable address gap in-between the first line and the second line.

LCD position	1	2	3	4	5	6	7	8	9	10	11	12	13	14	15	16
DDRAM address	00h	01h	02h	03h	04h	05h	06h	07h	08h	09h	0Ah	0Bh	0Ch	0Dh	0Eh	0Fh
	40h	41h	42h	43h	44h	45h	46h	47h	48h	49h	4Ah	4Bh	4Ch	4Dh	4Eh	4Fh

Figure 9.2. DDRAM address allocation for the 2 x 16 character display [12].

Character Generator ROM (CGROM)
The character generator ROM can generate either 5x8 or 5x11 dot character patterns.

Character Generator RAM (CGRAM)
Character Generator RAM (CGRAM) can be used to create user defined character patterns. For 5 x 8 dots, users can create eight-character patterns. For 5 x 11 dots, users can create four-character patterns.

Instruction Table
A summary of the selected instruction table is shown Table 9.3. For *"Clear Display"*, both *RS* and *R/W* need to be low, and the value of the command is 0x01. It may take about 1.52 ms to process it. So, this is not a trivial delay. This is the reason why the frequent use of the clear display is not recommended.

Users can set the LCD position. For instance, if they want to write characters on the 2nd line of the LCD. They can choose *"set DDRAM address,"* and use 0x40 as the address counter. Then, it will result in the command code of 0xC0.

		Instruction								Description
RS	R/W	DB7	DB6	DB5	DB4	DB3	DB2	DB1	DB0	
0	0	0	0	0	0	0	0	0	1	Clear display
0	0	0	0	0	0	0	0	1	-	Return home
0	0	0	0	0	0	0	1	I/D	SH	Entry mode set
0	0	0	0	0	0	1	D	C	B	Display ON/OFF
0	0	0	0	0	1	S/C	R/L	-	-	Cursor/Display shift
0	0	0	0	1	DL	N	F	-	-	Function set
0	0	0	1	AC5	AC4	AC3	AC2	AC1	AC0	Set CGRAM addr.
0	0	1	AC6	AC5	AC4	AC3	AC2	AC1	AC0	Set DDRAM addr.
0	1	BF	AC6	AC5	AC4	AC3	AC2	AC1	AC0	Read Busy flag & address counter
1	0	D7	D6	D5	D4	D3	D2	D1	D0	Write data
1	1	D7	D6	D5	D4	D3	D2	D1	D0	Read data

Table 9.3. Selected instruction table [12].

LCD test program

An LCD test code is shown in Program 9.1 This is the implementation using a pseudo code given by the manufacturer. This code was written to be *functional* for a breadboard prototype environment. This means that extra time delays were added, and this code is not written for a good performance. Users can make modifications according to your own discretion and the connection settings of their system.

There are three subroutines. They are *LCD_command*, *LCD_write*, and *LCD_init*. For *LCD_command*, it is related to sending a command to the LCD module. *LCD_write* is related to sending a character data. *LCD_init* is to initialize the LCD. After running this code successfully, users can see "Test" characters that will be displayed on their LCD module.

```
#include "msp.h"
void LCD_command(unsigned char);
void LCD_write(unsigned char);
void LCD_init(void);
void main(void) {
    WDT_A->CTL = WDT_A_CTL_PW | WDT_A_CTL_HOLD;  // hold the watchdog timer
    P2->DIR |= 0xFF;  // output direction for P2
    P2->OUT &= ~0xFF;
    P6->DIR |= 0xC1;  // output direction for P6
    P6->OUT &= ~0xC1;
    LCD_init();  // LCD init.
    LCD_write('T');  // write test a character on the LCD module
    LCD_write('e');
    LCD_write('s');
    LCD_write('t');
    while(1) {
        __no_operation();
    }
}

void LCD_command(unsigned char in) {
    P2OUT = in;
    P6OUT &= ~BIT7;  // clear RS
    P6OUT &= ~BIT6;  // clear R/W
    P6OUT |= BIT0;  // set E
    __delay_cycles(300);
    P6OUT &= ~BIT0;  // clear E
}

void LCD_write(unsigned char in) {
    P2OUT = in;
    P6OUT |= BIT7;  // set RS
    P6OUT &= ~BIT6;  // clear R/W
    P6OUT |= BIT0;  // set E
    __delay_cycles(300);
    P6OUT &= ~BIT0;  // clear E
```

```
}
void LCD_init() {
  P6OUT &= ~BIT0;  // clear E
  _delay_cycles(15000);
  LCD_command(0x30);  // wake up
  _delay_cycles(500);
  LCD_command(0x30);
  _delay_cycles(500);
  LCD_command(0x30);
  _delay_cycles(500);
  LCD_command(0x38);  // function set: 8 bit/2-line
  LCD_command(0x10);  // set cursor
  LCD_command(0x0F);  // display on, cursor on
  LCD_command(0x06);  // entry mode set
  LCD_command(0x01);  // clear display
  _delay_cycles(5000);
}
```

Program 9.1. LCD test program.

Chapter 10. Analog to Digital Converter

Digital signals have a finite set of possible values. Analog signals can be converted to digital signals. An Analog to digital converter (ADC) can perform this conversion. For instance, analog audio signals can be converted to digital signals, and they can be stored in a portable SD memory card. This ADC unit is useful in various applications. Most of modern MCUs have at least one integrated ADC. An MSP432P401R has one 14-bit ADC with 24 channels. In this chapter, we will study basics of ADCs, and the use of the ADC module in an MSP432P401R MCU.

Sampling and Quantization

The ADC conversion process can be understood as sampling and quantization. Sampling converts analog signals into discrete time signals. These discrete time signals are defined at discrete times and the amplitude values are continuous. The discrete time signals can be obtained at uniformly spaced times. The period of the uniformly spaced times is related to a sampling rate. Next, the sequence of the finite numbers from the continuous amplitudes can be obtained by a quantization process. This sequence of the finite numbers is related to digital signals. Some of the relevant quantization levels are 256 (8 bit), 4,096 (12 bit), and 16,384 (14 bit).

Nyquist Sampling Theorem

A sufficient sampling rate (f_S) for a band limited signal (B) is higher than $2B$ according the nyquist sampling theorem. For instance, an audible frequency range is about 20 to 20 kHz. Based on the Nyquist sampling theorem, the sampling frequency needs to be higher than 40 kHz. In digital audio, 44.1 KHz is common sampling frequency, which is used in CD (compact disc) digital audio. Some ADC have implemented a sampling (f_S) rate close to $2B$. These are Nyquist ADCs. However, practically, it is common to find ADCs to perform oversampling by choosing higher frequency than $2B$.

14-bit SAR ADC

One of the common ADCs that can be found in an MCU is a successive approximation (SAR) ADC. A SAR ADC is a reasonable choice for an application that needs a decent resolution and conversion speed. It is suitable for a low power application, and the size of the SAR ADC on a chip is relatively small. Therefore, SAR ADCs can be found in many modern MCU ICs.

A SAR ADC has a DAC that can generate reference voltages in a binary fashion. The comparator can generate the output comparing the input voltage with these reference voltages in sequence. The SAR ADC implements a binary search algorithm. The binary output values in sequence from the comparator will be the converted digital data.

A conceptual block diagram of a 14-bit SAR with 24 input channels is shown in Figure 10.1. Let us suppose the first channel is selected properly. Then, the analog signal passes an analog multiplexer (mux) and the signal will be sampled. The sampled value is compared to the reference voltage generated by the 14-bit DAC. The output of the comparator gets stored in one of the bits in a 14-bit register. Let us assume this 14-bit DAC can generate the relevant binary weighted voltages. This process will be repeated until it can fill the rest of the bits in the 14 bit-register.

In this block diagram, there is one SAR ADC core, but it can receive 32 analog inputs through the analog mux component. This functional description is similar to the SAR ADC in MSP432P401R. It has one 14-bit SAR ADC core with up to input 24 channels. For the MSP432P401R model, it was implemented to have up to 24 channels.

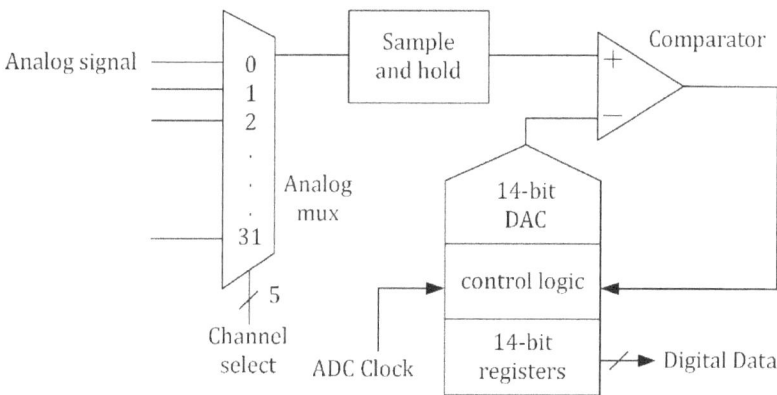

Figure 10.1. A conceptual block diagram of a14-bit SAR with 32 input channels.

Sigma Delta Converter

An MSP432P401R has an integrated SAR ADC. There are other types of ADCs such as Sigma Delta Converters. These Sigma Delta Converter can typically provide a higher sampling frequency and higher resolution. If your project needs this requirement, a designer can choose a different MCU with an integrated sigma delta converter, or the designer can use an additional standalone Sigma Delta Converter IC. The key technique of a Sigma Delta Converter is a sigma delta modulation. The delta-sigma modulator includes a quantizer and an integrator. The quantizer in the modulator generates a sequence of the digital signals.

ADC14

An MSP432P401R has an integrated ADC14 module. This a 14-bit SAR ADC and the module with up to 24 input channels. Figure 10.2 shows the simplified functional block diagram of the ADC14 module. The ADC core can covert analog signals to 14-bit digital signals. The programmable voltages of V_{R+} and V_{R-} are the upper and lower limit of the conversion. The full scale of the digital output (N_{ADC}) is 0x3FFF.

V_{in} is an input analog voltage. Then, the conversion formula of the 14-bit ADC for a single-ended mode is as follows:

$$N_{ADC} = 16383 \times \frac{V_{in} - V_{R-}}{V_{R+} - V_{R-}}$$

Using this equation, a designer can estimate the digital output (N_{ADC}) from the input voltage (V_{in}). Likewise, the input voltage (V_{in}) can be estimated by the digital output (N_{ADC}).

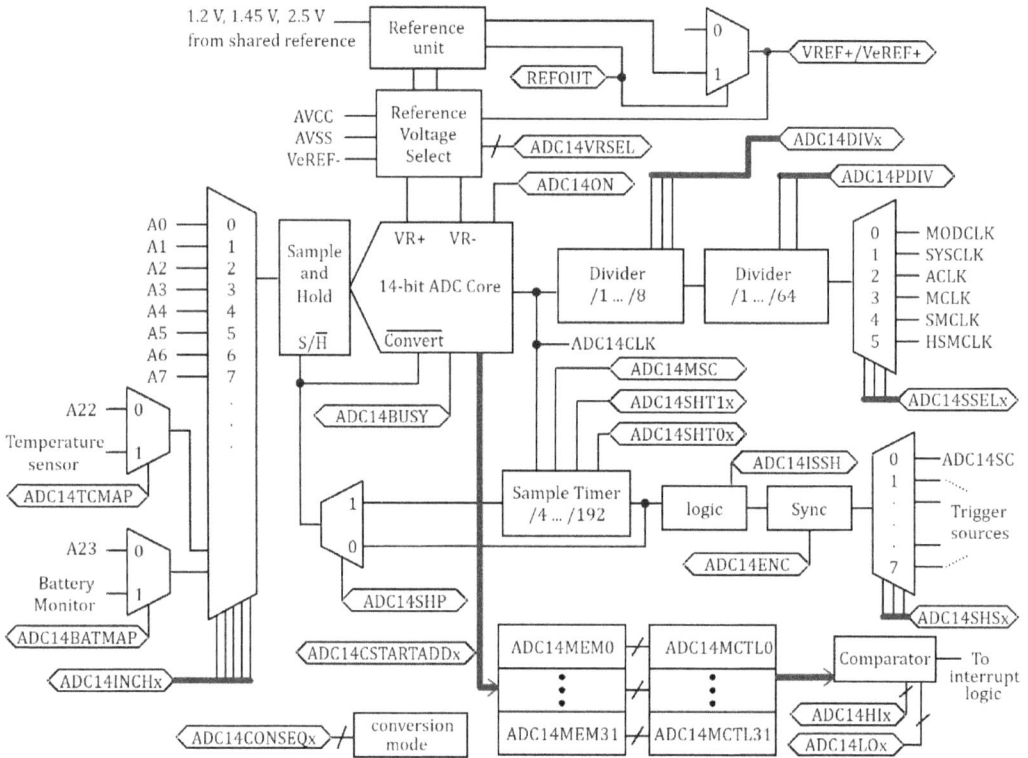

Figure 10.2. Simplified functional block diagram of ADC14 [6].

The converted digital data gets stored in the memory buffer. The memory buffer has memory registers of ADC14MEM[0]~ ADC14MEM[31]. The ADC conversion process can be initiated by ADC14SC bit. In this section, we will study the "single-channel single-conversion mode." In order to perform the test, a test circuit is configured as shown in Figure 10.3.

Readers can use a generic 1kΩ potentiometer for an experiment. The 10 Ω resistor that is connected in series was added for protection. For a BH EDU board, this potentiometer application circuit is already implemented. A user can simply connect P4.2 to a proper header on the BH EDU board.

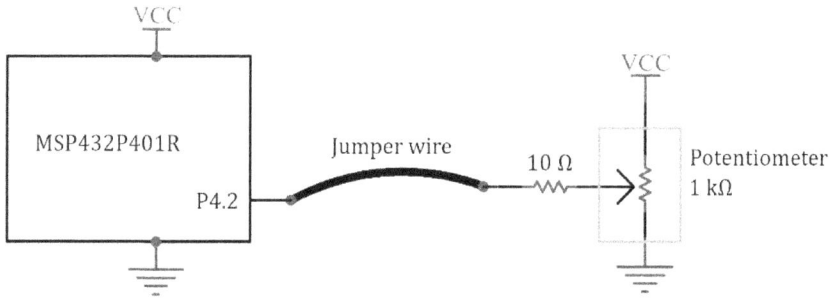

Figure 10.3. Simplified functional block diagram of ADC14.

ADC Test Example (Polling)

Program 10.1 shows an ADC test example. P4.2 is configured for the channel A11 by setting P4SEL1 and P4SEL0 bits. In the following line of the code, the ADC14->CTL0 is configured to turn the ADC on, and it also configures the timing of the ADC unit.

ADC14_CTL1_RES_3 was chosen to store the converted 14-bit data. The channel A11 was selected by configuring ADC14MCTL[0]. In the while loop, the ADC conversion is initiated by *ADC14_CTL0_SC*. There is another while loop that checks whether the ADC busy flag is set or not. The program stays in this while loop until the ADC conversion is completed. Then, the ADC result can be read using ADC14MEM[0], and it will be copied to *adc_raw*. Next, it can toggle a RED LED. This behavior of the ADC conversion and toggling an LED will be repeated in the loop.

```
#include "msp.h"
unsigned int adc_raw;
void main(void) {
    WDT_A->CTL = WDT_A_CTL_PW | WDT_A_CTL_HOLD;   // hold the watchdog timer
    P1->DIR |= 0x01;   // output direction for P1
    P4->SEL1 |= BIT2;   // alternative function, A11
    P4->SEL0 |= BIT2;   // alternative function, A11
    ADC14->CTL0 = ADC14_CTL0_SHT0_6 | ADC14_CTL0_SHP | ADC14_CTL0_ON;
                                                   // ADC14CTL0, ADC14ON
    ADC14->CTL1 = ADC14_CTL1_RES_3;   // 14 bit
    ADC14->MCTL[0] = ADC14_MCTLN_INCH_11;   // channel selection
    while(1) {
        ADC14->CTL0 |= ADC14_CTL0_ENC | ADC14_CTL0_SC;   // start conversion
        while ((ADC14->CTL0 & ADC14_CTL0_BUSY)!=0);   // busy flag check
        adc_raw=ADC14->MEM[0];   // read ADC
        P1->OUT ^= 0x01;   // toggle an LED
        _delay_cycles(50000);
    }
}
```

Program 10.1. ADC test example (Polling based).

Since the ADC result was copied to a global variable, *adc_raw*. There are many ways to check this value. One of them is to suspend the program in Code Composer Studio and move the cursor over the variable. Then, the value in stored in this variable will be displayed.

ADC Test Example (ISR)

The example code in the previous section was based on a polling method. It would be useful to write a ISR based code that can perform a similar task. Therefore, this ISR based ADC example code was written as shown in Program 10.2.

```
#include "msp.h"
unsigned int adc_raw;
void main(void) {
    WDT_A->CTL = WDT_A_CTL_PW | WDT_A_CTL_HOLD;  // hold the watchdog timer
    P1->DIR |= 0x01;  // output direction for P1
    P4->SEL1 |= BIT2;  // alternative function, A11
    P4->SEL0 |= BIT2;  // alternative function, A11
    ADC14->CTL0 = ADC14_CTL0_SHT0_6 | ADC14_CTL0_SHP | ADC14_CTL0_ON;
                                                // ADC14CTL0, ADC14ON
    ADC14->CTL1 = ADC14_CTL1_RES_3;  // 14 bit
    ADC14->MCTL[0] = ADC14_MCTLN_INCH_11;  // channel selection
    ADC14->IER0 |= ADC14_IER0_IE0;  // ADC ISR setup
    NVIC->ISER[0] = 1 << ((ADC14_IRQn) & 31);  // NVIC setup
    _enable_irq();  // enable global interrupt
    while(1) {
        ADC14->CTL0 |= ADC14_CTL0_ENC | ADC14_CTL0_SC;  // start conversion
        P1->OUT ^= 0x01;  // toggle an LED
        _delay_cycles(50000);
    }
}

void ADC14_IRQHandler(void) {
    adc_raw=ADC14->MEM[0];  // read ADC
}
```

Program 10.2. ADC test example (ISR based).

This code is similar to the example code previously shown in Program 10.1. The major difference is related to an ISR set up and the ISR. The interrupt configuration for the ADC ISR was performed using the code lines as follows:

```
ADC14->IER0 |= ADC14_IER0_IE0;
NVIC->ISER[0] = 1 << ((ADC14_IRQn) & 31);
```

The ADC interrupt is enabled by setting *ADC14_IER0_IE0* bit in *ADC14ISER0*, and the NVIC bit is set properly. For a reference, *ADC14_IRQn* is 24. The ISR name is "*ADC14_IRQHandler*".

In this ISR code, the ADC result will be copied to a global variable, *adc_raw*. As you have done in the previous example, you can check this variable to find out whether the ADC conversion was successful or not. Another indication of the completion of the ADC conversion is to check whether the Red LED keeps bilking or not.

Chapter 11. ADC Applications

Many embedded system applications have been using ADCs. For instance, the ADCs can be used in processing analog signals from various sensors. It is common to find sensors showing variations in resistance values or voltage levels with respect to physical states of the sensors. Let us consider temperature sensor applications. The variations of the values in resistances or voltages can be observed when the sensors are exposed to different temperatures. With the use of proper interface circuits, the variations can be measured using ADCs. The MCUs can provide digital communication interfaces for other embedded systems, and the digital sensor data can be transferred to another system. This configuration can be typically found in a temperature sensor application. As we have studied previously, an MSP432P401R MCU has an ADC module. In this chapter, we will study temperature sensor and accelerometer applications. The techniques can be applied to other ADC applications.

Temperature Sensors

The temperature measurements in embedded systems are common and there are many different temperature sensor applications. It can be easy to overlook the needs of understanding the physical characteristics of temperature sensors and the considerations of the testing environment. To analyze the temperature data properly, it is recommended to obtain the knowledge about the sensor characteristics and their limitations.

In this chapter, we will study four temperature sensor types. They are *Resistance Temperature Detector*, *Thermocouple*, *Thermistor*, and *Semiconductor-based temperature sensors*. They are briefly summarized in the following sections.

Resistance Temperature Detector (RTD)

A resistance temperature detector (RTD) sensor can measure temperatures based on the resistance variations in a metal wire. The RTD wire is commonly made of a pure material such as platinum, nickel, or copper. Platinum RTDs can provide high accuracies, and a typical operating range is –200 °C to 600 °C.

Thermocouple

Thermocouple temperature sensor type consists of two wires that are made of different metals. There are several types of Thermocouples. Wires at one side are connected each other, and they form a hot junction. The wires at the other side are connected each other to form a cold junction. Typically, the hot junction is a measuring point. The varying voltages that can be measured due to the use of the different metals are associated with the temperature variations. The measurements can be found to be nonlinear; therefore, it needs a proper conversion. The accuracy is a bit low, but the thermocouple sensors can be used in the application that needs a wide temperature range. The temperature ranges vary by type, and one of example operating ranges is −200 °C to 1750 °C.

Thermistor

A thermistor is a thermally sensitive resistor that shows the value of resistance can change as the temperature changes. There are two types of the thermistors. They are *Negative Temperature Coefficient (NTC) thermistor* and *Positive Temperature Coefficient (PTC) thermistor*. Typically, NTC thermistors are used as temperature sensors. The resistance of NTC thermistors will decrease as the temperature increases. NTC Thermistors shows non-linear resistance variations with respect to the temperature variations. NTC thermistors are suitable for various applications. An example operating temperature range is −50 °C to 250 °C.

PTC thermistors are also temperature sensitive, but the resistance will increase as the temperature increases. PTC Thermistors are typically used in circuit protection applications. A certain level of the overcurrent through a PTC can cause a high temperature on the PTC. The resistance of the PTC will increase significantly. When the cause of the overcurrent is eliminated and the PTC sensor is cooled down, the resistance will be decreased, and the circuit will work again. This is like a resettable fuse, and this can be used in a circuit protection application.

Semiconductor-based Temperature Sensor

Temperature sensors can be designed and placed on integrated circuits (ICs). They are often implemented by diodes and transistors. It can be grouped as *voltage output*, *current output*, *resistance output*, *digital output* and *diode* types. Semiconductor temperature sensors are implemented on a chip, and the chip is placed inside of the IC packages. IC packages are not necessarily designed for a thermal conduction. Therefore, there can be limitations in making a good thermal contact. In general, semiconductor-based temperature sensors are commonly found in embedded system applications. These sensors are low cost, and the sizes of the sensors are small. However, in general, they may not be suitable for the temperature applications that need high accuracy and a wide operating range. An example operating range is −40 °C to 120 °C.

Integrated Temperature Sensor in an MSP432P401R MCU

An MSP432P401R MCU has a built-in temperature sensor. The temperature sensor data can be accessed. This temperature sensor can be enabled by setting *ADC14TCMAP* bit in the *ADC14CTL1* register and clearing *REFTCOFF* bit in the *REF_A* module. The *REF_A* module is a reference system that can be used to generate references voltages. In an MSP432P401R MCU, this integrated temperature sensor is connected to the channel A22. Therefore, the voltage that is relevant to the temperature sensor can be read through the channel A22.

The manufacturer provides calibration data measured at 30°C ±3°C and 85°C ±3°C under certain internal voltage reference states of 1.25 V, 1.45, and 2.5 V. The temperature in Celsius degree (°C) can be calculated using the characteristic equations as follows:

$$Temp(°C) = (adc\_raw - Ref\_T30) \times \left(\frac{85 - 30}{Ref\_T85 - Ref\_T30}\right) + 30$$

The temperature data in Fahrenheit degree (°F) can be obtained by a simple mathematical formula. An integrated temperature sensor test code is shown in Program 11.1.

In this code, the 2.5-V internal reference voltage is enabled. The temperature sensor calibration data for the 2.5-V reference voltage was read from the MCU. ADC14_CTL1_RES_3 was chosen to store the converted 14-bit data. Moreover, the *ADC14CTL0, ADC14CTL1*, and *ADC14MCTL[0]* registers are configured as we have studied previously. In the while loop, the ADC value is read and converted to the corresponding temperatures in Celsius degree (°C).

```
#include "msp.h"
unsigned int adc_raw;
float TempDegC;
void main(void) {
    WDT_A->CTL = WDT_A_CTL_PW | WDT_A_CTL_HOLD;  // hold the watchdog timer
    P1->DIR |= 0x01;  // output direction for Red LED
    P8->DIR &= ~BIT3;  // input direction for P8.3 (optional)
    while(REF_A->CTL0 & REF_A_CTL0_GENBUSY);  // wait until the busy flag is cleared
    REF_A->CTL0 |= REF_A_CTL0_VSEL_3 | REF_A_CTL0_ON;  // enable internal 2.5V ref.
    REF_A->CTL0 &= ~REF_A_CTL0_TCOFF;  // enable temperature sensor
    int32_t Ref_T30=TLV->ADC14_REF2P5V_TS30C;  // temp. cal. (30degC/2.5V/14bit)
    int32_t Ref_T85=TLV->ADC14_REF2P5V_TS85C;  // temp. cal. (85degC/2.5V/14bit)
    ADC14->CTL0 = ADC14_CTL0_SHT0_6 | ADC14_CTL0_SHP | ADC14_CTL0_ON;
                                                                    // ADC CTL0
    ADC14->CTL1 = ADC14_CTL1_RES_3;  // 14 bit
    ADC14->CTL1 |= ADC14_CTL1_TCMAP;  // select ADC14TCMAP channel
    ADC14->MCTL[0] = ADC14_MCTLN_VRSEL_1 | ADC14_MCTLN_INCH_22;
                                          // V(R+) = VREF buffered, ADC channel selection
    while(1) {
        ADC14->CTL0 |= ADC14_CTL0_ENC | ADC14_CTL0_SC;  // ADC, Start conversion
        while ((ADC14->CTL0 & ADC14_CTL0_BUSY)!=0);  // wait until busy flag is cleared
        adc_raw=ADC14->MEM[0];  // read ADC
        TempDegC = (((float) adc_raw - Ref_T30) * 55) / (Ref_T85 - Ref_T30) + 30.0;
                                                        // temperature conversion
```

```
        P1->OUT ^= 0x01;    // toggle an LED
        __delay_cycles(50000);
    }
}
```

Program 11.1. Integrated temperature sensor test example.

Accelerometers

An accelerometer sensor can measure acceleration. For instance, when an accelerometer is at rest on the surface of the earth toward upwards, the acceleration will be measured approximately as +g ($\approx$ 9.81 m/s). When an accelerometer is in free fall, the acceleration will be measured approximately as zero.

Accelerometers have used in many applications such as the vibration detection, tilt detection, and shock detection. Accelerometers are also used in flight control applications and robot applications.

It is typical to find them as a part of an inertial measurement unit (IMU). An IMU can measures force, angular rate, and orientation of an object. For instance, it can be a combination of accelerometers, gyroscopes, and magnetometers. There are several types of accelerometers. In the following sections, we will learn about the accelerometers on a chip.

Accelerometer ICs

MEMS stands for micro-electromechanical system. It is a miniature mechanical and electro-mechanical element made by using the microfabrication techniques. It has been merged with other technologies including integrated circuits. These techniques make it possible to create accelerometer ICs that are suitable for many compact sized embedded systems. Many standalone accelerometer IC models and IMU IC models are available.

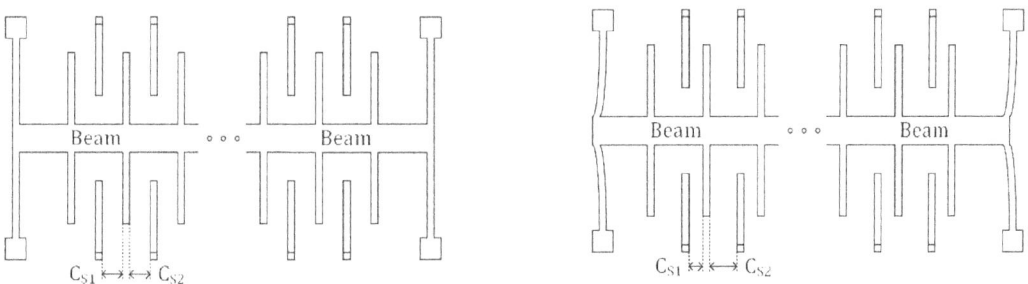

Figure 11.1. Simplified accelerometer MEM sensor example.

Let us consider a simplified accelerometer MEM sensor example as shown in Figure 11.1. The size of the sensor is assumed very small. On the left side, it shows the beam and finger structure. The gaps between beam and the fingers are associated with the capacitors of C_{S1} and C_{S2}. In this case, the beam is in the middle, the capacitors of C_{S1} and C_{S2} are assumed to be equivalent. In this MEM sensor, the beam is a moving mass. On the right side, the beam was shifted to the left side. In this case, the capacitors of C_{S1} and C_{S2} show the variations that are related to the acceleration. These variations can be read and can be converted to the voltage output as shown in Figure 11.2. This figure shows a simplified accelerometer MEM sensor block diagram for one axis.

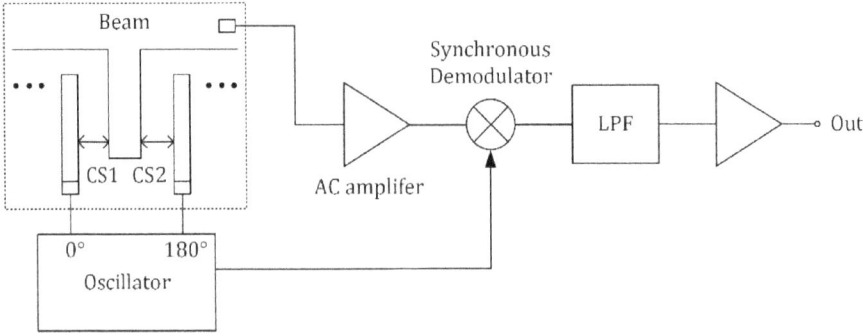

Figure 11.2. Simplified generic accelerometer block diagram for one axis.

It has an oscillator block that can generate two RF signals with 180-degree phase difference. They are applied to the fingers and the beam. The output from the beam is amplified. This amplified signal is demodulated and filtered. Then, it is properly amplified to provide the proper output level to be read by other system. This is a generic explanation for one axis. It can be extended for other axes with corresponding interface circuits.

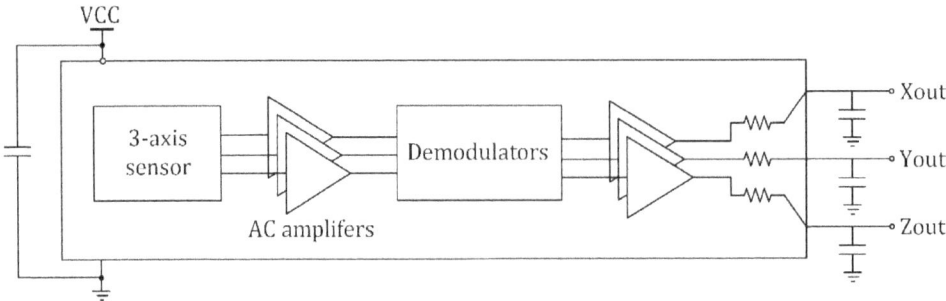

Figure 11.3. Simplified block diagram of ADXL355 accelerometer sensor IC [14].

For an experiment and further explanations, an ADXL335 module was chosen. A simplified block diagram of ADXL335 [14] accelerometer sensor IC is shown in Figure 11.3.

There is a 3-axis sensor block on the left side. The output signals are amplified and demodulated. Then, the amplifiers provide proper levels for Xout, Yout, and Zout. Typical zero g bias levels are almost the half of the supply voltage. However, the actual value might vary by sensor. The AXDL335 IC can be operated at 3.3 V. This sensor generates three output analog signals. They can be read through the ADC module in an MSP432P401R MCU.

Let us connect this ADXL335 and the MSP432P4 MCU. The connection diagram is shown Figure 14.4. The output signals of X, Y, and Z are connected to P4.2, P4.1, and P4.0, respectively. The alternative functions of the P4.2, P4.1 and P4.0 are related to A11, A12, and A13. The directions of the X, Y, and Z are marked on the PCB. In the following sections, we will study how to read multiple channel ADC values.

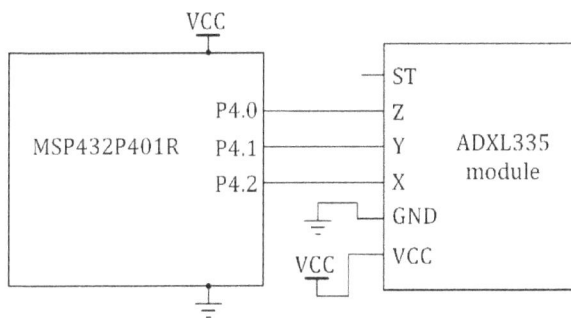

Figure 11.4. Connection example of an ADXL335 module [15].

Readers can find several ADXL335 modules available from different companies. If they have chosen an equivalent module instead, they need to refer to the documentation to determine the proper connections. On the BH EDU board, the ADXL335 IC is mounted on the PCB. Users can access the accelerometer outputs through the proper header pins.

ADC Conversion Modes

There are four ADC conversion modes. They are *Single-channel single-conversion*, *Sequence-of-channels*, *Repeat-single-channel*, and *Repeat-sequence-of-channels.* Previously, we have used a *Single-channel single-conversion* mode.

A *sequence-of-channels* mode is also called *autoscan* mode. Multiple channels can be sampled and covered once in sequence. We will use this mode in the multiple channel conversion example in the following section.

In addition, there are repeated modes for the continuous sampling and conversions. They are *Repeat-single-channel* mode and *Repeated-sequence-of-channels* (*Repeated autoscan*)

Multiple Channel Conversion

Depending on the sensors and the complexity of an embedded system, it is common to find the needs of reading multiple ADC channels. Given the test set up in Figure 11.4, we can write a program that can read three ADC channels for X, Y, and Z. The example code is shown in Program 11.2.

```
#include "msp.h"
unsigned int adc_raw[3]; // array
void main(void) {
    WDT_A->CTL = WDT_A_CTL_PW | WDT_A_CTL_HOLD; // hold the watchdog timer
    P1->DIR |= 0x01; // output direction for Red LED
    P4->SEL1 |= 0x07; // alternative function (A11, A12, A13)
    P4->SEL0 |= 0x07; // alternative function (A11, A12, A13)
    ADC14->CTL0 = ADC14_CTL0_SHT0_6 | ADC14_CTL0_SHP | ADC14_CTL0_ON;
                                                        // ADC CTL0 set up
    ADC14->CTL1 = ADC14_CTL1_RES_3; // 14 bit
    ADC14->CTL0 |= ADC14_CTL0_MSC | ADC14_CTL0_CONSEQ_1;
                        // multiple sample conversion, sequence of channel mode
    ADC14->MCTL[0] = ADC14_MCTLN_INCH_11; // multiple channel selection
    ADC14->MCTL[1] = ADC14_MCTLN_INCH_12;
    ADC14->MCTL[2] = ADC14_MCTLN_INCH_13 | ADC14_MCTLN_EOS;
                                                        // end of sequence

    while(1) {
        ADC14->CTL0 |= ADC14_CTL0_ENC | ADC14_CTL0_SC; // ADC. Start conversion
        while ((ADC14->CTL0 & ADC14_CTL0_BUSY)!=0); // wait until busy flag is cleared
        adc_raw[0]=ADC14->MEM[0]; // read ADC
        adc_raw[1]=ADC14->MEM[1];
        adc_raw[2]=ADC14->MEM[2];
        P1->OUT ^= 0x01; // toggle an LED
        __delay_cycles(50000);
    }
}
```

Program 11.2. Multiple channel conversion example.

The *ADC14CTL0* register is configured for multiple sample conversion and *sequence of channel* mode. The multiple sample conversion is enabled by setting *ADC14MSC* bit and the sequence of channel mode is selected by configuring *ADC14CONSEQ* bits.

In order to store multiple values, the *adc_raw* variable is defined as an array. *ADC14MCTL[0], ADC14MCTL[1], ADC14MCTL[2]* registers are configured for A11, A12, and A13, respectively. *ADC14_MCTLN_EOS* is added to the last channel of the sequence. In the while loop, the program waits until the ADC14BUSY flag is cleared to determine the completion of the conversion. Then, the converted data gets stored in the *adc_raw* array.

The raw reading of the ADC values may need to be converted to the corresponding voltages or angles. Users can modify this code to perform their proper conversions of the values. This multiple channel example can be modified and applied to other applications where it is necessary to read ADC values from multiple channels. For instance, the system in development may need to analog voltages related to a temperature sensor, a battery level monitor, and an analog tuning knob.

An MSP432P401R MCU can be configured to read many channels. If users need to use many ADC channels, they can find the specific pin numbers associated with the ADC channels in the datasheet [1]. For the MSP432P401R Launchpad, the pinout information can be found in the document [1]. Some of the analog channels available to be accessed through the 40-pin headers, and the ADC channels include A3 ~ A6, A8 ~ A11, and A13 ~ A14.

Chapter 12. Embedded Software Architectures

In general-purpose computer systems, speed or throughput is one of the key performance parameters. You can imagine a laptop or a PC as an example of a general-purpose computer system. This speed or throughput is also a key performance parameter in embedded systems. Throughput is the amount of data to be processed in a given amount of time. In addition, there are other key performance parameters such as response time and power consumption. Since embedded system is a special purpose system, the emphasis on performance parameters might vary depending on the applications.

Moreover, in some embedded systems, performance parameters may not only be the major factors but, other factors can be important such as reliability of the system or cost. In some cases, the cost associated with hardware and software can be a major consideration in some embedded systems.

Designers and programmers may need to understand the hardware and software requirements of the project in development. Then, they can choose a suitable hardware and an embedded software architecture for the project.

Embedded systems can be implemented without the use of any kernel or an embedded system operating system. In this case, these specific embedded systems simply do not have a kernel or a scheduler. In some other embedded systems, they are implemented using embedded system operating system such as real-time operating systems (RTOSs). In this chapter, we will study five embedded systems architectures. They are *Round Robin*, *Round Robin with Interrupts*, *Function-Queue scheduling*, and *Real-time operating system* [16].

Some embedded systems are built based on a Linux kernel. Embedded Linux operating systems have been widely accepted in embedded systems. Embedded Linux operating systems may process complex tasks and provide user-friendly environments. For instance, an Android™ operating system that are used in smartphones is this type of embedded Linux operating systems. An Android operating system is a mobile operating system, and it is based on a Linux kernel. Similarly, there are many variants of embedded operating systems based on a Linux kernel.

Embedded systems are becoming more powerful and complex. Some of those complex embedded systems can be found as embedded Linux operating systems. And, they are similar to low performance general-purpose computers. However, embedded Linux systems and general-purpose computers are not the same because embedded Linux systems are targeted to service specific purposes. There are several embedded Linux operating systems that are suitable for educational environments. Educational Embedded Linux Systems will be briefly introduced in the Chapter 28.

Scheduler and Kernel

A *scheduler* is in charge of changing *ready* state to *running* of a task or process. When the task or the process is running, it means it is using the associated system resources. It is typical to manage multiple tasks. *Scheduling* is a method that assigns or distributes computer resources to perform tasks. There are many scheduling algorithms. A scheduler is typically a part of a *kernel*. A kernel is a part of an *operating system*. The kernel is a core of an operating system, and typically, it is the program loaded into the memory on boot, and it manages the process of starting up the system.

Round Robin

Some of the embedded systems can be implemented without the need of a kernel. They may have several tasks to be performed. If the tasks do not need to be processed concurrently, they can be processed in sequence in an infinite loop. This embedded software system structure is called a *round robin* architecture. This structure can be seen as *cyclic executives or super loop*. This implementation is simple and easy. It may not suffer from a shared memory problem across multiple tasks.

Let us consider a pseudo code for the round robin architecture shown in Program 12.1. There are four tasks defined in the program. The first task is "*read-button*" task. The system reads the status of buttons. In this case, we assume the system has multiple buttons. The second task is "*read-ADC*" task. It reads the ADC values from the module and perform the associated calculations. The third task is "*control*" task. The program performs proper actions according to the system status including button and ADC status. The fourth task is "*display*" task. It manages to show data on a display module. The fifth task is "*send-data*" task. It sends data over a serial communication interface. In this program, a variable, *function,* is used in switching a running task. Initially, this variable is configured to run the *read-button* task at the start. Then, in the while loop, all of the four tasks are running in sequence repeatedly. A *volatile* keyword is used for this *function* variable. In this case, this *volatile* keyword is used to try to prevent an unexpected optimization by the compiler.

```
#include "msp.h"
volatile unsigned int function=0;
void main(void){
    # Initialization code
    function=0;
    while (1) {
```

```
    if (function==0) {
        # read-button task code
        function++;
    }
    if (function==1) {
        # read-ADC task code
        function++;
    }
    if (function==2) {
        # control task code
        function++;
    }
    if (function==3) {
        # display task code
        function++;
    }
    if (function==4) {
        # send-data task code
        function=0;
    }
  }
}
```

Program 12.1. Pseudo code for Round Robin.

In this program, each task can be processed one at a time. If there are data variables that are shared between the tasks, they do not suffer from shared memory problems. The shared memory is the memory area that can be accessed by multiple tasks; but, it cannot be accessed simultaneously. In this Round Robin architecture case, the shared memory is not accessed simultaneously by multiple tasks.

Since there can be other tasks to perform between the *read-button* task and the control task such as read-ADC task in this example, there is a chance that this program may suffer from a response-time problem. If the *read-button* task has a certain deadline like an emergency button and other tasks in-between could take longer time than the deadline. In this scenario, it may cause missing a deadline. A missed deadline might cause a serious system failure. In order to overcome this issue, we can use interrupt service routines in this Round Robin architecture described in the following section.

Round Robin with Interrupts

There can be several variants of Round Robin. In this section, let us consider an architecture of Round Robin with Interrupts. For the *read-button* task and the *read-ADC* task, they can be processed in the interrupt service routines (ISRs) as shown in Program 12.2. These two tasks can be processed when they are requested. As they have a higher priority, these tasks may interrupt a running task in the while loop. In this while loop, the *control* task, *display* task, and *send-data* task are running in sequence repeatedly. When buttons are pressed, a running task in the while loop is going to be interrupted. Then, the associated ISR, *PORT1_IRQHander*, is going to be processed. This method may resolve the response time problem that we have considered in the Round Robin example. In addition, this program does not need to wait until the ADC conversion and the relevant calculation are completed. When the ADC interrupt is requested, the *read-ADC* task can interrupt a task in the while loop. Then it can process the *read-ADC* task. After the *read-ADC* task is completed, the program will run *control* task, *display* task, and *send-data* task in sequence repeatedly.

```
#include "msp.h"
volatile unsigned int function=0;
void main(void){
    # Initialization code
    function=3;
    while (1) {
        if (function==3) {
            # control task code
            function=4;
        }
        if (function==4) {
            # display task code
            function=5;
        }
        if (function==5) {
            # send-data task code
            function=3;
        }
    }
}

void PORT1_IRQHandler(void) {
    // function 1
    # read-button task code
}
void ADC14_IRQHandler(void) {
    // function 2
    # read-ADC task code
}
```

Program 12.2. Pseudo code for Round Robin with Interrupts.

This variant of Round Robin is a good candidate to resolve the response time problem. However, there are some other conditions to be considered. While the system is in processing the *read-ADC* task, the other *read-button* task requests could be triggered multiple times. For an MSP432P401R MCU, an ADC14 ISR has a higher priority than a Port 1 ISR as we have studied previously in NVIC. In this case, there is a chance to miss the multiple read-button task requests. In addition, let us suppose other tasks in the while loop are higher priority tasks than the *read-button* or the *read-ADC* tasks. If ISRs have been dominating the processor time, the other tasks in the while loop cannot be running. This would be the reason that it is recommended to write ISR short. Next, let us consider a scheduling system to tackle this problem in the following section

Function-Queue Scheduling

We have studied simple example of Round Robin and a variant of Round Robin in the previous sections. Using a circular queue, we can implement a simple scheduling system. A circular queue can store data, and its data structure is based on FIFO (First In First Out). The last position of the data is connected back to the first position of the data, and it forms a circular buffer. Function pointers for tasks can be stored in the circular queue. Let us say that there is a program routine that checks whether the function pointer has any data or not. If it has the data, then the program reads the queue and calls the associated function.

An example of this type of the program with a circular queue is shown in Program 12.3. In this program, it is assumed that the circular queue is already implemented separately. This circular queue is not a part of a standard library; but a user can simply implement it, or a use can find relevant queue library in other software package. In this example program, there are five functions that are defined, and they are associated with five tasks we have studied previously.

```
#include "msp.h"
void function1(void);
void function2(void);
void function3(void);
void function4(void);
void function5(void);
// subroutine Header
void clearQueue(void);
void enQueue(unsigned int);
unsigned int deQueue();
unsigned char QueueIsNotEmpty();
// circular queue is assumed to be already implemented
void (*fcnPtr)(void); // function pointer with no parameter
void main(void){
   # Initialization
   clearQueue();
   enQueue(&function3);
   while (1) {
     while (QueueIsNotEmpty()) {
       fcnPtr = deQueue();
       (*fcnPtr)();
     }
```

```
    }
}

void PORT1_IRQHandler(void) {
    # minimum code to handle a read-button task
    enQueue(&function1);
}

void function1(void){
    # remaining code to complete the read-button task
}

void ADC14_IRQHandler(void) {
    # minimum code to handle a read-ADC task
    enQueue(&function2);
}

void function2(void){
    # remaining code to complete the read-ADC task
}

void function3(void){
    # control task code
    enQueue(&function4);
}

void function4(void){
    # display task code
    enQueue(&function5);
}

void function5(void){
    #send-data task code
    enQueue(&function3);
}
```

Program 12.3. Pseudo code for Function Queue Scheduling.

For a Port 1 ISR, it can process minimum actions to handle a *read-button* task, and the remaining actions to complete the *read-button* task can be processed in the *function1* sub-routine. An ADC ISR is handling minimum actions for a *read-ADC* task, and the *function2* has the remaining actions for the *read-ADC* task to be performed. The *function3*, *function4*, and *function 5* are the sub-routines related to *control* task, *display* task, and *send-data* task, respectively. The *function3*, *function4*, and *function5* will be running in sequence in a normal condition repeatedly in this example program. If there is any interrupt request from the Port1 or ADC, this cycle can be interrupted, and the relevant code and function will be running first. This example program is capable of catching task requests reasonably fast, and it could resolve the problems discussed in the previous example.

The function pointers that need to be executed are stored in the circular queue, and the program runs the relevant functions by reading function pointers from the queue. This is a function-queue scheduling, which is a simplified example of scheduling

Let us consider a scenario. If *function3*, *function4*, or *funcion5* is supposed to be low priority tasks and there have been many requests recorded in the queue, then, the chance of running higher priority tasks fully and properly gets lower. This might be relevant to the need of a capability to selectivity run a task from the task requests stored in the queue. In addition, this program treated as the same priorities for all functions except the tasks described in ISRs. In this function-queue example, we have not described the method of assigning different priorities. These complex cases can be handled by using a real-time kernel that is a part of a real-time operating system.

Real-time Operating System

A real-time kernel is a core of a real-time operating system. It manages booting, task scheduling, and resources of an MCU. A real-time operating system (RTOS) includes a real-time kernel and other higher level and additional services. An RTOS is designed to meet strict deadlines. In addition, an RTOS includes a large set of libraries that are suitable for various embedded system applications.

A pseudo code example for an RTOS is shown in Program 12.4. Fives tasks are defined. *Task3*, *Task4*, and *Task5* are for a *control* task, *display* task, and *send-data* task, respectively. They are running in sequence repeatedly by the synchronization using signals. There are two more tasks that are configured to be triggered by interrupts. They are *Task_GPIO_btn0* and *Task_ADC_callback0*. In the main program, it begins with the custom initializations including task definitions. Then, the BIOS (Basic Input Output System) gets started. Once the BIOS started, RTOS system will take over the system. As you can notice, this program style is different from the ones without an O/S. At the same time, it is also different from an application program for a general-purpose O/S because the application programing in a general-purpose O/S typically gets loaded and running after the booting process. However, in this RTOS, the initialization of the tasks run first. Developers add their custom code before the operating system runs. After this initialization, the kernel will be running, and it will run defined tasks. The pseudo code shown in Program 12.4 is a simplified version for the ease of explanation.

```
#include "msp.h"
#include "stdbool.h"
void Task1(void) {
    while (true) {
        # wait for Signal T1
```

```
        # read-button task code
        # clear Signal T1
    }
}
void Task2(void) {
    while (true) {
        # wait for Signal T2
        # read-ADC task code
        # clear Signal T2
    }
}

void Task3(void) {
    while (true) {
        # wait for Signal T3
        # control task code
        # clear Signal T3, set Signal T4
    }
}
void Task4(void) {
    while (true) {
        # wait for Signal T4
        # display task code
        # clear Signal T4, set Signal T5
    }
}
void Task5(void) {
    while (true) {
        # wait for Signal T5
        # send-data task code
        # clear Signal T5, set Signal T3
    }
}
void Task_GPIO_btn0(void) {
    # set Signal T1
    # minimum code to process the read-button task request
}
void Task_ADC_callback0((void) {
    # set Signal T2
    # minimum code to process the ADC task request
}
void main(void){
    Board_init();
    # custom initialization code including task definitions
    # initialization to run a default task at the start
    BIOS_start();
}
```

Program 12.4. Pseudo code for RTOS.

RTOS supports task scheduling and multitasking as we have seen previously. RTOS provides various methods for a multitasking environment such as mutexes. The mutexes are objects that can be used as signaling and they may be used in resolving a conflict in shared resources. Mutexes are binary semaphores with a method to resolve priory inversions. In addition, RTOS provides more methods that are suitable for a multitasking environment.

There are many RTOSs available, and the license options vary by RTOS. Texas Instruments provides a TI-RTOS. The TI-RTOS has a TI-RTOS kernel that was formerly called SYS/BIOS. Later in Chapter 24, we will study simple TI RTOS examples.

Architecture Selection

An embedded system is a special purpose system. It is up to the developers to determine a proper embedded system architecture for their targeted system. The decision is typically dependent on the project requirements and desired specifications. In this respect, it is recommended for developers to understand their project requirements in order to choose proper hardware and software architectures for their embedded systems. At the same time, they need to understand the limitations of their choice of the software architecture. In some applications, their embedded systems are relatively simple, and they can be implemented without the use of any scheduler or operating system. In some other applications, they may need to use embedded operating systems such as RTOSs.

As it was mentioned, some embedded systems have rich resources. They are suitable to run complex operating systems based a Linux kernel and Microsoft's Windows kernel as well as a macOS® kernel. In high-end embedded systems, the programming environment is similar to an application program in general-purpose computing systems. These systems may be still considered embedded systems since they were designed to perform specific tasks and for the specific purposes.

Chapter 13. Pulse Width Modulation

A Pulse Width Modulation (PWM) is a method of generating an analog signal using digital data. A PWM signal can control the duration of logical high or low states of a periodic digital signal. PWM signals are used in many applications including controlling DC motors, valves, and pumps as well as controlling the brightness of LEDs. There are two major parameters determining the behavior of PWM signals. They are a duty cycle and a frequency. Previously, we have studied how to generate variable frequency signals. In this section, we will learn how to generate variable duty cycle signals.

PWM signals

A duty cycle of a PWM signal can be determined by the percentage obtained by the fraction of the "ON" time and the period of the PWM signal. Let us suppose that a logical high signal is an ON state. Now, a duty cycle (%) can be obtained as follows:

$$Duty\ Cycle\ (\%) = \frac{T_{ON}}{T_{Period}} \times 100 = \frac{T_{ON}}{T_{ON} + T_{OFF}} \times 100$$

PWM signal examples with different duty cycles are shown in Figure 13.1. It shows the duty cycle of 50% at the top. In this case, the ON time is assumed to be the half of the period of the signal. We have studied variable frequency generator examples in the previous chapters. The duty cycles were 50% and they were not variable. In this section, we will learn about the method of how to vary the duty cycles.

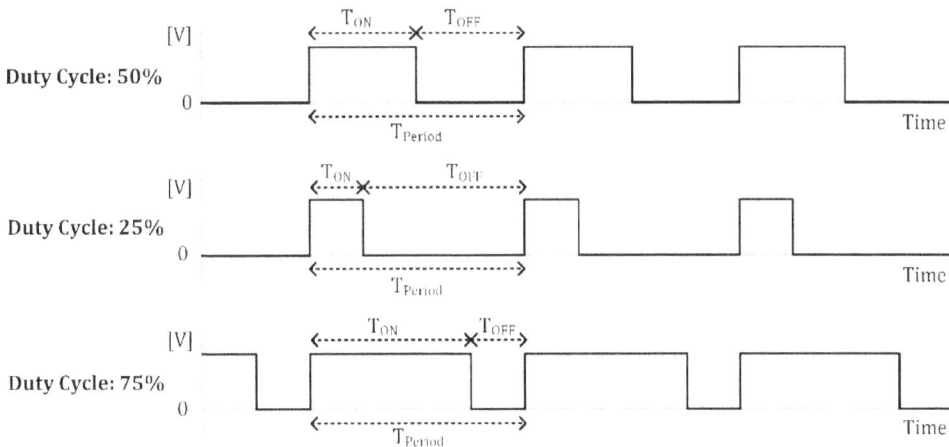

Figure 13.1. PWM signals.

In the middle of Figure 13.1, the duty cycle of a PWM signal is 25%. In this case, the ON time is smaller than the half of the period. The ON time is 1/4 of the period. At the bottom of Figure 13.1, it shows the case of the duty cycle of 75%. In this case, the

ON time is bigger than the half of the period. The ON time is 3/4 of the period. Next, let us use CCR0 and CCR1 of a Timer_A0 module to create PWM signals.

At the top of Figure 13.2, it shows a case where TA0CCR1 is the half of TA0CCR0. The counter is operating in *up mode*. Let us say that we can set an output signal when the counter reaches at TA0CCR0. Moreover, the output signal can be reset when the counter reaches at TA0CCR1. Then, the output signal alternating ON/OFF states can be generated. Since TA0CCR1 is the half of the TA0CCR0, the duty cycle is close to 50%.

In comparison, this method is different than the one we used in Chapter 7. Previously, the output signals were simply toggled at each time when the counter reaches at TA0CCR0. That is the reason that the frequency generated by this method in this chapter would be twice higher than the one in Chapter 7.

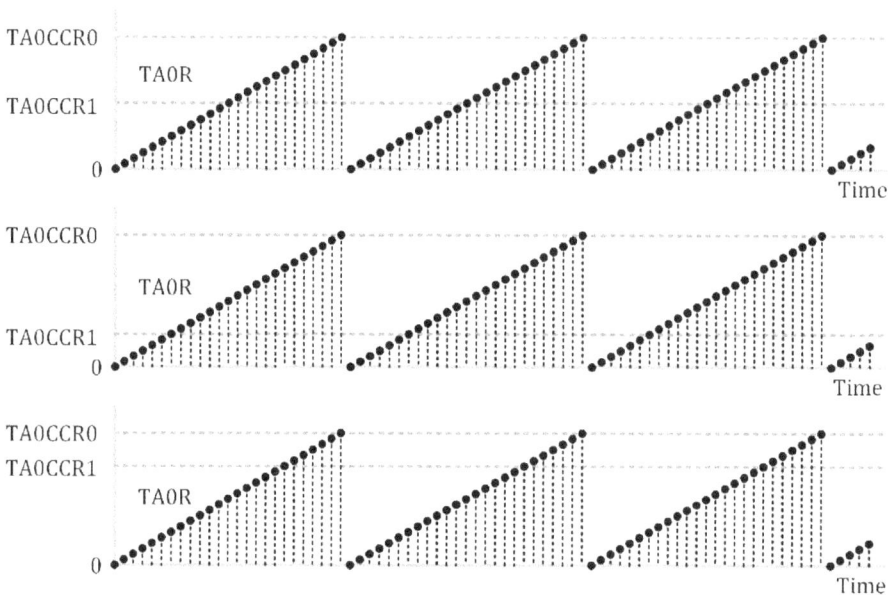

Figure 13.2. PWM generation using TA0CCR0 and TA1CCR1.

In the middle of Figure 13.2, it shows the case where TA0CCR1 is smaller than the half of the TA0CCR0. In this case, the duty cycle of a PWM signal is less than 50%. If TA0CCR1 is 1/4 of TA0CCR0, the duty cycle is close to 25%.

At the bottom of Figure 13.2, it shows the case where TA0CCR1 is bigger than the half of the TA0CCR0. In this case, the duty cycle of a PWM signal is higher than 50%. If TA0CCR1 is 3/4 of TA0CCR0, the duty cycle is close to 75%. Using TA0CCR0 and TA0CCR1, we have seen that it is possible to vary the duty cycle of a PWM signal.

Software PWM

Using a timer_A0 and a GPIO port, we can write a program that can generate PWM signals. We call this technique as a software PWM in this section. The code example of the software PWM using CCIFG flag is shown in Program 13.1. The values of TA0CCR0 and TA0CCR1 are configured as 5000 and 1250, respectively. Both TA0CCTL0 and TA0CCTL1 interrupts are enabled. *TA0_0_IRQn* and *TA0_N_IRQn* are used in setting up NVIC. *TA0_0_IRQHandler* and *TA0_N_IRQHandler* are the names of the interrupt service routines. The code in *TA0_0_IRQHandler* can check whether the CCIFG for TA0CCR0 is set or not. If the CCIFG is set, the P2.4 will be set. Moreover, the code in *TA0_N_IRQHandler* can check whether the CCIFG for TA0CCR1 is set or not. If the CCIFG is set, the P2.4 will be cleared. Based on the TA0CCR1 and TA0CCR0 ratio, the duty cycle of this PWM signal is 25%.

```
#include "msp.h"
void main(void) {
    WDT_A->CTL = WDT_A_CTL_PW | WDT_A_CTL_HOLD;  // hold the watchdog timer
    P1->DIR |= BIT0;  // output direction for an LED
    P2->DIR |= BIT4;  // output direction
    TIMER_A0->CCR[0] = 5000;  // set the value of TA0CCR0
    TIMER_A0->CCR[1] = 1250;  // set the value of TA0CCR1
    TIMER_A0->CTL = TIMER_A_CTL_TASSEL_2 | TIMER_A_CTL_MC_1 |
TIMER_A_CTL_CLR;  // TA0CTL setup
    TIMER_A0->CCTL[0] = TIMER_A_CCTLN_CCIE;  // enable CCIE interrupt
    TIMER_A0->CCTL[1] = TIMER_A_CCTLN_CCIE;  // enable CCIE interrupt
    _enable_irq();  // enable global interrupt
    NVIC->ISER[0] = 1 << ((TA0_0_IRQn) & 31);  // NVIC setup
    NVIC->ISER[0] |= 1 << ((TA0_N_IRQn) & 31);  // NVIC setup
    while(1) {
        P1->OUT ^= BIT0;  // toggle an LED
        _delay_cycles(500000);  // delay
    }
}

void TA0_0_IRQHandler(void) {
    if((TIMER_A0->CCTL[0] & TIMER_A_CCTLN_CCIFG)!=0) {  // check CCIFG flag
        P2->OUT |= BIT4;  // set P2.4
        TIMER_A0->CCTL[0] &= ~TIMER_A_CCTLN_CCIFG;  // clear CCIFG flag
    }
}

void TA0_N_IRQHandler(void) {
    if((TIMER_A0->CCTL[1] & TIMER_A_CCTLN_CCIFG)!=0) {  // check CCIFG flag
        P2->OUT &= ~BIT4;  // clear P2.4
        TIMER_A0->CCTL[1] &= ~TIMER_A_CCTLN_CCIFG;  // clear CCIFG flag
    }
}
```

Program 13.1. S/W PWM program using CCIFG flag (ISR).

Another program example of the software PWM using TAIFG flag is shown in Figure 13.2. The set-up process is similar; but there are differences. TA0CCTL and TA0CCTL1 interrupts are enabled. Only *TA0_N_IRQn* is used in setting up NVIC. *TA0_N_IRQHandler* is the name of the interrupt service routine.

In the subroutine, the code can check whether the TAIFG is set or not. If the TAIFG is set, the P2.4 will be set. Moreover, it can check whether the If the CCIFG of TA0CCR0 is set or not. If the CCIFG is set, the P2.4 will be cleared. Similar to the previous example, based on the TA0CCR1 and TA0CCR0 ratio, the duty cycle of this PWM signal is also 25%.

```
#include "msp.h"
void main(void) {
    WDT_A->CTL = WDT_A_CTL_PW | WDT_A_CTL_HOLD;  // hold the watchdog timer
    P1->DIR |= BIT0;  // output direction for an LED
    P2->DIR |= BIT4;  // output direction
    TIMER_A0->CCR[0] = 5000;  // set the value of TA0CCR0
    TIMER_A0->CCR[1] = 1250;  // set the value of TA0CCR1
    TIMER_A0->CTL = TIMER_A_CTL_TASSEL_2 | TIMER_A_CTL_MC_1 |
TIMER_A_CTL_CLR;  // TA0CTL setup
    TIMER_A0->CTL |= TIMER_A_CTL_IE;  // enable TAIE interrupt
    TIMER_A0->CCTL[1] = TIMER_A_CCTLN_CCIE;  // enable CCIE interrupt
    _enable_irq();  // enable global interrupt
    NVIC->ISER[0] |= 1 << ((TA0_N_IRQn) & 31);  // NVIC setup
    while(1) {
        P1->OUT ^= BIT0;  // toggle an LED
        _delay_cycles(500000);  // delay
    }
}

void TA0_N_IRQHandler(void) {
    if((TIMER_A0->CTL & TIMER_A_CTL_IFG)!=0) {  // check  TAIFG flag
        P2->OUT |= BIT4;  // set P2.4
        TIMER_A0->CTL &= ~TIMER_A_CTL_IFG;  // clear TAIFG flag
    }

    if((TIMER_A0->CCTL[1] & TIMER_A_CCTLN_CCIFG)!=0) {  // check CCIFG flag
        P2->OUT &= ~BIT4;  // clear P2.4
        TIMER_A0->CCTL[1] &= ~TIMER_A_CCTLN_CCIFG;  // clear CCIFG flag
    }
}
```

Program 13.2. S/W PWM program using TAIFG flag (ISR).

Both software PWM programs can generate similar PWM signals. However, internal operations are different. One of the benefits of using a software PWM generator is that programmers can apply a custom operation pattern using any of the GPIO pins. However, in order to provide more stable PWM signals, a hardware based PWM signal generation method can be used instead. This is supported by an MSP432P401R MCU. We will learn a hardware PWM generation method in the following sections.

Hardware PWM

We have studied software PWM methods. While the program can generate PWM signals, there can be a chance that interrupt routines with higher priorities need to be running. In this case, the accuracy of the PWM signals may suffer. In some applications such as motor applications, it can be critical, and it recommended to use a stable and accurate PWM signals.

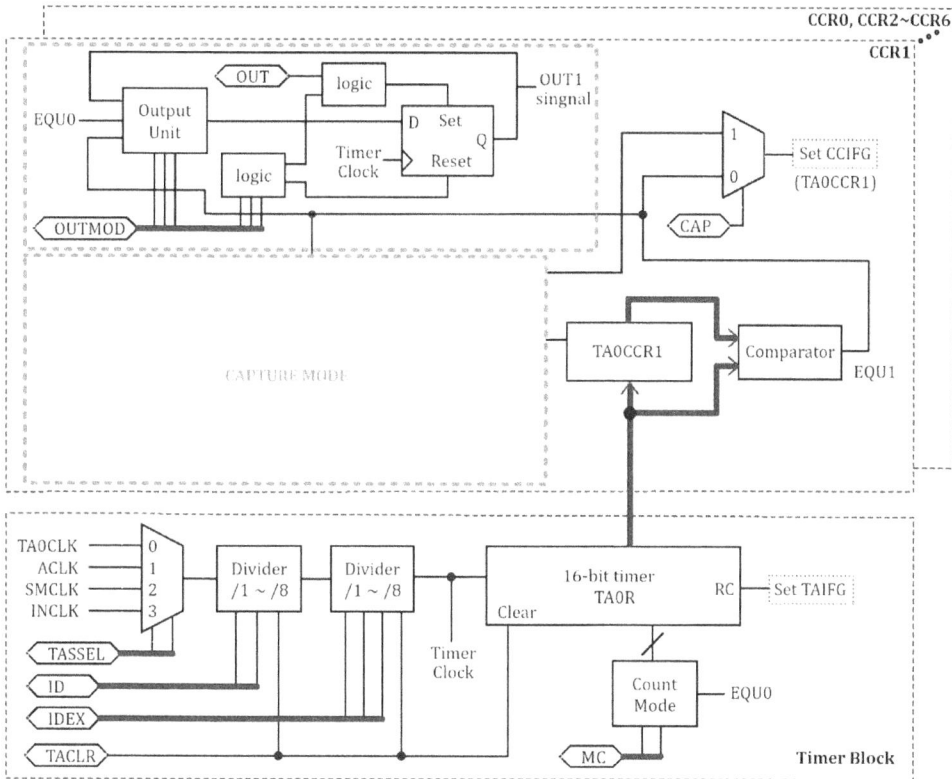

Figure 13.3. Simplified Timer_A0 block diagram showing the CCR1 block [1].

Timer_A modules in an MSP432P401R MCU have output units and relevant components that can be used in hardware PWM generations. A simplified Timer_A0 block diagram displaying the CCR1 block is shown in Figure 13.3. In this figure, the OUTPUT MODE box is disclosed. And, it is still enclosed with a thick dotted line, and it shows the output unit and relevant components. Each capture/compare block has these output unit and the relevant components.

Output Unit and Output Modes

There are seven capture and compare blocks in the Timer_A0 module. Each capture/compare block has an output unit. The output unit can be used in generating PWM signals. There are eight operating modes supported by the output unit as shown in Table 13.1. This table shows a specific case of TA0CCR0 and TA0CCR1. However, users can extend it other cases such as TA0CCR0/TA0CCR2, TA0CCR0/TA0CCR3, and so forth. One of the output modes can be selected by the configuration of OUTMOD bits.

Mode	OUTMOD bits	Description
Output	0	The output signal is updated according to the corresponding OUT bit.
Set	1	The output signal is set when the timer counts to TA0CCR1.
Toggle/Reset	2	The output signal is toggled when the timer counts to TA0CCR1, and it is reset when the timer counts to TA0CCR0.
Set/Reset	3	The output signal is set when the timer counts to TA0CCR1, and it is reset when the timer counts to TA0CCR0.
Toggle	4	The output signal is toggled when the timer counts to TA0CCR1.
Reset	5	The output signal is reset when the timer counts to TA0CCR1.
Toggle/Set	6	The output signal is toggled when the timer counts to TA0CCR1, and it is set when the timer counts to TA0CCR0.
Reset/Set	7	The output signal is reset when the timer counts to TA0CCR1, and it is set when the timer counts to TA0CCR0.

Table 13.1. OUTPUT modes (TA0CCR0/TA0CCR1) [6].

We have used a specific signal generation pattern in the previous software PWM examples. This pattern is based on the output mode 7. In this output mode 7, the output signal is reset when the counter reaches at TA0CCR1, and the output signal is set when the counter reaches at TA0CCR0. When it is properly configured, the hardware units and components perform this signal pattern generation. Users can generate different PWM signal pattern by using different output modes.

Output examples in *up mode* of the Timer_A0 is shown in Figure 13.4. In this example, TA0CCR1 is smaller than the half of the TA0CCR0. Given the configuration, output modes of 2, 3, 6, or 7 can generate PWM signals. However, the patterns and the duty cycles are different. The duty cycles can be varied by changing the value of TA0CCR1. Also, it is worth of mentioning that we have examined the case of the *up mode* only in this chapter. This is one setting out of other combinations. The other cases may involve other timer modes such as *continuous* mode and *up/down* mode.

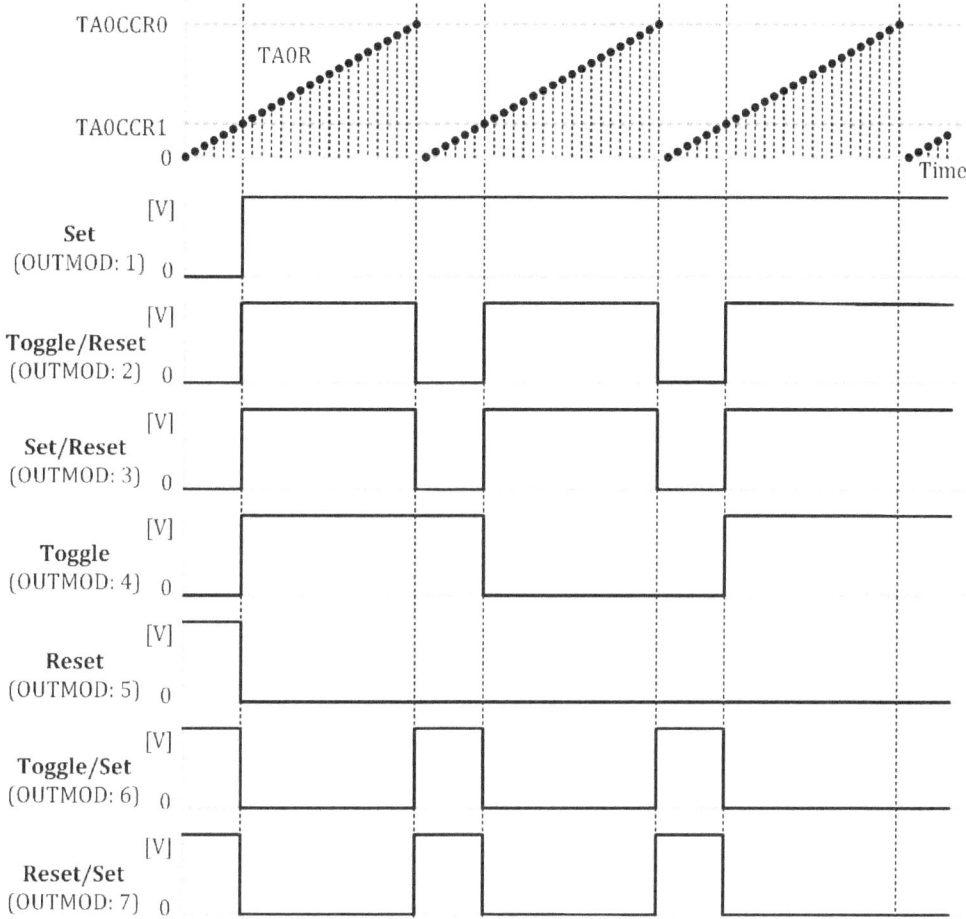

Figure 13.4. Output Example – Up mode [6].

Pin Functions

The pin function needs to be configured properly in order to generate an output. A certain pin has its pre-defined functions. The hardware connection varies by the MCU model. Table 13.2 shows the pin functions for P2.4 in an MSP432P401R MCU.

Pin	P2SEL1	P2SEL0	P2DIR	Description
P2.4	0	0	0	GPIO (Input)
	0	0	1	GPIO (Output)
	0	1	1	TA0.1

Table 13.2. Pin functions of P2.4 in an MSP432P401R MCU [6].

In order to generate output signals using the output unit and the relevant components, the P2SEL1 and P2SEL0 need to be configured properly for the alternative function of TA0.1. The output direction needs to be configured properly. Then, the output signals through the pin associated with P2.4 will be the output signals generated by the output unit of the Timer_A0.

H/W PWM example

The hardware PWM example is shown in Program 13.3. The P2.4 pin has been configured for an alternative function. The output signals through the P2.4 pin are related to the output unit of the Timer_A0. The TA0CCTL is configured for the output mode 7. The configuration is simpler than the one in the previous software PWM examples. This program example can generate hardware (H/W) based PWM signals with varied frequency and duty cycle through the P2.4 pin. In the following chapter, we will learn about a DC motor driver, and we will use the H/W PWM signals to control a DC motor.

```
#include "msp.h"
int main(void) {
  WDT_A->CTL = WDT_A_CTL_PW | WDT_A_CTL_HOLD;  // hold the watchdog timer
  P1->DIR |= BIT0;  // output direction for an LED
  P2->DIR |= BIT4;  // output direction
  P2->SEL1 &= ~BIT4;  // TA0.1 selection
  P2->SEL0 |= BIT4;  // TA0.1 selection
  TIMER_A0->CTL = TIMER_A_CTL_TASSEL_2 | TIMER_A_CTL_MC_1 |
TIMER_A_CTL_CLR;  // TA0CTL setup
  TIMER_A0->CCR[0] = 5000;  // set the value of TA0CCR0
  TIMER_A0->CCR[1] = 1250;  // set the value of TA0CCR1
  TIMER_A0->CCTL[1] = TIMER_A_CCTLN_OUTMOD_7;  // output mode 7
  while(1){
    P1->OUT ^= BIT0;  // toggle an LED
    __delay_cycles(500000);  // delay
  }
}
```

Program 13.3. H/W PWM generation program.

Chapter 14. DC Motor Control

A DC motor is an electromechanical component that transforms direct current electrical energy into mechanical energy in form of rotation. DC motors are widely used. Small-sized motors are used in handheld tools, toys, and small appliances. Large-sized DC motors are used in electric vehicles and industrial equipment. In this chapter, we will learn about the DC motor control method that can be used in embedded systems.

DC Motor Control and Practical Consideration

A DC motor and a switch are shown on the left side in Figure 14.1. This switch is open in this state initially. In the middle of the figure, it shows the case where the switch will be closed. In this state, the current flows through the motor. It causes the DC motor to rotate. Next, when it is rotating, the switch can be controlled to be open as shown on the right side of the figure. Then, it will cut off the power and the rotation of the DC motor will be eventually stopped. However, there is a possible coition that a high voltage could be induced, and it might cause arc through the air gap. This voltage spike could be occurred because the current flowing through the inductance of the motor was changed suddenly. You can consider an equation of an inductor as follows:

$$V_L = L\frac{di_L}{dt}$$

As you can see from the equation, the voltage of an inductor can be very high, if there is a sudden current change for a very short time. This voltage spike or Arc is not a desired condition because any spark can be hazardous, and the high voltage could damage electronics components. Therefore, it needs a protection method from the arc and unwanted high voltage. One of the methods is to use a flyback diode.

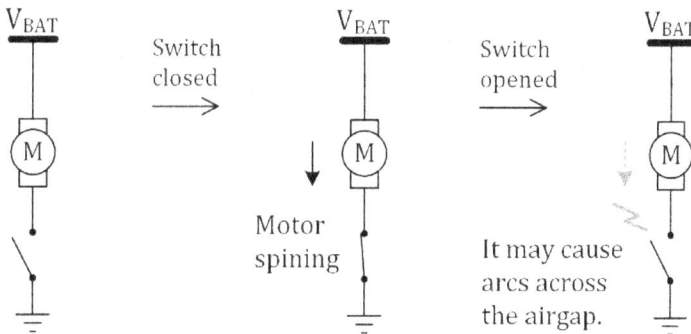

Figure 14.1. Simplified DC motor control and the practical consideration.

Flyback diode

A flyback diode is a diode connected in parallel to an inductor, and the flyback diode is placed with the reverse polarity from the power. The inductor could be a relay or motor. A flyback diode can be used to reduce the practical problem in causing an arc or a high voltage. It has other names such as a kickback diode, snubber diode, and so forth. Let us consider a case shown on the left side of Figure 14.2. This is a similar condition when the current is flowing, and the motor is operating. However, the difference is that this circuit has a diode connected across the motor.

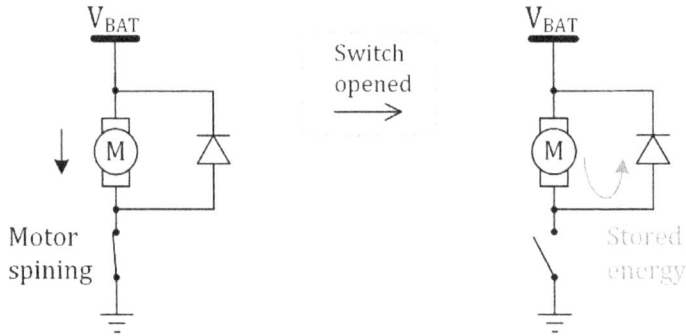

Figure 14.2. Simplified DC motor control circuit with a flyback diode.

When the motor is rotating, counter-electromotive force also known as back electromotive force (EMF) can be induced. This is because the motor is also like a generator. Back EMF can be measured as a voltage that appears in the opposite direction to the current flow. The voltage of the back EMF is related to the speed of the motor. Back EMF is not necessarily bad because the current consumption of a motor drops while the motor is spinning. Now, the switch can be turned off as shown on the right side of the figure. In this case, there is a still path through the diode. Therefore, the remaining current can flow through the path of the flyback diode. Flyback diodes are commonly used in many cases where an inductive device can be switched ON or OFF. Relay and motor driver circuits have used the flyback didoes.

Basic DC Motor Control Circuit

The switch can be implemented using a power transistor. A basic DC motor control circuit using an NPN power transistor is shown in Figure 14.3. A base resistor is used between the GPIO pin and the base of the transistor. This base resistor is an essential component for an NPN transistor. When the output of the GPIO pin is logical high, the significant current can flow through the motor. It causes the motor to rotate. When the output of the GPIO port is local low, the current across the motor is very small. It can make the motor stop eventually. During the transition from an ON to an OFF state, the remaining current has a path through the diode. Then, the motor current decays. This is a practical circuit example of controlling a DC motor in an embedded system. One of the GPIO pins of an MSP432P401R MCU can be used to control the DC motor.

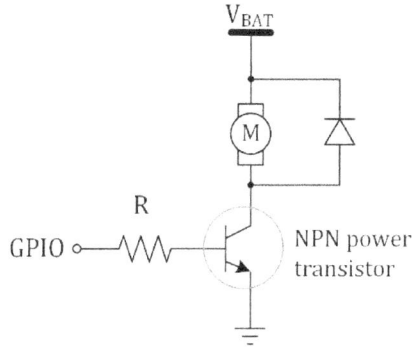

Figure 14.3. Basic DC motor control circuit.

This basic DC motor control circuit can control the motor to rotate or stop. However, it cannot change the direction of the rotation. If users want to control the direction of the rotation of the motor, an H-bridge configuration can be used.

H-bridge Motor Control Driver

An H-bridge is a circuit configuration that can switch the polarity of the voltage across a load. In this case, the load is a DC motor. An H-bridge circuit with ideal switches is shown on the left side of Figure 14.4. Four ideal switches and one motor are used in the circuit. As you can see, the graphical representation of the circuit is similar to the letter H.

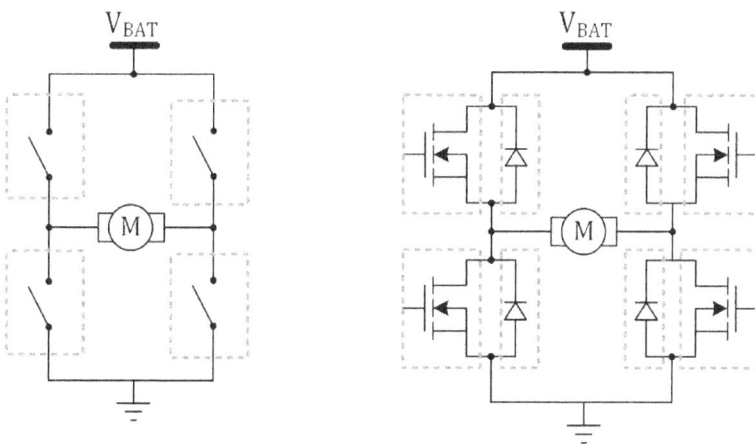

Figure 14.4. H-bridge circuits.

An ideal switch can be implemented using a N-channel power MOSFET (metal–oxide–semiconductor field-effect) transistor and a diode that is a flyback diode. All switches were replaced with this N-channel MOSFET power transistors and diodes as shown on the right side of Figure 14.4. To compare the cases of an NPN power transistor and a N-channel MOSFET, there is no need to use a resistor at the gate of the MOSFET transistor. This H-bridge circuit is a basic H-bridge configuration that we will study further in this section.

Let us consider the case where two transistors are turned ON and the rest of transistors are remained turned OFF as shown on the left side of Figure 14.5. In this case, the current can flow through the motor and two of the transistors at each side. On the right side of the figure, it shows the other case where the other two transistors are turned ON instead. In this case, the current can flow through the motor as well. However, the current directions in these two cases are different. Thus, the direction of the rotation can be switched by controlling the transistors. If we say that the first case is related to a forward direction, the other case is related to a reverse direction.

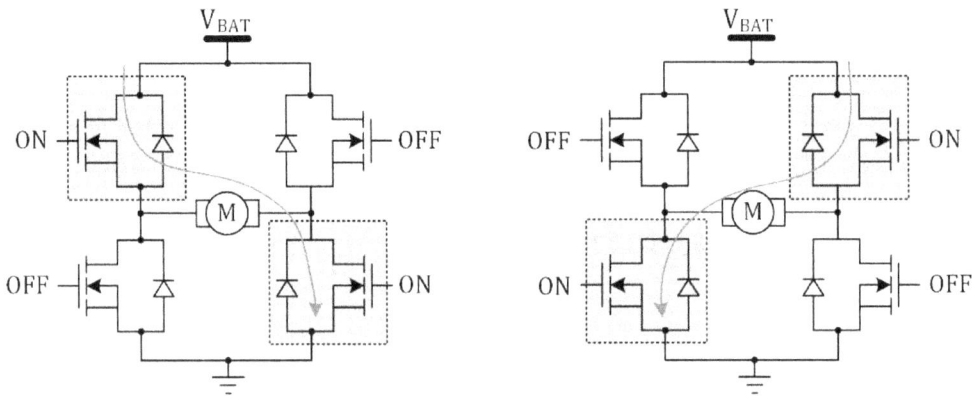

Figure 14.5. Forward and reverse directions.

Decay Modes

As shown on the left side of Figure 14.6, if the H-bridge driver is configured for the forward direction, the motor can spin. Then, let us say we want to stop spinning. The figure in the middle shows the condition that all of the transistors are turned OFF. In this case, as we have discussed earlier, there is a path of the current through the flyback diodes. This is a behavior of turning all transistors OFF during the dead time in this example. However, this behavior during the dead time can be determined differently by the manufacturer. Let us examine different decay modes for stop conditions.

One of the decay modes is a *fast decay* mode. In order to stop the motor, the motor driver can turn the opposing transistors ON as shown at the top right side of Figure 14.6. These transistors are turned ON until the current decays to zero or during a fixed short amount of time. The current in this mode is made to decay faster than other decay modes.

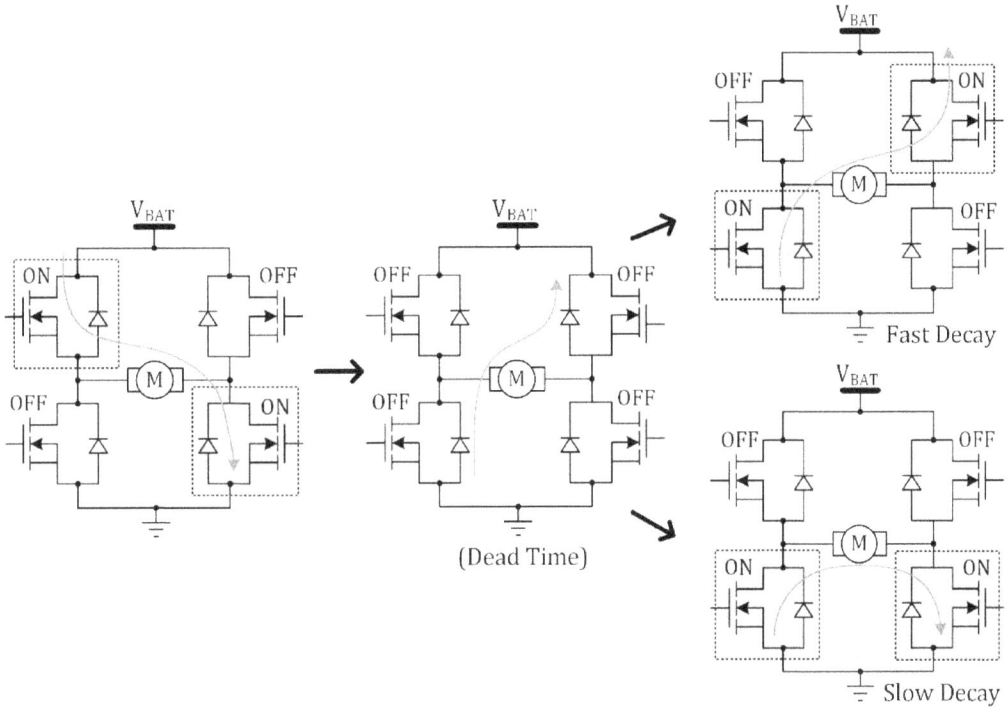

Figure 14.6. Decay modes.

Another decay mode is a *slow decay* mode. To stop a motor, the motor driver can turn two of the low side transistors ON as shown at the bottom right side of Figure 14.6. In this configuration, there would be a back EMF involved across the motor. Shorting the back EMF causes a very quick rotor stop. This is also known as a short brake.

In some motor drivers, they support *mixed decay* mode. For instance, a fast decay mode can be applied for a certain duration. Then, a slow decay mode can be applied for another duration. The ratio of the durations in these two modes may vary by the motor driver. The *mixed decay* mode can be useful in stepper motor driver applications.

Shoot-through

When the transistors are controlled, a shoot-through condition should be avoided. An example of a shoot-through condition is shown in Figure 14.7. If both of two transistors are turned ON at the same side as shown in the figure, it might cause an excessive current flow and a catastrophic damage. It is common to use an H-bridge motor driver IC instead of using individual components. One of the advantages in using an H-bridge motor driver IC is that some of the H-bridge driver IC models support the shoot-through protection or prevention features.

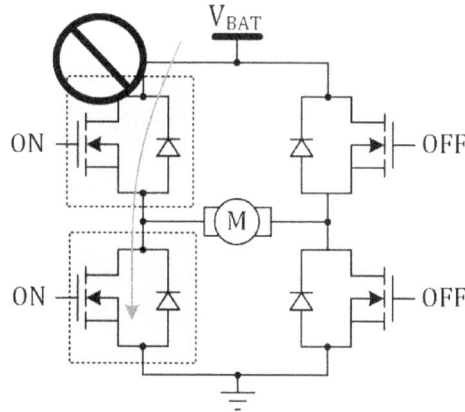

Figure 14.7. Shoot-through.

DRV8833 H-bridge Motor Driver

There are many H-bridge motor driver ICs. Developers need to find a suitable one for their project. In this book, as an example, a TI DRV8833 H-bridge motor drive IC is chosen [17]. The DRV8833 can be powered with the supply voltage of 2.7 V to 10.8 V. The DRV8833 IC provides two H-bridge drivers. Each H-bridge driver can provide the current up to 1.5-A RMS and 2A peak.

A simplified block diagram is shown in Figure 14.8. Two H-bridge drivers can be found on the right side, and they are connected to two DC motors. AIN1 and AIN2 input pins are used to control the state of one of the H-bridge drivers. The other set of the input pins are BIN1 and BIN2. An MPS432P401R can be used to connect to this IC. There is a logic and gate driver block that control the behavior of the H-bridge drivers including decay modes. The H-bridge logic for a DRV8833 IC is shown in Table 14.1.

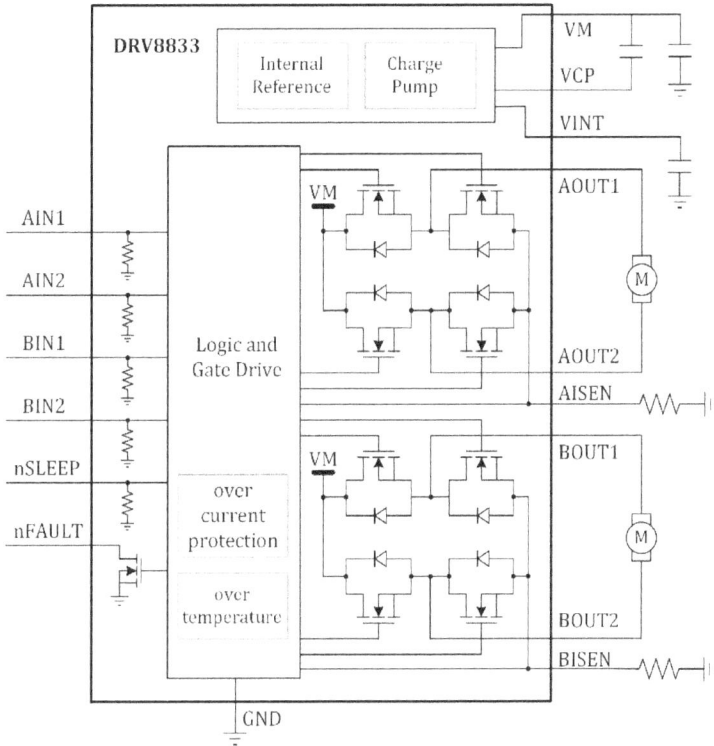

Figure 14.8. Simplified block diagram of a DRV8833 IC [17]

The H-bridge logic table shows the relevant functions according to the input signals. If the logic levels of AIN1 and AIN2 are high and low, respectively, the motor will spin. Let us say this is a forward direction. If the logical levels of AIN1 and AIN2 are low and high, the motor will spin but, the direction of the motor will be the opposite. This is a reverse direction.

AIN1(BIN1)	AIN2 (BIN2)	Description
0	0	Fast decay
0	1	Reverse
1	0	Forward
1	1	Slow decay (Short brake)

Table 14.1. H-bridge logic.

When the motor is spinning, both of the AIN1 and AIN2 can be controlled to be either low or high. Then, the motor is going to stop spinning. If both of the AIN1 and AIN2 are low, the current gets decayed in a *fast* decay mode. On the other hand, if both of AIN1 and AIN2 are high, the current gets decayed in a *slow* decay mode. In the fast decay, the current decays faster. In the slow decay, due to the effect of shorting back EMF, the rotor stops quickly.

In order to control the speed of the motor, PWM (Pulse Width Modulation) signals can be applied. Table 14.2 shows the functions when the PWM singles are applied.

AIN1(BIN1)	AIN2 (BIN2)	Description
0	PWM	Reverse (PWM) / fast decay
PWM	0	Forward (PWM) / fast decay
1	PWM	Forward (PWM) / slow decay
PWM	1	Reverse (PWM) / slow decay

Table 14.2. PWM Control.

If the logical level of AIN1 is low and PWM signals are applied to AIN2, the reverse and fast decay states will be alternating. By controlling the average power delivered to the motor, the motor speed can be controlled. When the PWM signal and the low logic level are switched, the direction of the motor will be reversed.

Likewise, if the logical level of AIN1 is high and PWM signals are applied to AIN2, the forward and slow decay states will be alternating. When the PWM signal and the high logic level are switched, the direction of the motor will be reversed. The speed of the motor can be varied by the PWM signals that can control the average power delivered to the motor.

A simplified DRV8833 connection example is shown in Figure 14.9. This example controls two DC motors. The DRV8833 motor driver is connected to the GPIO pins of an MSP432P401R MCU.

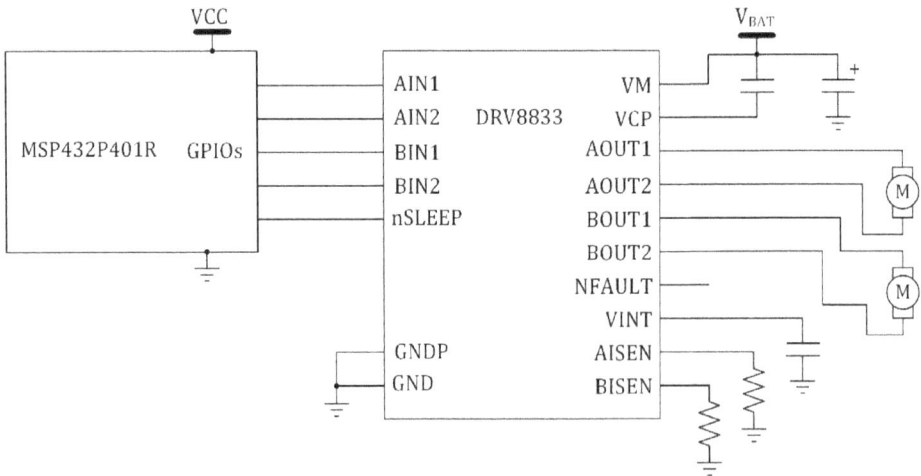

Figure 14.9. Simplified DRV8833 connection diagram for two DC motors.

As it can be seen, the supply voltage of a DRV8833 IC can be higher than the supply voltage of an MSP432P401R MCU. Four GPIO pins are used for AIN1, AIN2, BIN1, and BIN2 pins, and one more GPIO pin is used for the nSLEEP pin. If the logic level is high at this pin, the motor driver will be activated. However, if the logic level is low at this pin, the motor driver enters a low-power sleep mode.

DRV8833 Motor Driver Module

Instead of using an individual DRV8833 IC, a DRV8833 motor driver module can be used. There are several modules available from different vendors. Readers can choose their DRV8833 module. One of the modules used in this section is Adafruit® DRV8833 module. Using this module, the connection can become simpler.

The connection diagram is shown in Figure 14.10. In this example, only one motor is connected. There is "VM" pin in the module. This is connected to the VM pin of the DRV8833 IC. In this module, there is a small screw fixed terminal block. This module supports a reverse polarity protection through this terminal block. And, it is internally connected to the VM pin. Either the terminal block or VM pin would work to supply voltage to the motor driver. However, it is preferred to supply the power through the terminal block due to the reverse polarity protection function.

For testing and safety purposes, a DC power supply can be used instead of batteries. The supply voltage to the DRV8833 module has to meet the specification of a DC motor. For instance, a DC gearbox motor may have a recommended operating range such as 3 V to 6 V DC. A user can choose 5 V that is within the operating range.

In this diagram, three pins are connected to an MSP432P401R MCU. The AIN1 and AIN2 pins are connected to P2.4 and P2.5, respectively. The SLP pin is the internally connected to nSLEEP pin of the DRV8833 IC. The SLP pin is connected to P5.0.

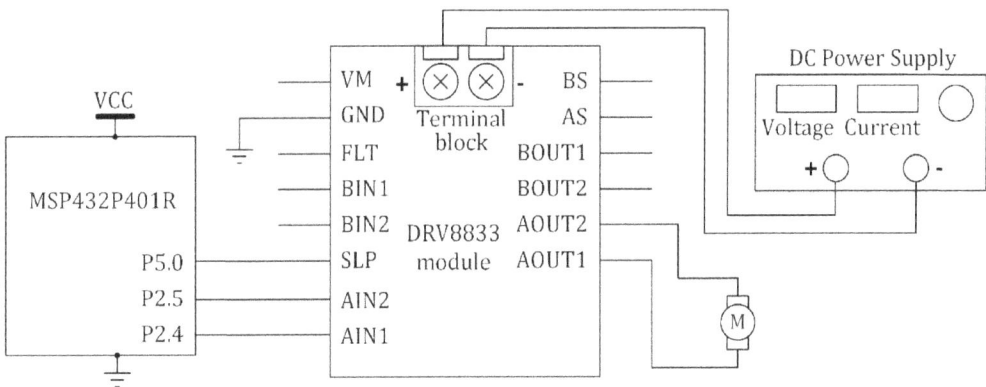

Figure 14.10. DRV8833 module connection diagram [18]

On the BH EDU board, an DRV8833 IC is mounted. A user simply needs to connect the control pins properly to header pins on the BH EDU board.

Pin functions

The pin functions of P2.4 and P2.5 are shown in Table 14.3. As we have studied in the previous chapter, P2SEL1, P2SEL0, and P2DIR need to be configured properly for the alternative function of TA0.1. As shown in the table, the alternative function of the P2.5 can be chosen. In order to generate PWM signals, we can select TA0.2. Similarly, P2SEL1, P2SEL0, an P2DIR need to be configured properly for the alternative function of TA0.2.

Pin	P2SEL1	P2SEL0	P2DIR	Description
P2.4	0	0	0	GPIO (INPUT)
	0	0	1	GPIO (OUTPUT)
	0	1	1	TA0.1
P2.5	0	0	0	GPIO (INPUT)
	0	0	1	GPIO (OUTPUT)
	0	1	1	TA0.2

Table 14.3. Pin functions of P2.4 and P2.5 in an MSP432P401R MCU [6].

DC Motor Control Example

A DC motor control program is shown in Program 14.1. This is based on the connection shown in Figure 14.10. In this code, the GPIO and the Timer_A0 are configured properly for the hardware PWM signals through P2.4 and P2.5. In the previous chapter, we have studied the code that can generate PWM signals at one pin. This code in this chapter can generate PWM signals through two separate pins.

The duty cycles of the PWM signals can be controlled by tweaking TA0CCR1 and TA0CCR2 values. In this case, TA0CCR1 and TA0CCR2 values are configured as 2500 and 5000, respectively. Since TA0CCR0 is 5000, the duty cycles for the PWM signals at P2.4 and P2.5 are about 50% and 100%. The ideal 100% PWM signal is simply like a logical high. It is worth of mentioning that it is not the same as a solid logical high signal. It may show some periodic glitches due to the output circuit behavior. Referring to Table 14.2, this example will show the operations of the reverse motor rotation and slow decay.

```
#include "msp.h"
int main(void) {
    WDT_A->CTL = WDT_A_CTL_PW | WDT_A_CTL_HOLD;  // hold the watchdog timer
    P1->DIR |= BIT0;  // output direction for an LED
    P5->DIR |= BIT0;  // output direction for P5.0
    P5->OUT |= BIT0;  // set the output of P5.0
    P2->DIR |= BIT4 | BIT5;  // output direction
    P2->SEL1 &= ~(BIT4 | BIT5);  // TA0.1 & TA0.2 selection
    P2->SEL0 |= (BIT4 | BIT5);  // TA0.1 & TA0.2 selection
    TIMER_A0->CTL = TIMER_A_CTL_TASSEL_2 | TIMER_A_CTL_MC_1 |
TIMER_A_CTL_CLR;  // TA0CTL setup
    TIMER_A0->CCR[0] = 5000;  // set the value of TA0CCR0
```

```
    TIMER_A0->CCR[1] = 2500;  // set the value of TA0CCR1
    TIMER_A0->CCTL[1] = TIMER_A_CCTLN_OUTMOD_7;  // output mode 7
    TIMER_A0->CCR[2] = 5000 ;  // set the value of CCR2
    TIMER_A0->CCTL[2] = TIMER_A_CCTLN_OUTMOD_7;  // output mode 7
    while(1){
      P1->OUT ^= BIT0;  // toggle an LED
      __delay_cycles(500000);  // delay
    }
}
```

Program 14.1. PWM DC motor control example.

Users can change the TA0CCR1 and TA0CCR2 values in order to create various conditions shown in Table 14.2. The value of TA0CCR0 can be tweaked and it may vary the frequency. While any of the PWM frequency can be chosen, it is preferred to choose a frequency that is higher than audible frequency range. This is because an audible noise in a motor can be problematic. However, if the PWM frequency gets too high, the motor driver may not be able to handle the signals properly. This is also related to the choice of the decay mode.

In Chapter 22, we will study the system integration and a simple educational robot as an example. This robot is a differential wheeled robot platform, which has two separately driven wheels with one or more caster wheels. To operate the two motors, users can modify this example to add two more PWM signals for other two pins of an MSP432P401R MCU.

Chapter 15. Servo Motor

A servo motor is an actuator that produces a rotary motion typically for precise control of angular position. Servo motors have been utilized in many applications. They are also used in industrial robotics, manufacturing equipment, and CNC (Computer Numerical Control) machines. Moreover, they can be small in size, and they are used in radio-controlled (R/C) cars, airplanes, and boats. In this chapter, we will learn about servo motors.

Open Loop Control System

A gear motor can be controlled by an open loop system as shown in Figure 15.1. In an open loop control system, the input is simply fed to a controller, and the controller controls the gear motor accordingly. To make it clear, the output of a system is not used as an input back to the system to determine whether the output has achieved the goal or not.

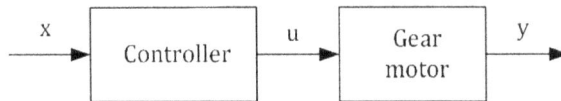

Figure 15.1. Open loop control.

The advantage of using an open loop control is the reduction of a system complexity. However, this open loop system cannot correct errors that may have caused by any disturbances. This open loop motor control behavior is similar to the one we have studied in the previous chapter. An MCU generates PWM signals according to the desired motor behavior. Then, a motor driver IC controls the DC motor based on the PWM signal inputs. However, any data about the rotation speed or the direction of the motor is not fed back to the MCU. In a normal condition, the output behavior may be close to the desired behavior or goal. However, in the presence of disturbances, there is a chance that the output behavior can be deviating from the goal.

Closed Loop Control

A gear motor can be controlled by a closed loop system as shown in Figure 15.2. In a closed loop control system, the output of a system has a feedback loop to the system and the output is used as an input to the system to determine whether the output has achieved the goal. A feedback controller controls the gear motor. The difference between the variable "x" and the sensor block output will be used as an input for the feedback controller. The sensor block converts a behavior of the gear motor such as rotation or angle to a proper format of signals or data. This closed loop system is more complex than the open loop system. However, in the presence of disturbances, the output behavior can be corrected to meet the goal and for the desired behavior. A servo motor is an example of a closed loop control system.

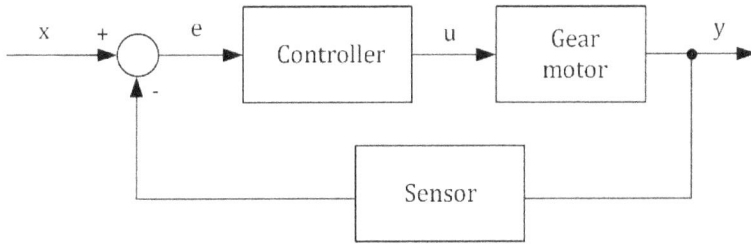

Figure 15.2. Closed loop control.

PID Control

The controller in Figure 15.3 has thee proportional (P), integral (I), and derivative (D) blocks. Their outputs are summed to provide the input to the motor module. This is an example of a proportional integral derivative controller (PID) controller. A PID controller continuously calculates an error between the goal and the measured value, and it applies corrections based on proportional, integral, and derivative terms. A PID controller has been widely used in control applications.

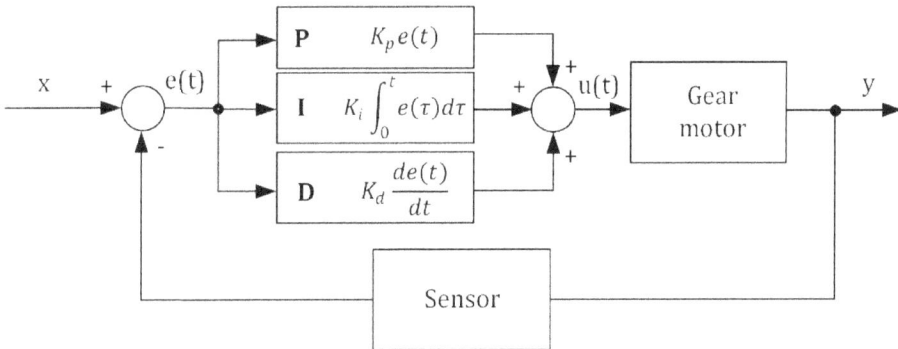

Figure 15.3. PID control.

The control function can be expressed by the equation as follows:

$$u(t) = K_p e(t) + K_i \int_0^t e(\tau)d\tau + K_d \frac{de(t)}{dt}$$

The first term is the proportional term. It contributes to the output that is proportional to the current error value. The rate of the change can be adjusted by a constant K_p. The second term is the integral term. The contribution to the output can be determined by the sum of instantaneous errors over time. The rate of the change can be adjusted by a constant K_i. The third term is the derivative term. The contribution is determined by the slope of the error over time. The rate of the change can be adjusted by a constant K_d. There are three control terms. In some applications, only one or two terms can be used depending on applications. Proportional and integration terms are chosen, which is known as a PI controller.

PID controllers can be found in many control applications including servo motor control systems. In a servo motion control system, it has a feedback loop, and a PID controller provides tuning of a control loop.

Servo Motor

Servo motors are used in industrial applications including industrial robots and industrial automation systems. Servo motors provide high precision positioning. A servo motor is shown in Figure 15.4. The servo motor is paired with an encoder which can be used to determine the speed and position. Depending on the servo motor model, a servo motor may provide several connectors including encoder and power connectors.

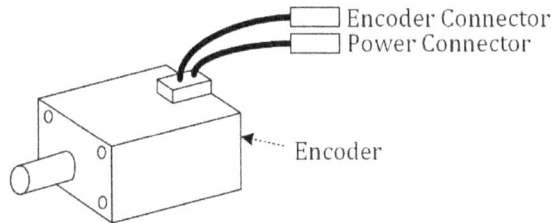

Figure 15.4. Servo motor.

Using this servo motor, a servo motor system is configured as shown in Figure 15.5. The servo motor is connected to a block with servo amplifier and the motion controller. It communicates with a computer. A custom application on the computer controls the position of the servo motor. For instance, it can control the servo motors that are used in a CNC machine.

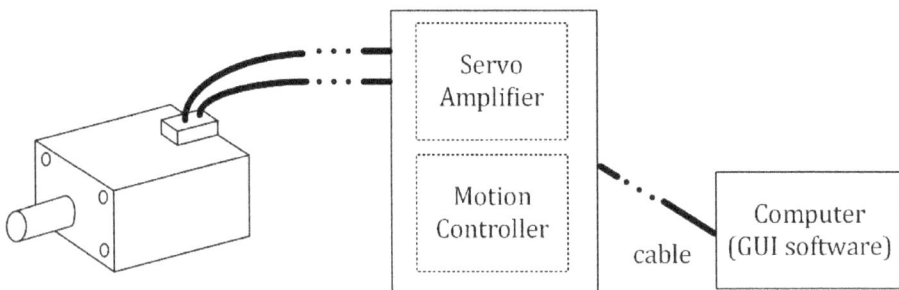

Figure 15.5. Servo motor system.

Hobby Servo Motor

In some small or simple electronics projects, hobby servo motors are used to provide the motion control. Typically, a servo motor system can be expensive. However, hobby servo motors are inexpensive, and developers can buy them off the self. It can reduce the effort in designing a custom control system. A micro servo and standard servo motors are shown in Figure 15.6. These servo motors are also called RC servos, and they are widely used in R/C cars and R/C airplanes. Standard servo motors are bigger than micro servo motors; however, typically, they can deliver higher torque. Hobby servo motors have been used in small-sized robotics projects.

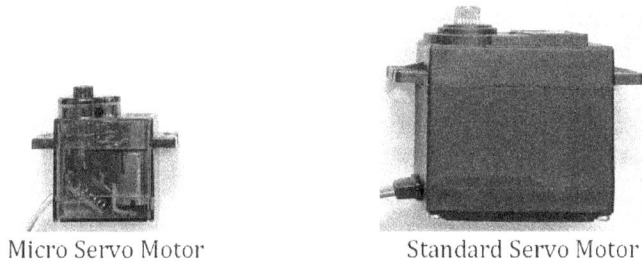

Micro Servo Motor   Standard Servo Motor

Figure 15.6. Hobby servo motors.

A simplified block diagram of a hobby servo motor is shown in Figure 15.7. A hobby servo motor is a smaller scale system than the industrial servo motor system we have studied previously. A hobby servo motor also has a feedback control, and the shaft position is measured by a potentiometer. PWM signals can be applied to a hobby servo motor, and the shaft of the hobby servo motor can hold a corresponding angular position.

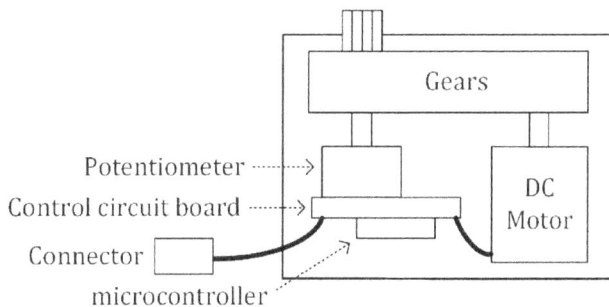

Figure 15.7. Simplified block diagram of a hobby servo motor.

Control of a Hobby Servo Motor

It is typical to find a 3-pin female header that is attached to a hobby servo motor. One of the pins is a control signal line. Digital signal pulse patterns can be applied through this pin to control the shaft position of the servo motor. Servo control signal pattern examples are shown in Figure 15.8. It shows the neural position case in the center of the figure. The ON time is 1.5 ms, and the period of the signal is 20 ms. When the servo motor receives this control signal pattern, the shaft of the hobby servo motor attempts to stay at the neural position. An MCU can generate this control signal pattern using 50-Hz digital signals with a proper duty cycle. The duty cycle can be varied to generate this 1-ms ON time pattern. Then, the shaft of the servo motor will be rotated by a 45 degree. Let us suppose we set the shaft of the servo motor back to the neural position. Next, we can change the duty cycle to generate the 2-ms ON time pattern. In this case, the shaft of the servo motor will be rotated to the other direction by a 45 degree. In this way, the servo motor position can be varied by applying proper PWM signals.

A typical range of the ON time extends from 1 ms to 2 ms. However, depending on a servo motor model, the servo motor position can travel further by applying a lower than 1-ms or higher than 2-ms ON time pattern. For instance, some of the servo motors can provide 180-degree range of motion. Moreover, if the ON time is out of the operating range, the servo motor may not respond. The specifications of servo motors may vary by manufacturer. Developers need to refer to the documentation from the manufacturer for the servo motor, and they may find the information such as operating ranges.

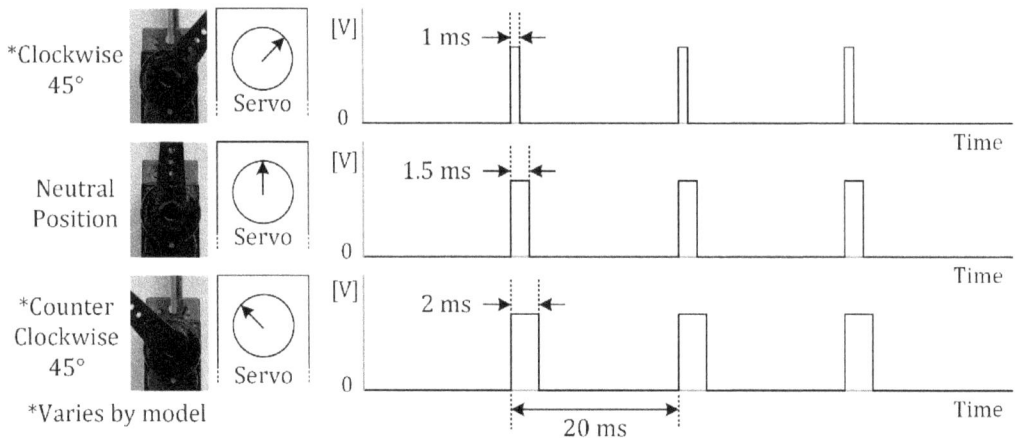

Figure 15.8. Control signal pattern examples.

There are continuous rotation servos. While a regular servo motor rotates the shaft within a certain rotation range, the shaft of these continuous rotation servos can spin continuously. In this case, the PWM control signals control the speed and direction of the servo motor.

Micro Servo Motor Example

SG90 servo models are widely used in RC helicopters and airplanes. There are several similar models with difference specifications. As an example, let us choose a TowerPro SG92R for an experiment, and the connection diagram is shown in Figure 15.9. A

TowerPro SG92R model is similar to SG90 model; but, SG92R has a higher torque. The color of the control signal is yellow or white depending on the model. This control line is connected to P5.6 of an MSP432P401R MCU. The Red color line is connected to the positive terminal and the Brown line is connected to the negative terminal of a power supply. The Brown line is a ground signal line, and the color of this line can be found Black depending on the model. The supply voltage for this servo motor is 5 V. It is worth of mentioning that the ground lines between the MSP432P401R and the servo motor may need to be connected each other.

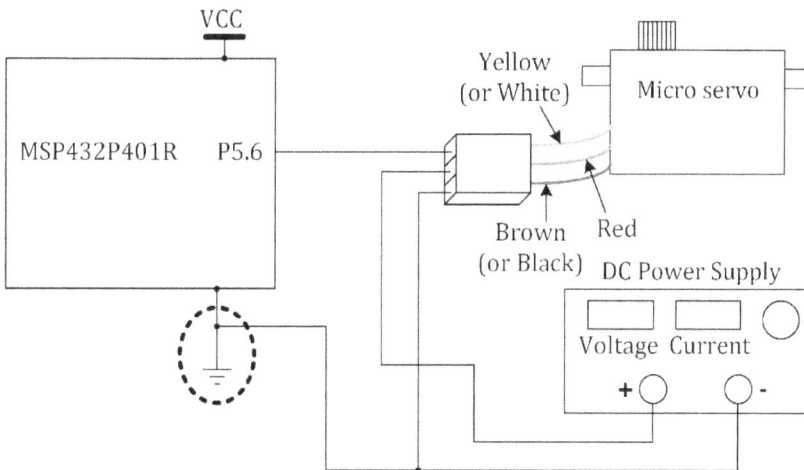

Figure 15.9. micro servo motor connection example.

Servo Motor Programming Example

A servo motor programming example is shown in Program 15.1 One of the alternative functions of P5.6 pin is TA2.1. This alternative function was configured in the program. Previously, we have used the Timer_A0. In this program, Timer_A2 was used instead. The timer configuration for Timer_A2 is very similar to the one for Timer_A0. The value of TA2CCR0 was calculated and a specific value was used to generate 50-Hz PWM signals. The output mode 7 is selected. TA2CCR1 was calculated and the proper value was entered to generate a 1.5 ms. Using this program, the position of the servo motor can be set as neutral. This program can be used in many servo models. The duty cycle can be varied as TA2CCR1 changes. As

TA2CCR1 varies within a proper range, the servo motor position will change accordingly.

```
#include "msp.h"
int main(void) {
  WDT_A->CTL = WDT_A_CTL_PW | WDT_A_CTL_HOLD;  // hold the watchdog timer
  P1->DIR |= BIT0;  // output direction for an LED
  P5->DIR |= BIT6;  // output direction
  P5->SEL1 &= ~BIT6;  // TA2.1 selection
  P5->SEL0 |= BIT6;  // TA2.1 selection
  TIMER_A2->CTL = TIMER_A_CTL_TASSEL_2 | TIMER_A_CTL_MC_1 |
TIMER_A_CTL_CLR;  // TA2CTL setup
  TIMER_A2->CCR[0] = 60000;  // set the value of TA2CCR0
  TIMER_A2->CCTL[1] = TIMER_A_CCTLN_OUTMOD_7;  // output mode 7
  TIMER_A2->CCR[1] = 4500;  // set the value of CCR1
  while(1){
    P1->OUT ^= BIT0;  // toggle an LED
    _delay_cycles(500000);  // delay
  }
}
```

Program 15.1. Servo motor programming example.

Chapter 16. Basics of Serial Communications and UART

Data communication refers to the transmission of data between systems. The communication links can be a point-to-point link or point-to-multiple links. Embedded systems typically utilize one or more communication modules to exchange data between microcontrollers and other external devices. In this chapter, we will learn about serial communications and the UART module on an MSP432P401R MCU.

Serial and Parallel

In digital communications, serial and parallel communications can be used to exchange data between devices. Data can be transmitted and received over a single channel in serial communications. Or, data can be transmitted and received simultaneously over multiple channels in parallel communications.

The examples of serial communications on computers are USB, Firewire, and SATA. The examples of parallel communications on computers are IDE (Integrated Drive Electronics) and PCI (Peripheral Component Interconnect).

Intuitively, it would seem the parallel communications might offer faster speed of data transfer compared to the serial communications. However, practically, this is not the case in modern systems. The serial communications offer faster speed of data transfer. There are many reasons. Firstly, the signals that travel along the multiple wires may not arrive at the destination at the same time. This difference may get more significant as the frequency gets higher. It may cause a problem in synchronization, and eventually, it will affect and limit the data transmission speed. Secondly, the parallel wires may suffer from crosstalk as well as inter symbol interference (ISI) due to noise. For these reasons, the parallel communications may result in lower speed than the serial communications.

Types of Communication Systems

Types of communications systems can be defined in several ways. Let us consider three types with respect to communication channels between two systems as shown in Figure 16.1. A simplex communication system is shown at the top. *System A* can send the data over a channel to *System B,* while the *System B* is unable to send data back to the *System A*. A simplex communication system transmit data in one direction only. An example is the communication between a radio broadcast station and a listener.

Duplex communication systems transmit data and receive data in both directions. In duplex communications, there are half-duplex and full-duplex communication systems. A half-duplex communication system is shown in the middle of Figure 16.1.

A half-duplex system can send and receive data between two systems but not simultaneously. *System A* and System B can exchange data, but it does not send and receive the data simultaneously. An example is a walkie-talkie, which is a two-way radio transceiver and only one radio on the channel can transmit at a time.

Simplex Communication

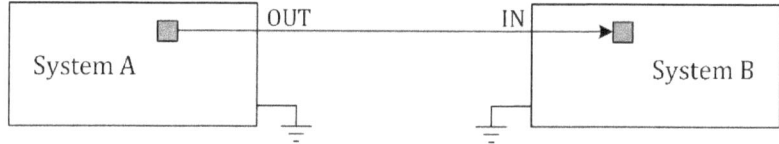

Duplex Communication

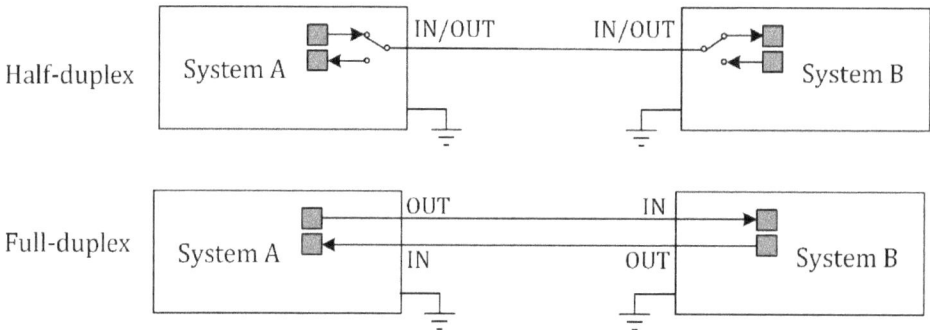

Figure 16.1. Types of communication systems with respect to communication channels.

A full-duplex communication system is shown at the bottom of Figure 16.1. A full-duplex system can send and receive data between two systems simultaneously. *System A* and System B can exchange simultaneously. An example of a duplex communication is a mobile phone communication.

Universal Asynchronous Receiver/Transmitter

Universal asynchronous receiver-transmitter (UART) peripherals are commonly found in microcontrollers. There can be multiple UART modules in an MCU. A UART provides asynchronous serial communication. It has been widely used in data communications between external ICs. An example is the UART communications between the MCU and an USB-to-UART IC. In this setting, the MCU can communicate with a computer over USB interface. An MSP432P401R Launchpad includes a XDS110-ET block that is a debug probe unit. This XDS110-ET provides a "backchannel" UART-over-USB connection. The backchannel term is used to differentiate the UART channel that is provided through the booster pack header pins. The microUSB connector is not only used to supply power to the MSP432P401R Launchpad board, but also to provide a serial communication between an MSP432P401R MCU and a computer.

UART Data Transmission

A baud rate is one of the important parameters that needs to be matched between systems in a UART communication. A baud rate is used to determine the speed of the serial communication. A baud rate is usually expressed in bits-per-second (bps). Standard baud rates include 1200, 2400, 4800, 9600, 19200, 38400, 57600, and 115200. Let us say that 9600 bps is chosen for the system. Each bit for the UART data transmission has a fixed time duration. If we calculate 1 divided by 9600 bps, we can obtain 104 µs per bit. This is the value associated with the time duration for a single bit to be sent or received.

A UART data frame format is shown in Figure 16.2. One bit is allocated for the start bit. The logic level of the start bit is low. One bit or two bits can be allocated for the stop bit(s). The logic level of the stop bit is high. Between the start and stop bits, there are data bits and a parity bit. The number of bits for data can be any choice between 5 and 9. The common choice is 7 or 8. Typically, data can be transmitted least significant bit (LSB) first. The use of the parity bit is selectable, which was expressed as the "0~1 bit" in the frame format.

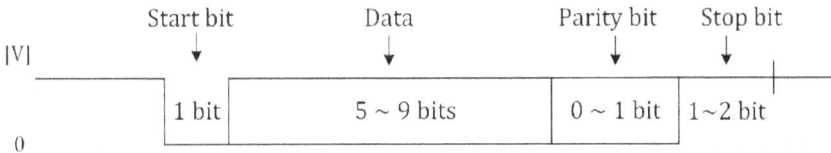

Figure 16.2. UART data frame format.

Let us consider a 9600 7E1 case. In this 9600 7E1 setting, the baud rate is 9600 bps. The number of data bits is 7, and the parity bit is enabled. The setting for the parity bit is even. One bit of the stop bit is selected. The 7E1 UART data frame case is shown in Figure 16.3.

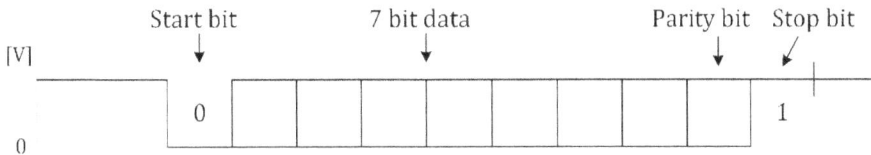

Figure 16.3. 7E1 UART data frame.

Now, let us suppose we want to send character **T**. Let us create this UART data packet. The ASCII (American Standard Code for Information Interchange) code for the character T is 0x54. We can send the bits of the data, and LSB can be sent first. The value of the parity bit is 1 because it can make the even number of 1s in the data packet excluding start and stop bits. One bit is used for the stop bit. This UART data packet is shown in Figure 16.4.

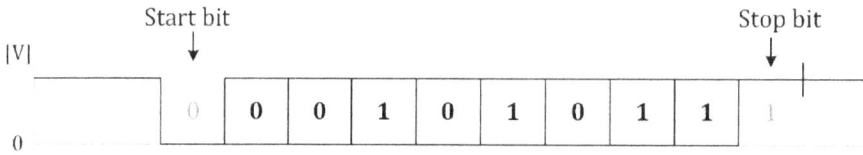

Figure 16.4. 7E1 UART data frame example for the character of T.

Another common choice is 8N1. In this 8N1 setting, the number of data bits is 8 and the parity bit is not used. The 8N1 UART data frame for the character T is shown in Figure 16.5. This is similar to the 7E1 case, but the difference is related to the parity bit. In this 8N1 setting, the location of the parity bit is used as a part of the data.

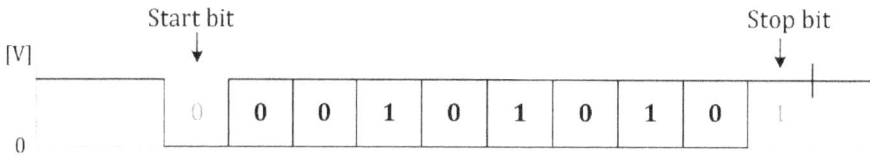

Figure 16.5. 8N1 UART data frame example for the character T.

UART Device Connection

A UART device connection example is shown in Figure 16.6. UART devices are typically connected using a crossover cable. The TX pin in *System A* is connected to the RX pin in *System B*, and the RX pin in *System A* is connected to the TX pin in *System B*. Additionally, we may need VDD and GND wires. Power line configuration may vary by system. The wires for RX and TX pins and additional power wires can be used for a basic connection via UART communications.

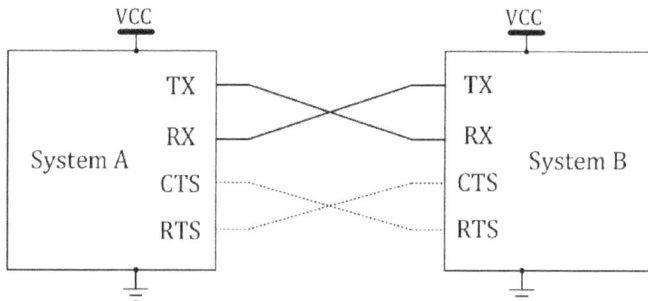

Figure 16.6. UART device connection.

Moreover, there are two more pins of RTS and CTS. They are used for a hardware flow control. In some applications, a handshaking process is needed to ensure the communication between systems or devices. RTS means *Request to Send*, and CTS means *Clear to Send*. RTS pin in *System A* is connected to CTS in *System B*, and CTS pin in *System A* is connected to RTS in *System B*. This is a typical connection of the hardware flow control. However, in some implementations, it can be found that RTS is connected to RTS and CTS is connected to CTS depending on their configuration.

UART connections are typically used in a point-to-point configuration as shown in Figure 16.6. There can be variants including a one-to-multiple configuration. However, the one-to-multiple configurations are not typical connection scheme.

Software UART

Without dedicated hardware, serial communications can be implemented simply using timers and GPIOs. This technique is called *bit-banging*. Using a *bit-banging* technique, we can implement a UART using two GPIO pins for transmit and receive channels. This can be called Software UART. We will learn about hardware UART in the following section, and the hardware UART is a preferred method. However, there could be the case where the software UART is needed depending on the applications.

An asynchronous communication is relatively easier to implement compared to a synchronous communication. A UART communication is an asynchronous communication because there is no external clock signal line used for synchronization.

Software UART Programming Example

Software UART program example is shown in Program 16.1. This program keeps sending the character T over a backchannel UART. P1.3 is used as TX in this program. This matches with the TX pin configuration in the backchannel UART. This means that data will be sent to a computer. The data can be read using a terminal window in Code Composer Studio or using other serial terminal software such as PuTTY.

An array of *TX_buf* has the pattern for the character T. It also includes the start and stop bits. This program reads the bit in sequence from this array, then, it sets or clears the output of the P1.3. Since it keeps repeating, the terminal will keep receiving the character T. The time duration between each bit is controlled by the line of *_dealy_cycles(300)*. The target time delay is 104 µs. This code line can result in roughly 104 µs. This means this is functional but, it is not accurate. In this program, a general-purpose timer is not utilized. To achieve a better software UART, a general-purpose timer can be used to generate the accurate time duration. As it was described, the time delay of 104 µs is related to 9600 bps. In order to receive the characters successfully, the terminal setting on a computer needs to be configure properly to match with 9600 8N1.

```c
#include "msp.h"
unsigned char TX_buf[10]={0,0,0,1,0,1,0,1,0,1}; // UART TX pattern for T
int main(void) {
    WDT_A->CTL = WDT_A_CTL_PW | WDT_A_CTL_HOLD;  // hold the watchdog timer
    P1->DIR |= BIT3 | BIT0;  // output direction for TX & LED
    unsigned char kp;  // variable
    while(1){
        for (kp=0; kp<10; kp++) {  // sending the pattern
            if (TX_buf[kp]!=0) P1->OUT |= BIT3;  // set P1.3
            else P1->OUT &= ~BIT3;  // clear P1.3
            __delay_cycles(300);  // delay (~104us)
        }
        P1->OUT ^= 0x01;  // toggle
        __delay_cycles(500000);  // delay
    }
}
```

Program 16.1. Software UART program (Sending characters).

This software UART programing example does not process received data from a terminal. If a user sends data over a terminal, it will be sent to P1.2. This P1.2 is related to RX in the back channel UART. However, as described, this program does not process the received data. An MSP432P401R MCU supports hardware UART communications. A hardware UART is a preferred method to provide a good communication between UART devices. The MSP432P401R UART communication module will be covered in the following sections. We will learn how to send data and how to process received data.

Hardware UART

An MSP432P401R MCU has eUSCI (Enhanced Universal Serial Communication Interface) modules. An eUSCI module includes eUSCI_A and eUSCI_B modules. An eUSCI_A supports UART and SPI modes. A simplified block diagram of eUSCI_A0 in UART mode is shown in Figure 16.7. On the left side, it shows a baud rate generator. The setting of these parameters is important in UART communications. BRCLK can be found in the figure. It is used as an input for the baud rate generator. The baud rate generator in an eUSCI_A module can provide signals for standard and non-standard baud rates. It supports two modes of operation that can be selected by a UCOS16 bit. The two modes are low-frequency baud rate and oversampling baud rate generation modes.

At the bottom of the figure, it shows the blocks associated with the transmit functions. The major blocks are *transmit state machine*, *transmit shift register*, and *transmit buffer.* The name of the transmit buffer is UCA0TXBUF. At the top of the figure, it shows the blocks associated with the receive functions. The major blocks are *receive state machine*, *receive shift register*, and *receive buffer*. The name of the receive buffer is UCA0RXBUF.

There are registers related to interrupt and interrupt flags in the USCI_A0 module. *UCA0IE* register is an interrupt enable register. It has *UCTXIE* and *UCRXIE* bits. *UCA0IFG* register is an interrupt flag register. It has *UCTXIFG* and *UCRXIFG* bits.

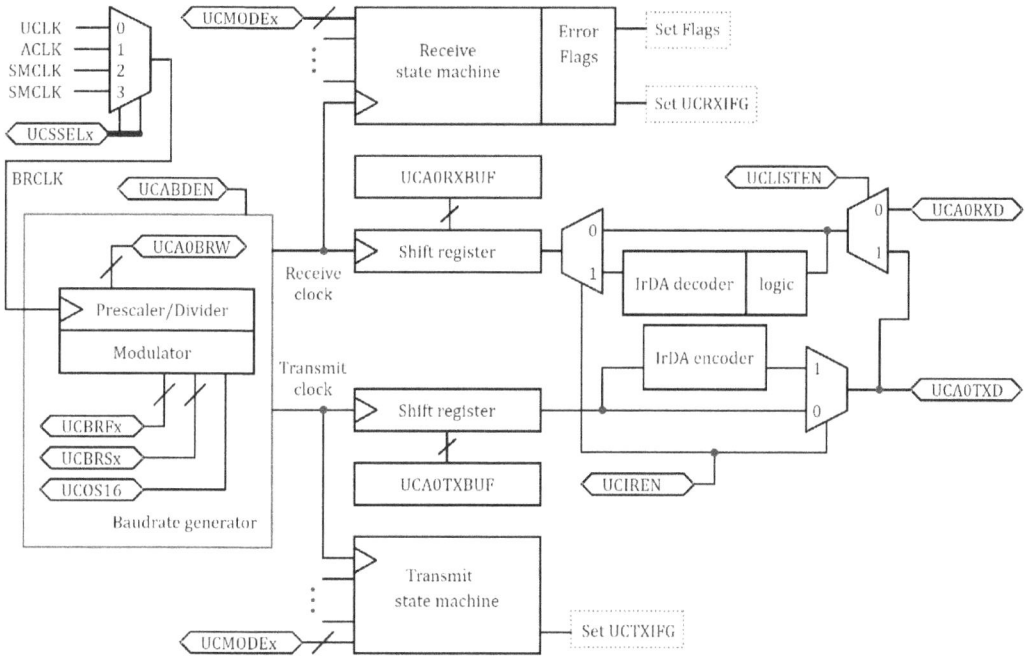

Figure 16.7. Simplified block diagram of eUSCI_A0 in UART mode [6].

eUSCI_A0 Initialization

Setting *USCWRST* bit can reset the eUSCI_A0 module. While keeping this bit set, we can configure the eUSCI_A0 by changing eUSCI_A0 registers. The port configuration can be processed. Once it is completed, eUSCI_A0 can operate in a normal mode by clearing *USCWRST* bit. This step of configuring eUSCI_A module is recommended to avoid an unexpected behavior. The initialization step is summarized below.

    (a) Set USCWRST
    (b) Initialize eUSCI_A0 registers (while USCWRST bit is set)
    (c) Port configuration
    (d) Clear USCWRST
    (e) If applicable, enable interrupts such as UCRXIE and UCTXIE

UART Baud Rate Generation

One of the low-frequency baud-rate and oversampling baud rate generation modes can be selected by a *UCOS16* setting. If the *UCOS16* bit is cleared, it operates in low-frequency baud rate generation mode. This mode is suitable for the signals from low frequency clock sources such as a 32.769 kHz crystal.

If the *UCOS16* bit is set, it can operate in an oversampling frequency baud rate generation mode. This mode is suitable for the higher frequency generation. It uses a modulator to generate an internal clock that is 16 times faster, and it results in a factor of 1/16 in UART baud rate parameter calculations. We will study how to determine parameters in the following sections.

Setting a Baud Rate

Using a BRCLK and baud rate, a division factor of N can be determined using the equation as follows:

$$N = \frac{f_{BRCLK}}{baud\ rate}$$

If N is equal or greater than 16, it is recommended to use an oversampling frequency baud rate generation mode. In this case, let us say *UCOS16* is 1. It means UCOS16 bit is set.

Low-frequency Baud rate Generation

In the low-frequency mode, we can say *UCOS16* is 0. It means the UCOS16 bit is cleared. We can obtain the integer portion of the divisor N that is relevant to the prescaler parameter as shown in the following equation.

$$UCBRx = Integer\ of\ N$$

Since *UCOS16* is 0, the UCBRFx is ignored. The fractional portion of N is relevant to the modulator parameter.

The value of *UCBRSx* can be obtained by using the table of "*UCBRSx Settings for Fractional Portion of N*" from the manufacturer's technical manual documentation [6], or performing an detailed error calculation based on the recommendation from the manufacturer.

For the value of UCBSRx, this book introduces another method as an option for readers. We can multiply the fraction portion of N by 10,000, and we can obtain the FN by taking integer portion of the product. The equation of FN is shown as follows:

$$FN = Integer\ of\ \left((fractional\ portion\ of\ N) \times 10^4\right)$$

Next, using the value of FN, we can obtain the value of UCBRSx from Table 16.1.

FN	UCBRSx	FN	UCBRSx	FN	UCBRSx
0 ~ 528	0	3335 ~ 3574	73	7001 ~ 7146	183
529 ~ 714	1	3575 ~ 3752	74	7147 ~ 7502	187
715 ~ 834	2	3753 ~ 4002	82	7503 ~ 7860	221
835 ~1000	4	4003 ~4285	146	7861 ~ 8003	237
1001 ~1251	8	4286 ~ 4377	83	8004 ~ 8332	238
1252 ~ 1429	16	4378 ~ 5001	85	8333 ~ 8463	191
1430 ~ 1669	32	5002 ~ 5714	170	8464 ~ 8571	223
1670 ~ 2146	17	5715 ~6002	107	8572 ~ 8750	239
2147 ~ 2223	33	6003 ~ 6253	173	8751 ~ 9003	247
2224 ~ 2502	34	6254 ~ 6431	181	9004 ~ 9169	251
2503 ~ 2999	68	6432 ~ 6666	182	9170 ~ 9287	253
3000 ~ 3334	37	6667 ~ 7000	214	9288 ~ 9999	254

Table 16.1. UCBRSx settings for FN [6].

The parameters obtained using this calculation can be used as initial values. However, these parameters are not necessarily fixed numbers, but they can be tweaked by system for better performance. Specifically, for instance, modulator parameter can be tweaked such as UCBRFx and UCBRSx to achieve better performance.

To assist the understanding of the low-frequency baud rate generations, the baud rate calculation example is shown in Exercise 16-1.

Exercise 16.1) *If the BRCLK is 32.768 kHz and the baud rate is 9600 bps, what are the reasonable parameter values for UCOS16, UCBRx, UCBRFx, and UCBRSx?*

Explanation) *We can obtain the division factor as follows:* $N = \frac{f_{BRCLK}}{baud\ rate} = \frac{32768}{9600} = 3.41$. *Since this is lower than 16, UCOS16 is selected as 0. This is a low-frequency baud rate generation mode setting. UCBRx can be obtained by the equation as follows: UCBRx = Integer of N = 3. UCBRFx is ignored because USCO16 =0. The fractional portion of N is 0.4133, and the value of FN is 4133. From Table 16.1, UCBRSx is 146.*

Oversampling Baud rate Generation
In the oversampling mode, we can say UCOS16 is 1. We can obtain the value of *UCBRx* using the equation as follows:

$$UCBRx = Integer\ of\ \frac{N}{16}$$

The first stage modulator parameter can be obtained by the equation as follows:

$$UCBRFx = round\left(\left(fractional\ portion\ of\ \frac{N}{16}\right) \times 16\right)$$

, where $fractional\ portion\ of\ \frac{N}{16} = \left(\frac{N}{16} - Integer\ of\ \frac{N}{16}\right)$

For the value of UCBRSx, it can be obtained from the same method described previously in Low-frequency baud rate Generation. One of the methods was to obtain the value of FN. Using the value of FN, we can obtain the value of UCBRSRx from Table 16.1.

The baud rate calculation example for the case of the oversampling baud rate generation shown in Exercise 16-2. The explanation is followed.

Exercise 16.2) *If the BRCLK is 3 MHz and the baud rate is 9600 bps, what are the reasonable parameter values for UCOS16, UCBRx, UCBRFx, and UCBRSx?*

Explanation) *We can obtain the division factor as follows:* $N = \frac{f_{BRCLK}}{baud\ rate} = \frac{3 \times 10^6}{9600} =$ *312.5. Since this is higher than 16, UCOS16 is selected as 1. This is an oversampling baud rate generation mode setting. UCBRx can be obtained by the equation as follows:* $UCBRx = INT(N/16) = 19$. *UCBRFx can be obtained by the equation described above. Thus, UCBRFx = 9. The fractional portion of N is 0.5, and the value of FN is 5000. From Table 16.1, UCBRSx is 85.*

Hardware UART Program

Previously, we have used a software UART. In this section, we can write a program that can perform a similar task using a hardware UART. This program example is shown in Program 16.2.

As you can see, there are code lines that initialize the eUSCI module. It starts with setting *EUSCI_A_CTLW0_SWRST* bit. The UART setting is 9600 8N1. We have studied this case in Exercise 16.2. The SMCLK is selected. In this setting, the BRCLK is 3MHz. As UCBRx was calculated as 19, we can put "EUSCI_A0->BRW" as 19. UCBRFx and UCBRSx were calculated as 9 and 85, respectively. The UCOS16 was 1. Thus, "EUSCI_A0->MCTLW" is configured to be (9 << EUSCI_A_MCTLW_BRF_OFS) | (85 << EUSCI_A_MCTLW_BRS_OFS) | EUSCI_A_MCTLW_OS16". Next, the port configuration for the UART functions has been added.

After the UART initialization, *EUSCI_A_CTLW0_SWRST* bit is cleared. In the while loop, the *UCA0TXIFG* flag is cleared. The character T will be stored in the *transmit buffer*. The name of the *transmit buffer* is TX *EUSCI_A0->TXBUF*. If the transmission is completed, the *UCA0TXIFG* flag will be set. Then, the program waits until *UCA0TXIFG* flag is set. Next, it will toggle an LED. This pattern keeps repeating, and it will result in keeps sending the character T to the computer through the back channel UART. You can check whether you can receive the character T through a serial terminal in Code Composer Studio, or through any other serial terminal software such as PuTTY.

```
#include "msp.h"
int main(void) {
  WDT_A->CTL = WDT_A_CTL_PW | WDT_A_CTL_HOLD;  // hold the watchdog timer
  P1->DIR |= 0x01;  // output direction for an LED
  EUSCI_A0->CTLW0 |= EUSCI_A_CTLW0_SWRST;  // eUSCI reset state
  EUSCI_A0->CTLW0 = EUSCI_A_CTLW0_SWRST | EUSCI_A_CTLW0_UCSSEL_2;  // SMCLK
  EUSCI_A0->BRW = 19;  // 9600 bps setting
  EUSCI_A0->MCTLW = (9 << EUSCI_A_MCTLW_BRF_OFS) | (85 <<
EUSCI_A_MCTLW_BRS_OFS) | EUSCI_A_MCTLW_OS16;  // 9600 bps setting
  P1->SEL1 &= ~(BIT2 | BIT3);  // UART function for P1.2 & P1.3
  P1->SEL0 |= BIT2 | BIT3;  // UART function for P1.2 & P1.3
  EUSCI_A0->CTLW0 &= ~EUSCI_A_CTLW0_SWRST;  // eUSCI operation state
  __delay_cycles(1000);  // delay
  while(1){
    EUSCI_A0->IFG &= ~EUSCI_A_IFG_TXIFG;  // clear UCA0TXIFG flag
    EUSCI_A0->TXBUF = 'T';  // store the character in UCA0TXBUF
    while ((EUSCI_A0->IFG & EUSCI_A_IFG_TXIFG)==0);  // wait until UCA0TXIFG is set
    P1->OUT ^= 0x01;  // toggle
    __delay_cycles(500000);  // delay
  }
}
```

Program 16.2. Hardware UART program (Sending characters).

UART Echo Program (Polling)

A UART "echo" program can be useful in testing UART communications between systems or devices. This is a loopback test. It can simply send back received data. Once the communication channel is established and verified, the program can be modified to describe complicated tasks.

The UART echo example is shown in Program 16.3. This code is based on a polling method. The initialization is the same as the one we have studied previously. In the while loop, it receives data and stores it in a byte variable. This process was described in *EUSCI0_UART_RX_*data subroutine. In the subroutine, it waits until data is coming to the UART channel by checking whether the *UCA0RXIFG* flag is set or not. If the *UCA0RXIFG* flag is set, the program reads data from the receive buffer. Then, clear the *UCA0RXIFG* flag. Next, it has sent the data. This process was described in *EUSCI0_UART_TX_*data subroutine. In the subroutine, it clears the *UCA0TXIFG* flag, and store the data in *UAC0TXBUF*. Then, it waits until the transmission is completed by checking whether *UAC0TXIFG* is set or not. This pattern of receiving data and sending it back keeps repeating with a certain time delay in the while loop.

As a result, for instance, when a user types a character on a serial terminal window, this character will be sent to the MSP432P401R MCU. Then, the data will be sent back to the computer so that it will be displayed on the serial terminal. This UART echo test is useful in checking and verifying the serial communication between the device and the computer.

```c
#include "msp.h"
void EUSCI0_UART_TX_data(unsigned char);
unsigned char EUSCI0_UART_RX_data(void);
volatile unsigned char ch; // byte variable
int main(void) {
    WDT_A->CTL = WDT_A_CTL_PW | WDT_A_CTL_HOLD; // hold the watchdog timer
    P1->DIR |= BIT0; // output direction for an LED
    EUSCI_A0->CTLW0 |= EUSCI_A_CTLW0_SWRST; // eUSCI reset state
    EUSCI_A0->CTLW0 = EUSCI_A_CTLW0_SWRST | EUSCI_A_CTLW0_UCSSEL_2; // SMCLK
    EUSCI_A0->BRW = 19; // 9600 bps setting
    EUSCI_A0->MCTLW = (9 << EUSCI_A_MCTLW_BRF_OFS) | (85 <<
EUSCI_A_MCTLW_BRS_OFS) | EUSCI_A_MCTLW_OS16; // 9600 bps setting
    P1->SEL1 &= ~(BIT2 | BIT3); // UART function for P1.2 & P1.3
    P1->SEL0 |= BIT2 | BIT3; // UART function for P1.2 & P1.3
    EUSCI_A0->CTLW0 &= ~EUSCI_A_CTLW0_SWRST; // eUSCI operation state
    __delay_cycles(1000); // delay
    while(1){
        ch=EUSCI0_UART_RX_data(); // receive a character
        EUSCI0_UART_TX_data(ch); // send a character
        P1->OUT ^= BIT0; // toggle
        __delay_cycles(500000); // delay
    }
}

void EUSCI0_UART_TX_data(unsigned char data) {
    EUSCI_A0->IFG &= ~EUSCI_A_IFG_TXIFG; // clear UCA0TXIFG flag
    EUSCI_A0->TXBUF = data; // store the character in UCA0TXBUF
    while ((EUSCI_A0->IFG & EUSCI_A_IFG_TXIFG)==0); // wait until UCA0TXIFG is set
}

unsigned char EUSCI0_UART_RX_data(void) {
    volatile unsigned char data;
    while ((EUSCI_A0->IFG & EUSCI_A_IFG_RXIFG)==0); // wait until UCA0RXIFG is set
    data = EUSCI_A0->RXBUF; // read UCA0RXBUF
    EUSCI_A0->IFG &= ~EUSCI_A_IFG_RXIFG; // clear UCA0RXIFG flag
    return data;
}
```

Program 16.3. UART Echo Example (Polling).

It is worth of mentioning that the *volatile* keyword was used to try to prevent unexpected optimizations by the compiler.

UART Echo Program (ISR)

A UART echo program can be useful in serial-port testing. We have studied a polling based UART echo program previously. The interrupt based UART echo program can be written. The UART echo program example based on ISR is shown in Program 16.4. The UART initialization is similar to the one in a polling based UART echo program. But, in this ISR based UART echo program, the UART interrupt is enabled, and the relevant NVIC set up is added. In the while loop, it blinks an LED.

The UART tasks have been processed in *USCIA0_IRQHandler*. In the ISR, it executes a relevant code block, if the *UCA0RXIFG* is set. This code block contains several lines of code. First, the data is read from *UCA0RXBUF*. The data will be stored in *UCA0TXBUF*. Then, it waits until the *UCA0TXIFG* flag is set. After the transmission is completed, both of *UCA0TXIF* and *UCA0RXIFG* flags are cleared. As a result, a UART echo program will perform a similar task as shown in the previous polling-based example.

```c
#include "msp.h"
int main(void) {
    WDT_A->CTL = WDT_A_CTL_PW | WDT_A_CTL_HOLD;   // hold the watchdog timer
    P1->DIR |= BIT0;   // output direction for an LED
    EUSCI_A0->CTLW0 |= EUSCI_A_CTLW0_SWRST;   // eUSCI reset state
    EUSCI_A0->CTLW0 = EUSCI_A_CTLW0_SWRST | EUSCI_A_CTLW0_UCSSEL_2;   // SMCLK
    EUSCI_A0->BRW = 19;   // 9600 bps setting
    EUSCI_A0->MCTLW = (9 << EUSCI_A_MCTLW_BRF_OFS) | (85 <<
EUSCI_A_MCTLW_BRS_OFS) | EUSCI_A_MCTLW_OS16;   // 9600 bps setting
    P1->SEL1 &= ~(BIT2 | BIT3);   // UART function for P1.2 & P1.3
    P1->SEL0 |= BIT2 | BIT3;   // UART function for P1.2 & P1.3
    EUSCI_A0->CTLW0 &= ~EUSCI_A_CTLW0_SWRST;   // eUSCI operation state
    EUSCI_A0->IE |= EUSCI_A_IE_RXIE;   // set UCA0RXIE
    NVIC->ISER[0] = 1 << ((EUSCIA0_IRQn) & 31);   // NVIC setup
    _delay_cycles(1000);   // delay
    _enable_irq();   // enable global interrupt
    while(1){
        P1->OUT ^= BIT0;   // toggle
        _delay_cycles(500000);   // delay
    }
}
void EUSCIA0_IRQHandler(void) {
    if ((EUSCI_A0->IFG & EUSCI_A_IFG_RXIFG)!=0) {   // check whether UCA0RXIFG is set
        EUSCI_A0->TXBUF = EUSCI_A0->RXBUF;   // read the data and send it back
        while ((EUSCI_A0->IFG & EUSCI_A_IFG_TXIFG)==0);   // waits until UCA0TXIFG is set
        EUSCI_A0->IFG &= ~EUSCI_A_IFG_TXIFG;   // clear UCA0TXIFG flag
        EUSCI_A0->IFG &=~ EUSCI_A_IFG_RXIFG;   // clear UCA0RXIFG flag
    }
}
```

Program 16.4. UART Echo Example (ISR).

This code can be modified for embedded system applications that needs the communication between the device and the computer.

ASCII control character

When we use a serial terminal, you may experience and wondering why it may show different behaviors than what you have type on the serial terminal.

For instance, you can send "\n" expecting that it may work similar to "enter key" on your keyboard. It may move the position to the next line on the serial terminal. But, the position may stay in the same row. This is related to the control characters. There are control characters in ASCII. Some of the useful control characters are summarized below.

8 is a backspace. We can use it by adding backslash; thus, it is "\b".

10 is a line feed. It can be used as "\n".

13 is a carriage return. It can be used as "\r".

27 is an escape. It can be used as "\e".

In order to move the position to the first line, "\r" is needed. Therefore, if a user wants to perform the function that is similar to "enter key" on a keyboard, two control characters are needed. They are "\n" and "\r".

Chapter 17. RS-232, RS-485, and USB

Digital output signals from typical GPIO pins of an MCU are not suitable for a long-distance communication due to the noise. For instance, UART signals from an MCU are typically for a short-distance communication. To extend the distance of the communication, line drivers and buffers can be used to improve the signal reliability and the noise immunity. RS-232 and RS-485 are widely used in personal computers and industrial applications. They can increase the range of the communications. In modern systems, many of the applications have been largely replaced by the USB technology. In this chapter, we will learn about the drivers and buffers including RS-232, RS-485, and USB.

RS-232

RS-232 is a standard protocol for serial communications. The RS-232 standard was introduced in 1962 and revised in 1969. EIA-232-D standard was developed in 1986. Many modern RS-232 ICs are based on TIA/EIA-232-E (1991) or TIA/EIA-232-F (1997). But, there is a more recent version of the RS232-standard. Physical serial ports on computers used to be widely used for RS-232 communications; but they are not used in personal PCs or laptops anymore. However, you may still find serial COM ports in a few industrial equipment and instrumentations to be compatible with old models or devices. TXD and RXD pins are for transmitter and receiver, respectively. In addition to these pins, RS-232 provides flow control functions using RTS and CTS as well as DCD, DTR, DSR, and RI.

Signal lines are unbalanced. The signals are simply voltages referred to the ground. For TXD and RXD signals, Logic 1 is represented as a negative voltage, and it is named as "mark". On the other hand, Logic 0 is represented as a positive voltage and it is named as "space". For control signals, they are defined differently. The "asserted" is a positive voltage and the "de-asserted" is a negative voltage.

The maximum speed is about 20kbit/s at a 50 ft cable length. Practically, some of the RS-232 devices can be operated faster these days. In addition, the length of the cable can play a role in the speed of communication.

There are many RS-232 ICs available. The operating voltage for a majority of the traditional RS232 IC models such as MAX232 is +5 V. In order to interface with a 3.3-V MSP432P410R MCU, it may need extra circuits such as a logic level converter. There are several RS232 ICs that can operate at +3.3 V. A MAX3232 IC is an example of this 3.3-V device. This IC support 2 receives and 2 drivers. Internal regulated charge pumps generate output voltages of ±5.5V.

RS-485

RS-485 is a standard protocol for serial communications. RS-485 is also known as EIA-485. The EIA-485 standard was approved in 1983. RS-485 support multipoint interconnections, and electrical signaling is balanced. RS-485 can be used in communications over a long distance in electrically noisy environments.

The maximum data rate is about 10 Mbit/s at a 40 ft cable length. This is much higher data rate than RS-232. Practically, some of the RS-485 devices can achieve higher data rate these days. The maximum cable length is 4000 ft.

RS-485 uses a balanced interface. Differential singling provides noise immunity because a majority of the common mode noise can be rejected. For instance, the ground shifts as noise signals can be nullified.

RS-485 can form a network, and it supports up to 32 transceivers on the bus. Depending on a RS-485 IC, it can be found that it can support more than 32 transceivers on the bus. Unlike a RS-232 application, RS-485 application circuits need termination resistors to avoid reflected signals. Typical resistor value is 120 Ω.

RS-485 can be either half-duplex or full-duplex system. If it is used in a half-duplex system, there are "enable" control pins. They need to be controlled properly. In a certain RS-485 ICs, the pin names are DE and $\overline{RE}$.

RS-485 is used as a physical layer of industrial control systems. One of the examples is Modbus. It is a serial communication protocol and originally published by Modicon® (now Schneider Electric®) in 1979 for programmable logic controllers (PLCs). It is commonly used in industrial electronic devices.

The operating voltage of the many of RS-485 ICs is +5V. For instance, a MAX485 [21] is a transceiver for the RS-485 communication. However, there are serval RS-485 ICs that works at +3.3 V. A MAX3485 IC is an example of a 3.3-V device. This IC support up to 32 transceivers on the bus.

Performance comparison

The performance comparison between RS-232 and RS-485 for selected parameters is shown in Table 17.1. If a simple configuration for the communication between two systems is needed, RS-232 can be selected. However, if the network between multiple systems is needed, RS-485 may be suitable because RS-485 can be used to connect up to 32 transceivers.

RS-232 signaling is unbalanced. It may have less noise immunity than RS-485. Thus, RS-232 can be found useful in the short distance communication application between two systems. For the systems that are separately more than 50 ft, RS-485 can be a reasonable choice.

Parameter	RS-232	RS-485
Cabling	Single-ended	Differential
Number of devices	1 transmitter 1 receiver	32 transmitters 32 receivers
Maximum cable length	50 feet	4000 feet
Signaling	Unbalanced	Balanced
Typical maximum data rate	~20 kbit/s at 50 ft cable length	~10 Mbit/s at 40 ft cable length
Typical logic levels	±5 to ±15 V	±1.5 to ±6 V

Table 17.1. Summarized characteristics of RS232 and RS485.

As it was mentioned, some of RS-232 and RS-485 communication modules are replaced by USB technology. Let us learn about USB in the next sections.

USB

Universal Serial Bus (USB) is an industry standard that provides a serial bus for connecting devices. USB 1.0 specification was introduced in 1996. USB became popular a few years later. USB 2.0 was introduced in 2001. USB ports are commonly found in desktop and laptop computers these days. The data rate has been improved significantly in USB 2.0. The summary of USB specifications is shown in Table 17.2.

	Release date	Maximum data rate	*Typical voltage	*Typical maximum current
USB 1.0	1996	12 Mbit/s	5 V	0.5 A
USB 2.0	2000	480 Mbit/s	5 V	0.5 A
USB 3.0	2008	5 Gbit/s	5 V	0.9 A
USB 3.1	2013	10 Gbit/s	5 V	0.9 A
USB 3.2	2017	20 Gbit/s	5 V	3.0 A
USB 4.0	2019	40 Gbit/s	5 V	-

Table 17.2. USB specifications. (*It excluded USB power delivery specification).

In USB 3.0, the data rate has been improved significantly. The power capacity is also increased. There are separate USB power delivery specifications since some of the USB ports are used primarily for supplying power. These were not included in Table 17.2. In USB 3.1, the speed has been increased. In USB 3.2, both speed and power have been improved. This power improvement is because of the use of USB-C connectors and cables.

USB-C can carry significantly more power, and USB-C can supply power to decent size electronics devices. The latest USB standard is USB 4.0. It is even faster than USB 3.2.

USB signaling is balanced. For instance, there are four wires in a USB 2.0 cable. There are +5V and ground wires. In addition, there are D+ and D- wires. They are for data signals, and the signaling is balanced. In USB 2.0 technology, the data encoding and decoding is based on NRZI (Non Return to Zero Inverted).

USB protocol layers are sophisticated. There are several ways to provide communications over USB in an embedded system. One of the easy methods is to use a USB-UART IC and to create a virtual COM port. Then, the system sends and receives data in a way that is similar to UART communications.

USB-to-UART IC

We will learn about open source electronics development platforms in Chapter 25. One of the popular open source electronics platforms is Arduino® [23]. Arduino Uno is one of the hardware models. In the earlier model of Arduino Uno, FT232RL IC was used as an USB-to-UART IC. Recent Arduino Uno model uses an ATMEGA16U2. The FT232RL IC is a dedicated IC for a USB-to-UART bridge function. The ATMEGA16U2 IC in an Arduino is an 8-bit MCU with an internal USB controller. Once the proper firmware is loaded on the MCU, ATMEGA16U2 IC works as a USB-to-UART bridge IC. A benefit of this approach is that it could be used to provide additional custom functions.

An MSP432P401R Launchpad comes with on-board XDS110. The core of this on-board XDS110-ET is a TM4C129 MCU. The TM4C129 MCU has an Arm Cortex-M4 core. The TM4C129 is a Tiva™ Series MCU. One of the important features of this MCU is an USB controller. It supports USB 2.0 standard. Using a high level TivaWare™, the USB controller can be easily accessible. If an MSP432P401R MCU sends a character over the backchannel UART, the data can be processed in the TM4C129 MCU and it can be sent over an USB to a computer. In addition, the TM4C129 IC is used to debug and program the MSP432P401R IC through JATG pins.

Chapter 18. Serial Peripheral Interface (SPI)

Various serial interfaces, buses, and protocols have been used in embedded systems. The serial peripheral interface (SPI) and Inter-integrated Circuit (I²C) bus are widely adopted in embedded systems. In this chapter, we will learn about SPI bus and the SPI communication in an MSP432P401R MCU.

Serial Peripheral Interface

The serial peripheral interface (SPI) was introduced by Motorola® in the late 1970s. It is one of the simple synchronous communication protocols. It has been widely accepted in embedded system applications. The connection of the master and slave SPI devices are shown in Figure 18.1.

The serial data out (SDO) pin of the master device is connected to the serial data in (SDI) pin of the slave device. This line is called MOSI, which stands for "Master Out, Salve In." The SDI pin of the master device is connected to the SDO pin of the slave device. This line is called MISO, which stands for "Master In, Salve Out." The master device provides clock signals through a serial clock (SCK) line to the slave device. The master device also provides chip enable (CS) or slave select (SS) signals using a control line. The control pin is active low. This means the slave device is selected by pulling this line low.

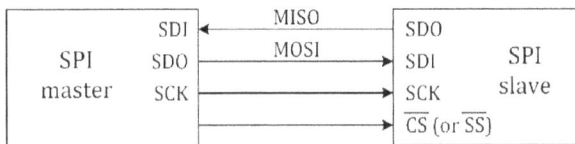

Figure 18.1. SPI, Master-Slave connection.

A simple SPI bus can be understood conceptually as communications between two modules with shift registries and buffers as shown in Figure 18.2. Let us suppose the data that needs to be transferred is 0x81 from the master device to the slave device. First, this data needs to be stored in the 8-bit shift register of the master device. Now, the most significant bit (MSB) is passed to the buffer. The buffer transmits it to the input of the 8-bit shift register of the slave device through the MOSI line. After repeating the process for the rest of the bits, the data can be sent to the 8-bit register of the slave device. Once the data transfer is completed, it can be seen that the data in the slave device is 0x81. Likewise, the data in the slave device can be sent to the master device. This is a simple conceptual description for the ease of understanding. However, an actual SPI unit is more complicated, and an internal state machine provides micro-operations that are needed for the SPI module.

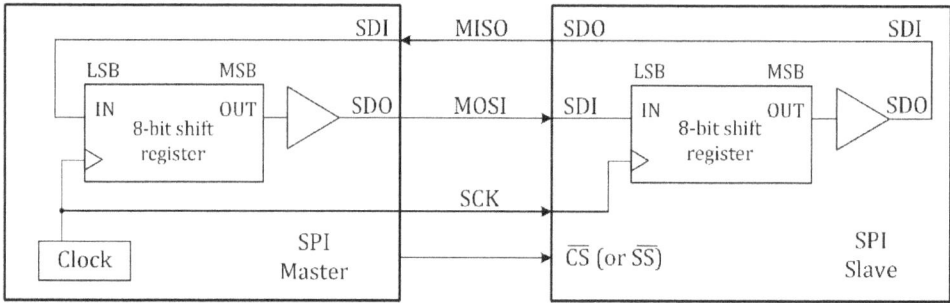

Figure 18.2. Simplified block diagram of a SPI bus.

An SPI is a simple serial communication compared to other serial communication interfaces and buses. A SPI bus can achieve higher throughput than an I²C bus. An SPI protocol is more flexible than an I²C protocol.

SPI Device Connection

Multiple slave devices can be connected to one master device. A typical SPI bus connection is shown in Figure 18.3. In this setting, one master SPI device communicates with two slave SPI devices. The slave-A device can be selected by the active low control signal at $\overline{CS}$ pin (SPI Slave A). Next, the slave-B device can be selected by the active low control signal at $\overline{CS}$ pin (SPI Slave B). This connection requires one *chip select* pin per slave device. As the number of the slave devices increases, this connection scheme may increase the hardware complexity due to the increasing number of *chip select* pins that are needed for the master device. In order to reduce the number of select pins, daisy chained connection can be considered as shown in Figure 18.4

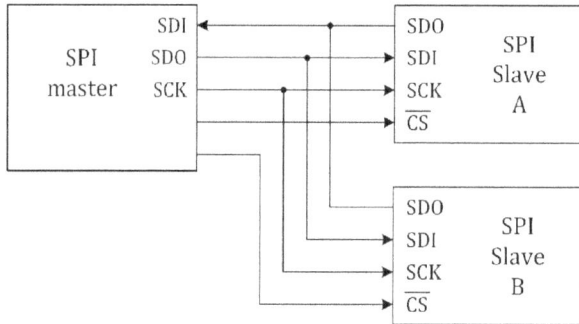

Figure 18.3. Typical SPI bus connection.

The daisy chained SPI bus does not need to use additional *chip select* pin. The *chip enable* signals are shared between slave devices. The data from the slave-A device can be transferred to the master directly. However, the data from the slave-B device needs to be transferred to the slave A-device first. Then, the data can be transferred to the master. In order to configure a daisy chained SPI connection, the slave devices should meet daisy chain requirements. You can check the datasheet to see whether a SPI device supports a daisy chain connection.

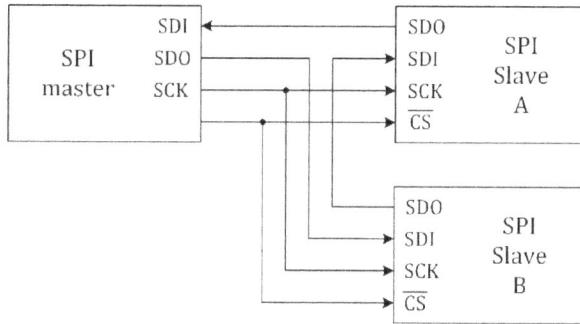

Figure 18.4. Daisy chained SPI bus connection.

SPI Mode

In an SPI bus, there are a few key parameters such as clock polarity (CPOL) and clock phase (CPHA). They are used to determine the clock format and associated timing of the data signals. These CPOL and CPHA as well as the waveforms are shown in Figure 18.5. The CPOL parameter determines whether the clock is active high or active low. CPHA determines whether the clock is out of phase with the data or in phase with the data. There are four SPI modes depending on the combinations of the CPOL and CPHA parameters.

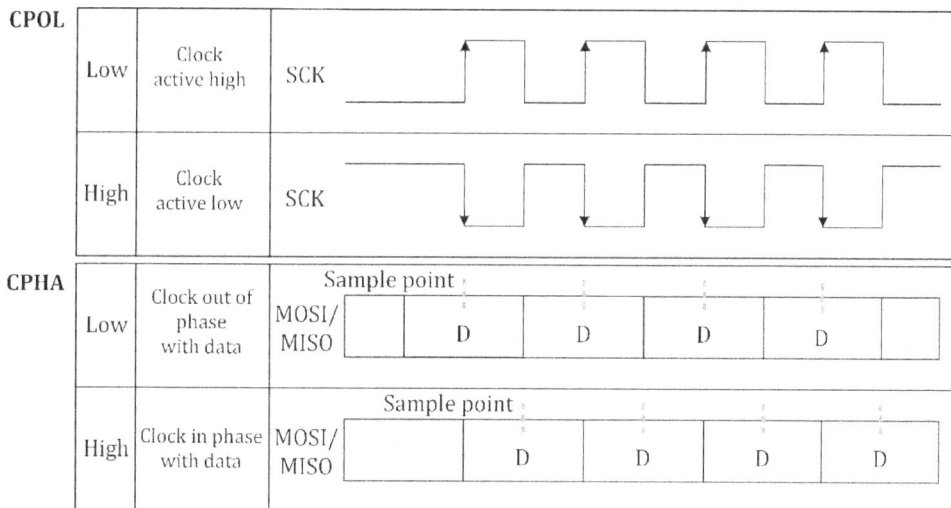

Figure 18.5. CPOL, CPHA, and waveforms.

The SPI transfer modes are shown in Table 18.1. The SPI mode in an MSP432P401R MCU is configurable. For the slave SPI ICs, the SPI mode information may be found in the datasheet, or it can be determined by examining the timing diagram in the datasheet.

CPOL	CPHA	SPI Mode
Low	Low	0
Low	High	1
High	Low	2
High	High	3

Table 18.1. SPI modes.

SPI Transactions

A simple SPI write transaction example is shown in Figure 18.6. This shows the case that sends an instruction and one-byte data. The transaction begins with pulling the Chip Select (CS) signal line low. For the MOSI line, the instruction is sent. Next, a data byte is sent. The MISO line in the salve device can be controlled to be high impedance. The transaction ends with pulling CS line high.

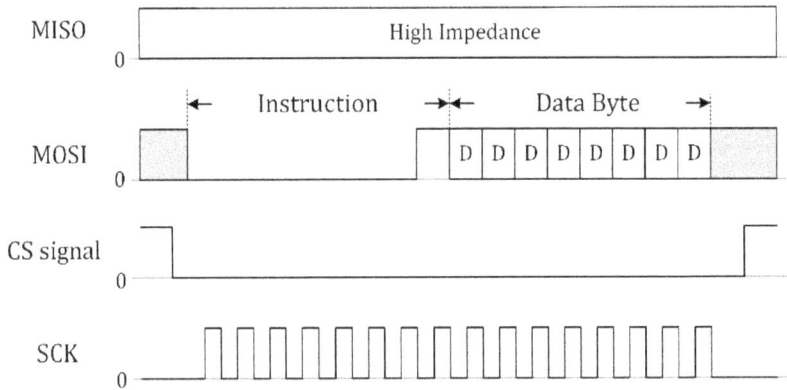

Figure 18.6. Simple SPI write transaction.

A simple SPI read transaction example is shown in Figure 18.7. This is the case that sends an instruction and receive one-byte data. Similarly, the transaction begins with pulling the CS signal line low. For the MOSI line, the instruction is sent. Since this is a read instruction, a data byte is sent from the slave deice to the master device through the MISO line. While receiving the data, the MOSI line on the master device side can be controlled to be high impedance. The transaction ends with pulling CS line high.

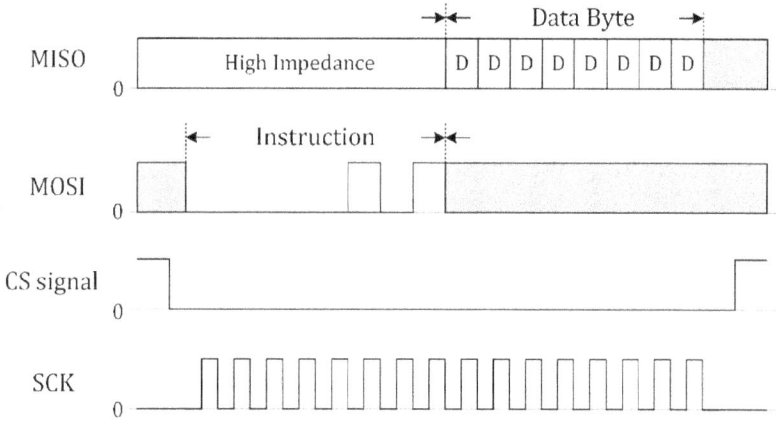

Figure 18.7. Simple SPI read transaction.

eUSCI – SPI Mode

Let us examine the SPI communication in an MSP432P401R MCU. The SPI mode is supported by both the eUSCI_A and eUSCI_B. There are several SPI units available in an MSP432P401R MCU. In this chapter, we have chosen an eUSCI_B0 unit. The simplified block diagram is shown in Figure 18.8.

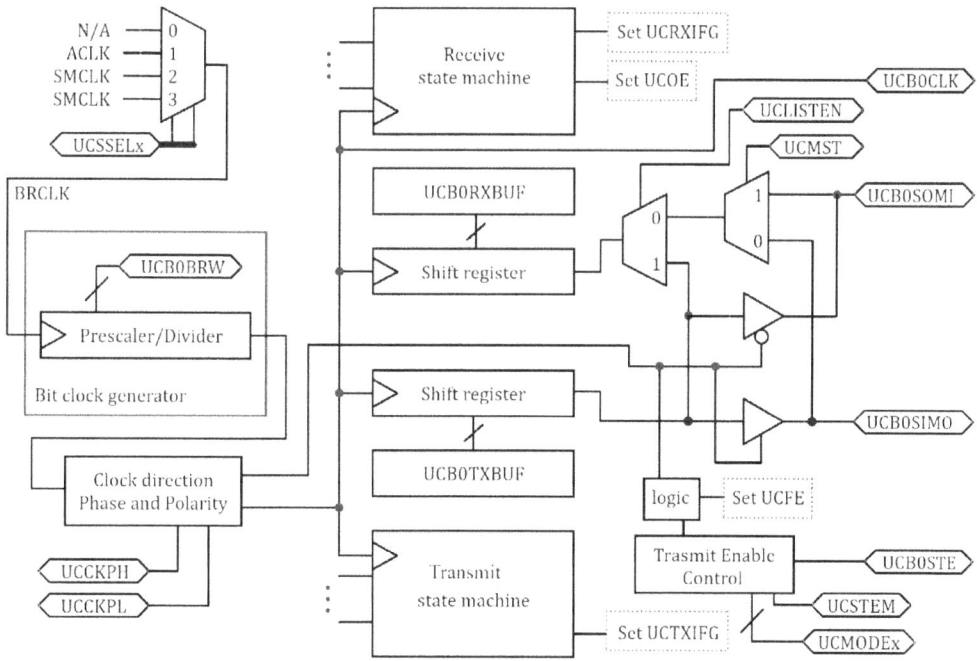

Figure 18.8. Simplified block diagram of eUSCI_B0, SPI mode [6].

There are four pins related to the SPI mode They are *UCB0SIMO*, *UCB0SOMI*, *UCB0CLK*, and *UCB0STE* pins. The SPI mode parameter can be configured by

UCMODE bits. Either 3-pin or 4-pin SPI operation can be chosen. For the 4-pin SPI operation, all four pins are used. However, for the 3-pin SPI operation, *UCB0STE* is not used. *UCB0STE* is a slave transmit enable. Master or slave modes are programmable. The master can be selected by setting *UCMST* bit. The parameter in data transmission whether the LSB or MSB first can be configured by *UCMSB* bit.

The clock direction phase can be configured by *UCCKPH* bit. This is related to *CPHA*. The clock polarity can be configured by *UCCKPL* bit. This is related to *CPOL*. These are the parameters configuring the SPI modes.

MCP3008 SPI Example

An MCP3008 IC is an 8-channel 10-bit A/D converter with an SPI serial interface [24]. There are several IC packaging options. One of them is a Plastic DIP (PDIP) package. The PDIP model of the MCP3008 IC can be mounted on a prototyping breadboard. Readers can perform their experiments in this way. On a BH EDU board, this MCP3008 IC is mounted, and the pins of the IC are accessible through header pins.

The connection diagram is shown in Figure 18.9. Since the MSP432P401R MCU has a 14-bit SAR ADC with many channels, an additional external 10-bit ADC IC may seem unnecessary. This configuration of using an external ADC is for an educational purpose to show an SPI example. It can be extended for the case where the MSP432P401R MCU needs to communicate with other external ADC module with a better specification. In general, this 10-bit ADC IC can be found useful for the microcontrollers with 8-bit ADC modules or the microprocessors that does not have any ADC module. In some cases, it can be found that more ADC channels are necessary where there are many analog sensors or analog voltages to read.

The MCP3008 IC has eight ADC channels. In this section, we will study an example code that can read the channel 0. The potentiometer is connected to the channel 0. The test voltage can be varied by tweaking the knob of the potentiometer. The input pin of the IC (DIN) is related to the MOSI line. It is connected to P1.6. The choice of the alternative function is *UCB0SIMO*. The output pin of the IC (DOUT) is related to the MISO line. It is connected to P1.7. The choice of the alternative function is *UCB0SOMI*, The CLK pin of the IC is connected to P1.5. The choice of the alternative function is *UCB0CLK*. The slave select pin for this SPI connection is *UCB0STE*. It is related to P1.4. However, the P1.4 has been already used by the right-side push-button switch (S2). Thus, P3.0 is selected as a custom chip select pin. This pin is connected to $\overline{CS}$ pin.

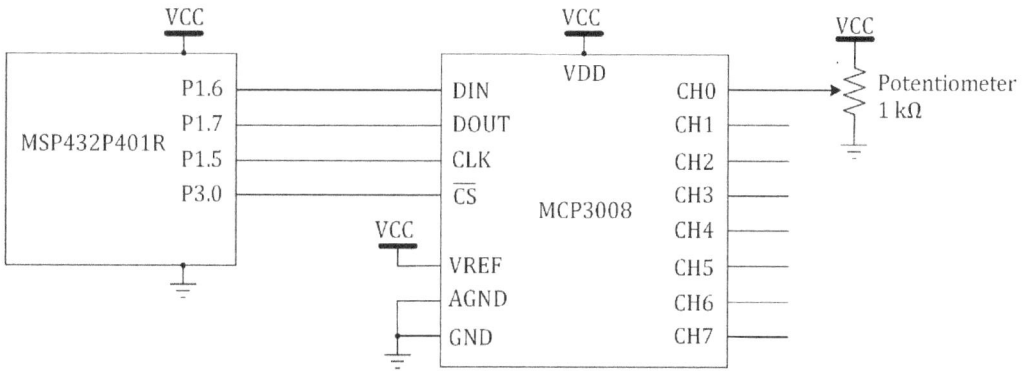

Figure 18.9. MCP3008 connection diagram.

The MCP3008 SPI example program is shown in Program 18.1. The selected SPI mode is 0. The SMCLK is selected as a clock source, and the SCK is about 100kHz. In the while loop, it read the data from the IC, and store it in *ADC_buf*. The pattern of receiving data from the IC over SPI communication keeps repeating.

The method of the SPI communications varies by IC. It is recommended to refer to the datasheet. For the MCP3008 IC, it performs several transmit and receive operations to read the ADC value form the IC. *EUSCI0_SPI_TX_data* and *EUSCI0_SPI_RX_data* subroutines are used to transmit or receive data.

```
#include "msp.h"
unsigned int ADC_buf;
unsigned char RXdata;
void EUSCIB0_SPI_TX_data(unsigned char);
unsigned char EUSCIB0_SPI_RX_data(void);
void main(void) {
    WDT_A->CTL = WDT_A_CTL_PW | WDT_A_CTL_HOLD;  // hold the watchdog timer
    P1->DIR |= 0x01;  // output direction for an LED
    P1->DIR |= BIT5 | BIT6;  // output direction for P1.5 & P1.6
    P1->SEL0 |= BIT5 | BIT6 | BIT7;  // SPI mode for P1.5, P1.6, P1.7
    P3->DIR |= BIT0;  // output direction for P3.0
    P3->OUT |= BIT0;  // set P3.0, custom SS pin
    EUSCI_B0->CTLW0 |= EUSCI_B_CTLW0_SWRST;  // eUSCI reset state
    EUSCI_B0->CTLW0 = EUSCI_B_CTLW0_SWRST | EUSCI_B_CTLW0_MSB |
EUSCI_B_CTLW0_MST | EUSCI_B_CTLW0_MODE_0 | EUSCI_B_CTLW0_SYNC |
EUSCI_B_CTLW0_UCSSEL_2;  // eUSCI 3-pin SPI mode, master
    EUSCI_B0->CTLW0 &= ~EUSCI_B_CTLW0_SWRST;  // eUSCI operation state
    EUSCI_B0->BRW = 30;  // ~100k
    _delay_cycles(2000);  // delay
    while(1) {
        P3->OUT &= ~BIT0;  // set P3.0, custom SS pin
        EUSCIB0_SPI_TX_data(0x01);  // send start bit
        RXdata=EUSCIB0_SPI_RX_data();  // receive data
        EUSCIB0_SPI_TX_data(0x80);  // send data with channel info
        RXdata=EUSCIB0_SPI_RX_data();  // receive data
```

```
        ADC_buf = (RXdata & 0x03) << 8;  // store data in ADC_buf (highest 2 bits)
        EUSCIB0_SPI_TX_data(0x00);  // send  data
        RXdata=EUSCIB0_SPI_RX_data();  // receive data
        ADC_buf |= RXdata;  // store data in variable (the rest of 8 bits)
        P3->OUT |= BIT0;  // clear P3.0
        P1->OUT ^= 0x01;  // toggle
        __delay_cycles(50000);  // delay
    }
}

void EUSCIB0_SPI_TX_data(unsigned char data) {
    EUSCI_B0->IFG &= ~EUSCI_B_IFG_TXIFG;  // clear UCB0TXIFG flag
    EUSCI_B0->TXBUF = data;  // store the character in UCB0TXBUF
    while ((EUSCI_B0->IFG & EUSCI_B_IFG_TXIFG)==0);  // wait until UCB0TXIFG is set
}

unsigned char EUSCIB0_SPI_RX_data(void) {
    unsigned char data;  // variable
    while ((EUSCI_B0->IFG & EUSCI_B_IFG_RXIFG)==0);  // wait until UCB0RXIFG is set
    data = EUSCI_B0->RXBUF;  // read data from UCB0RXBUF
    EUSCI_B0->IFG &= ~EUSCI_B_IFG_RXIFG;  // clear UCB0RXIFG flag
    return data;  // return the data
}
```

Program 18.1. MCP3008 SPI example program.

Chapter 19. Inter-integrated Circuit (I²C)

The integrated Circuit (I²C) bus is versatile, and it is widely used in embedded systems. There are several variants of I²C serial communication interfaces; however, they are typically compatible each other. There are many sensor ICs with I²C serial interfaces. In this chapter, we will learn about an I²C peripheral in an MSP432P401R MCU.

Inter-integrated Circuit

I^2C was developed by PHILIPS®. It has been widely used in embedded systems. This is a serial communication based on two wires. The patent of this two-wire bus system was filed on 1981, and the date of the patent is August 25, 1987 [25]. The original I²C patent was already expired. The hardware and the software protocol structures are relatively simple. It provides a simple universal bus, and many manufactures provide ICs with the I²C bus interfaces.

Each device on the I²C bus is identified by its own address. The master device initiates communication providing the clock signal. There is a maximum clock frequency. However, the minimum clock speed is not defined.

The master device can "poll" the device with a specific address. It can be used to check whether a specific device is present or not. This allows designers to build a system that can support easily adding or removing I²C slave devices.

A System Management Bus (SMBus) is also a two-wire interface, which is based on the principles of operation of the I²C bus. The SMBus was defined by Intel® in 1995. The SMBus and I²C buses are very similar and they can be interoperable in general. However, there are a few differences in specifications including *VDD & threshold voltage* and *address acknowledge*, and etc.

Two Wire Interface (TWI) was introduced by Atmel® and other companies. This bus is almost identical to I^2C, but it has a few differences such in high-speed mode. Generally, TWI devices are compatible with I^2C devices.

A simple I²C bus example is shown in Figure 19.1. There are two I²C devices. Any of these two can be used as either master or slave device. It is typical to have one master device on the I²C bus. However, it is not common; but, it is possible to have multiple masters on the I²C bus. A master device can initiate the I²C communication.

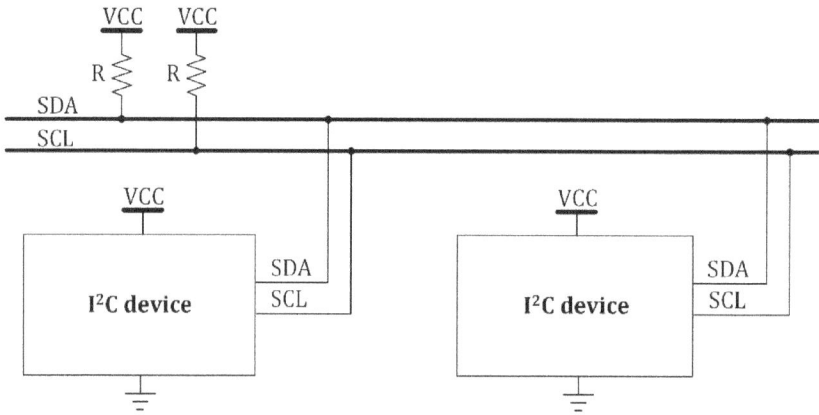

Figure 19.1. Simple I²C bus example.

In Figure 19.1, you can find SDA and SCL lines. SDA means "serial data." This line is used to send and receive data. SCL means "serial clock." This line is used to provide the clock signal. There are two pull-up resistors connected to these lines. These resisters are required components. The value of the resisters may not need to be precise. Common choices of the values are 1 kΩ, 4.7 kΩ, and 10 kΩ. Designers can choose a reasonable value. The resistance may affect the communication speed, therefore, in some applications, the choice of the value can be important.

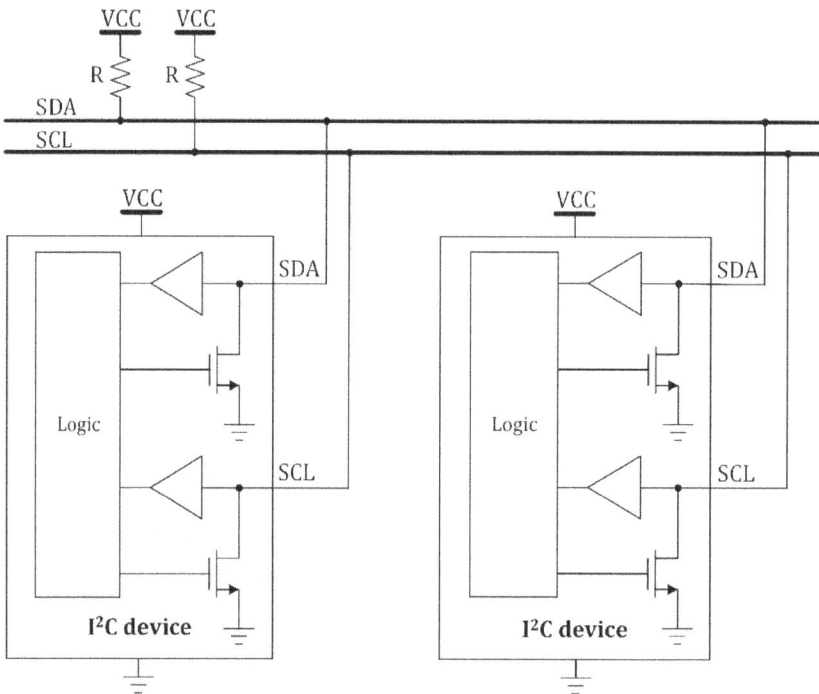

Figure 19.2. Simplified I²C block diagram on the I²C bus.

A simplified I²C block diagram on the I²C bus is shown in Figure 19.2. This conceptual I²C device block is consisted of buffers, Field effect transistors (FETs), and a control logic. This is an open-drain configuration. This is the reason that the external pull-up resistors are essential.

Each I²C device can read the digital values on the bus. Each device can pull the bus lines low, or it can release the bus lines. The example of puling the bus line low or releasing the bus is shown in Figure 19.3. The figure on the left shows the case of controlling the FET to be the ON state from the OFF state. When the FET is OFF, the bus line generates a logical high output since it is pulled up. When the FET is controlled to be ON, the bus line is pulled low and the logical output is low. Next, as shown on the right side of the figure, the FET is controlled to be OFF. In this case, the bus line is released, and the logical output is back to high. This bus configuration is applied to both SDA and SCL lines.

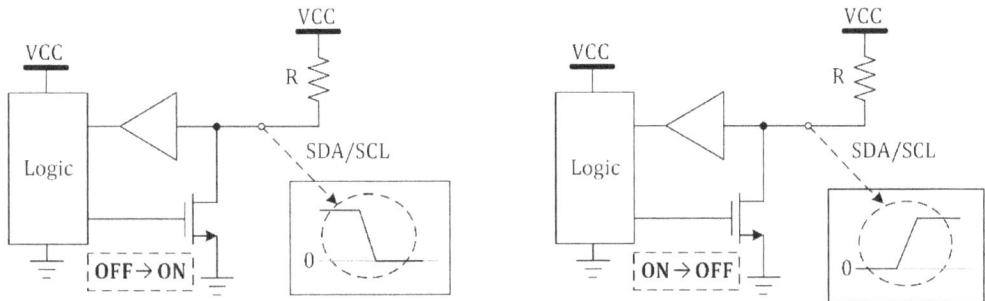

Figure 19.3. Open-drain driver pulls the line low or releases the line.

In the previous example, it shows only two devices. You can connect multiple I²C devices. The connection example is shown in Figure 19.4.

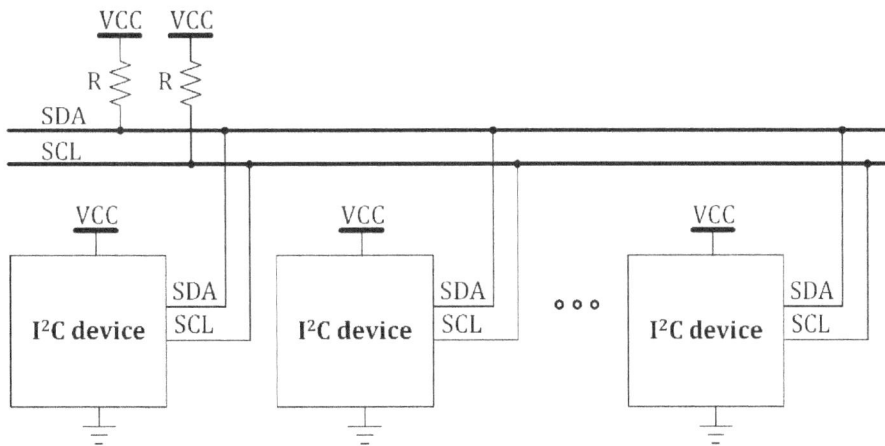

Figure 19.4. Multiple devices on the I²C bus.

The multiple I²C devices can share the SDA and SCL lines, and the connection of multiple I²C devices is straightforward and simple. However, the designers need to make sure to use pull-up resisters properly. Moreover, each device needs to have a unique address on the bus.

In embedded system applications, it is common to find a system that uses multiple supply voltage levels such as 3.3 V and 5V. Let us suppose there are two 3.3-V I²C devices and two 5-V I²C devices, and we want them to be the I²C bus. One of the example connections in this case is shown in Figure 19.5. We can use a bi-directional logic converter that is at the top of the figure. It provides an interface between 3.3-V and 5-V signals. One channel of the bi-directional logic converter is consisted of one N-channel MOSTFET and two pull-up resistors. There are several "bidirectional logic level converter" modules available. One of bidirectional logic level converters module will be used for interfacing 3.3-V and 5-V signals in the next chapter.

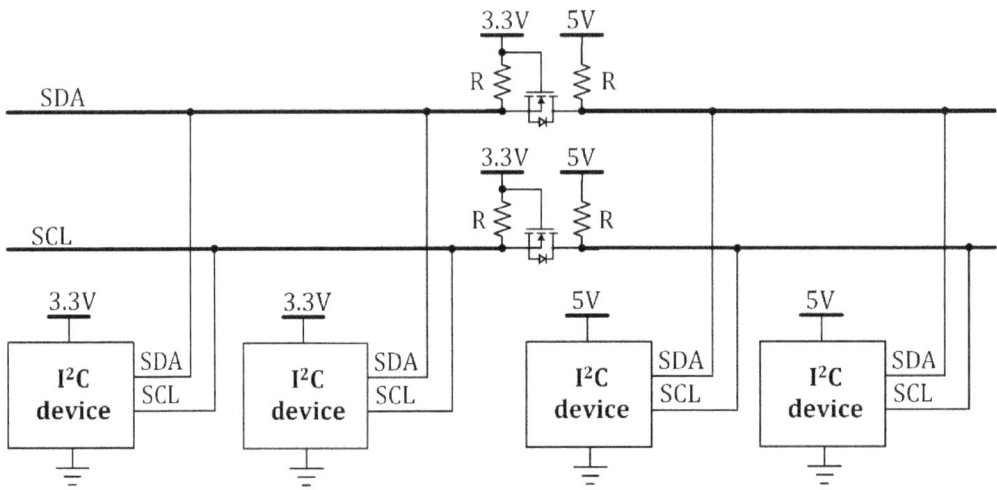

Figure 19.5. 3.3-V and 5-V I²C devices on the I²C bus.

I²C Message Format and Transactions

An I²C message example is shown in Figure 19.6. The message starts from the "start condition (ST)." It can be generated when the SDA line pulled low while the SCL is held high. Next, a 7-bit address is sent. The data is valid, while the SCL line is held high. The change of the data is possible, while the SCL line is pulled low. The 8th bit is R/$\overline{W}$. It indicates whether it is a read or write operation.

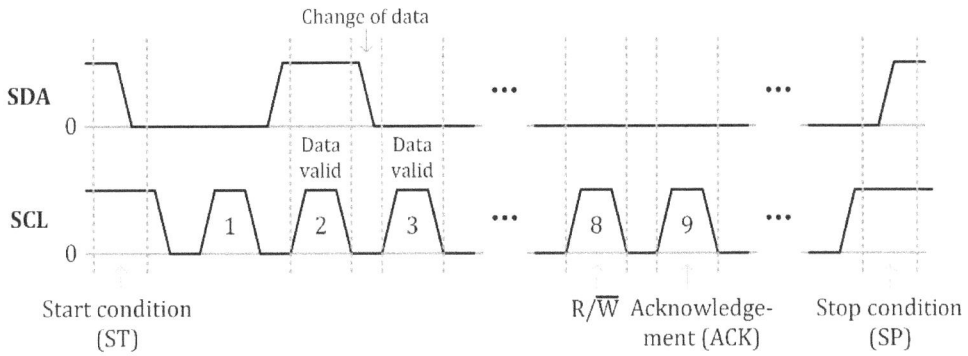

Figure 19.6. I²C message example.

The 9th bit is an acknowledgement (ACK) signal. The SDA line is pulled low. This means that the logic level is 0. This ACK is generated by the receiver side. It can be used to check whether the data is sent successfully. If not, NACK bit can be sent instead. NACK means "Not Acknowledgement." In this case, the SDA line is released. This means the logical level is 1. NACK can be used in other cases including the condition to halt communication followed by the stop condition in a repeated start transaction. The stop condition (SP) is shown at the end of the message. It can be generated, when the SDA line pulled high during the SCL is held high.

An I²C write transaction example is shown in Figure 19.7. The start condition is sent. Next, 8 bits are sent. It is consisted of a 7-bit address and one bit of R/$\overline{W}$. In this case, R/$\overline{W}$ bit is logical low. It is followed by receiving acknowledgement. Next, 8-bit data is sent, and it received acknowledgment. Then, it generates a stop condition. This transaction initiates the communication and sends a byte data to the slave device.

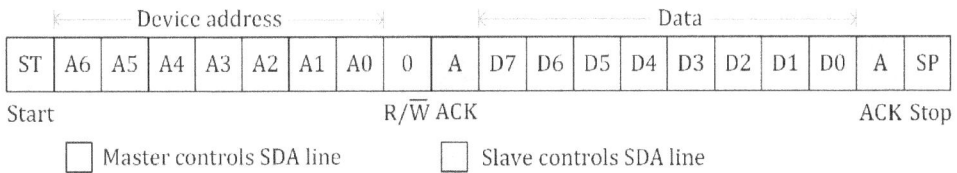

Figure 19.7. I²C write transaction example.

Next, an I²C read transaction example is shown in Figure 19.8. As it was done in the previous case, the start condition is sent. Next, 8 bits are sent. It is consisted of a 7-bit address and one bit of R/$\overline{W}$. This is a read operation. Thus, R/$\overline{W}$ bit is logical high. Then, it is followed by receiving acknowledgement. Now, 8-bit data will be sent from the slave deice, and the master receives the 8-bit data. Next, the master device sends acknowledgment and stop condition. This transaction initiates the communication and receive a byte data from the slave device.

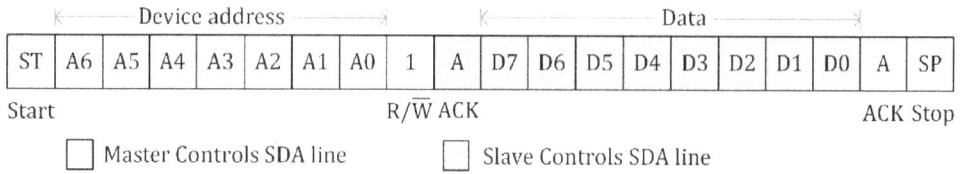

	Device address										Data									
ST	A6	A5	A4	A3	A2	A1	A0	1	A	D7	D6	D5	D4	D3	D2	D1	D0	A	SP

Start   R/$\overline{W}$ ACK   ACK Stop

☐ Master Controls SDA line   ☐ Slave Controls SDA line

Figure 19.8. I²C read transaction example.

I²C read and write operations can be performed by a combined transaction as shown in Figure 19.8. First, it performs an I²C write optation. However, it does not send a stop condition. Instead, it sends a repeated start, and it performs an I²C read optation. Instead of ACK, the master device sends NACK. Next, it sends a stop condition. This transaction sends a byte to the slave device first, and it receive a byte from the slave device.

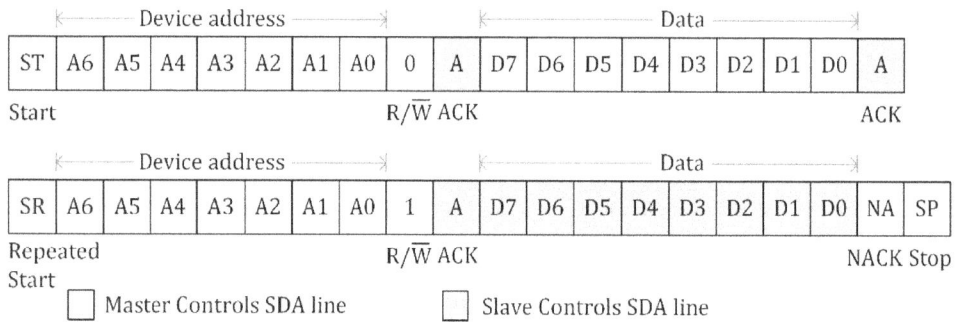

	Device address										Data							
ST	A6	A5	A4	A3	A2	A1	A0	0	A	D7	D6	D5	D4	D3	D2	D1	D0	A

Start   R/$\overline{W}$ ACK   ACK

	Device address										Data								
SR	A6	A5	A4	A3	A2	A1	A0	1	A	D7	D6	D5	D4	D3	D2	D1	D0	NA	SP

Repeated   R/$\overline{W}$ ACK   NACK Stop
Start

☐ Master Controls SDA line   ☐ Slave Controls SDA line

Figure 19.9. Combined I²C write and read transaction example.

eUSCI – I²C Mode

The eUSCI_B module supports I²C mode and provides an interface to communicate with I²C devices. A simplified block diagram of eUSCI_B1 – I²C mode is shown in Figure 19.10. Open drain transistors were used and they are connected to the *UCB1SDA* and *UCB1SCL* lines. The *UCB1SCL* line is associated with the clock circuit block. The *UCB1SDA* line is associated with transmit and receive data blocks. The I²C state machine block controls the operations of the I²C module.

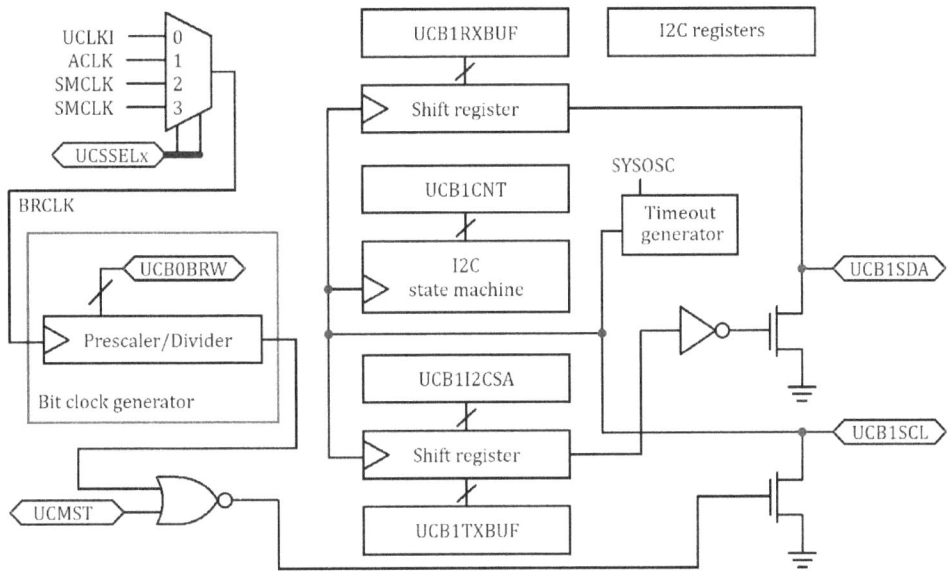

Figure 19.10. Simplified block diagram of eUSCI_B1 – I²C mode [6].

PCF8574 I²C Example

Some of the embedded system applications use many GPIOs. These cases include keyboard and LED matrix applications. In some cases, the number of GPIOs available in an MCU may not be enough, and the developers may choose to use GPIO expanders. Theses GPIO expanders provide a method of adding extra I/Os. As an example, a GPIO expander with an I²C interface can be used to control a parallel interface LCD. In this case, the LCD can be controlled by the I²C bus. It can free up many GPIO pins of an MCU.

A PCF8574 IC is an 8-bit GPIO expander via an I²C bus [26]. The operating voltage range is 2.5 V to 6 V. It works with a 3.3-V device such as an MSP432P401R IC. The PCF8574 has 8-bit quasi-bidirectional I/O ports. Three address pins of the IC can be used to provide 8 slave addresses. The active low open drain interrupt output ($\overline{INT}$) can be used to indicate whether the input status of the IC has changed or not.

A connection diagram of a PCF8574 IC is shown in Figure 19.11. The alternative functions for the P6.4 and P6.5 are associated with SDA and SCL lines, respectively. P4.7 is used to read an interrupt output from the IC. Pull-up resistors are connected to these lines. The address is selected by the three pins (A2 ~ A0). Two I/O ports are connected to LEDs.

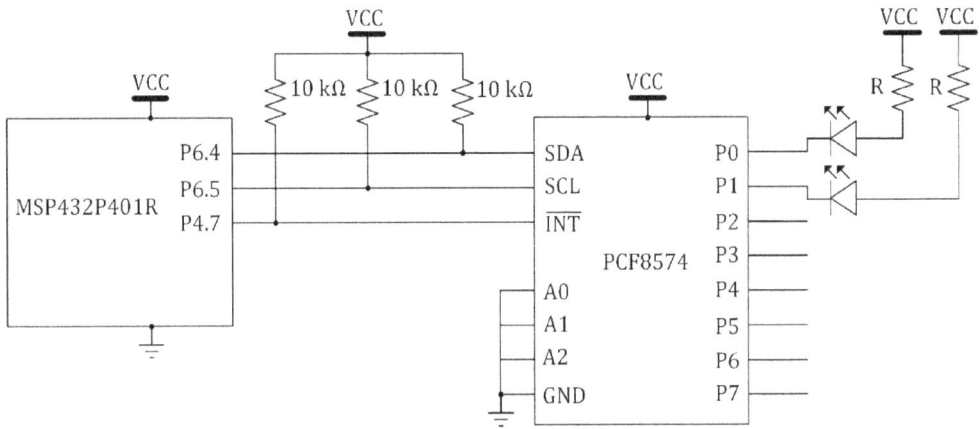

Figure 19.11. PCF8574 connection diagram.

The PCF8574 ICs are offered in many packaging types. They include a Dual In-line Package (DIP). This DIP IC can be mounted on a prototyping breadboard. Readers can perform the experiment using a prototyping breadboard. On the BH EDU board, the PCF8754 was mounted, and users can access the IC pins through header pins.

Based on this connection, a programming example of the PCF8574 is written as shown in Program 19.1. The P6.4 and P6.5 pins are configured properly to provide the I²C alternative functions. Next, eUSCI B1 is configured to operate in I²C mode. The slave address is 0x20 in this setting. The automatic stop generation function is selected. It is configured to generate a stop condition after processing one byte. In the while loop, the program generates the start condition in the master transmitter mode. Next, it waits until *UCB1TXIFG* is set. Then, the data will be stored in *UCB1TXBUF*. The next line is to ensure the stop condition. Now, the I²C transmit transaction is completed, and the LEDs connected to the I/O port gets to be turned ON or OFF according to the received data. *TXdata* variable was initialized as 0x01, and two bits are toggled in the loop. This will result in blinking two LEDs alternatively.

For some versions of BH EDU boards, a different version of PCF8574 such as PCF8754A may have been used instead. The difference is the device address. The relevant line of the code is as follows: "EUSCI_B1->I2CSA = 0x20". For the PCF8754A IC, this line can be modified to change the device address to 0x38.

```
#include "msp.h"
unsigned char TXdata=0x01; // initialize variable
int main(void) {
    WDT_A->CTL = WDT_A_CTL_PW | WDT_A_CTL_HOLD;  // hold the watchdog timer
    P4->DIR &= ~BIT7;  // Input direction for P4.7
    P6->SEL1 &= ~(BIT4 | BIT5);  // I²C function for P6.4 & P6.5
    P6->SEL0 |= BIT4 | BIT5;  // I²C function for P6.4 & P6.5
```

```
EUSCI_B1->CTLW0 |= EUSCI_B_CTLW0_SWRST; // eUSCI reset state
EUSCI_B1->CTLW0 = EUSCI_B_CTLW0_SWRST | EUSCI_B_CTLW0_MODE_3 |
EUSCI_B_CTLW0_MST | EUSCI_B_CTLW0_SYNC | EUSCI_B_CTLW0_UCSSEL_2;
                                        // configure USCIB1 control register
EUSCI_B1->BRW = 30;  // ~100kHz
EUSCI_B1->I2CSA = 0x20;  // slave address
EUSCI_B1->CTLW1 |= EUSCI_B_CTLW1_ASTP_2;
                        // automatic stop generated after TBCNT is reached
EUSCI_B1->TBCNT = 0x01;  // threshold (TBCNT)
EUSCI_B1->CTLW0 &= ~EUSCI_B_CTLW0_SWRST;  // eUSCI operation state
_delay_cycles(2000);  // delay
while (1) {
  EUSCI_B1->CTLW0 |= EUSCI_B_CTLW0_TR | EUSCI_B_CTLW0_TXSTT;
                                        // I2C start, transmitter
  while ((EUSCI_B1->IFG & EUSCI_B_IFG_TXIFG)==0);  // wait until UCB1TXIFG is set
  EUSCI_B1->TXBUF = TXdata;  // store data inUB1TXBUF
  while (EUSCI_B1->CTLW0 & EUSCI_B_CTLW0_TXSTP);  // ensure stop condition
  TXdata ^= 0x03;  // toggle two bits
  _delay_cycles(500000);  // delay
}
}
```

Program 19.1. PCF8574 I^{2}C example program.

There is a wide range of ICs and modules with I^{2}C interfaces. Particularly, many I^{2}C compatible sensor ICs can be found. Readers can choose some of the sensors with I^{2}C interface and extend their knowledge for learning purposes and for their own embedded systems.

Chapter 20. Time Measurement

There are embedded systems using sensors based on the measurement of the relative time between events. In an MSP432P401R MCU, the capture mode in a Timer_A module can be used in recording and processing timer events. We will learn about capture mode, ultrasonic distance sensor, and IR communication in this chapter.

Capture Mode in Timer_A

Timer events can be captured by several methods. An MSP432P401R MCU supports capturing timer events using Timer_A modules. A simplified block diagram of a Timer_A2 displaying the CCR2 block is shown in Figure 20.1. The CAPTURE MODE box was hidden previously, in this figure, this CAPTURE MODE box is disclosed, and it is enclosed with a thick dotted line.

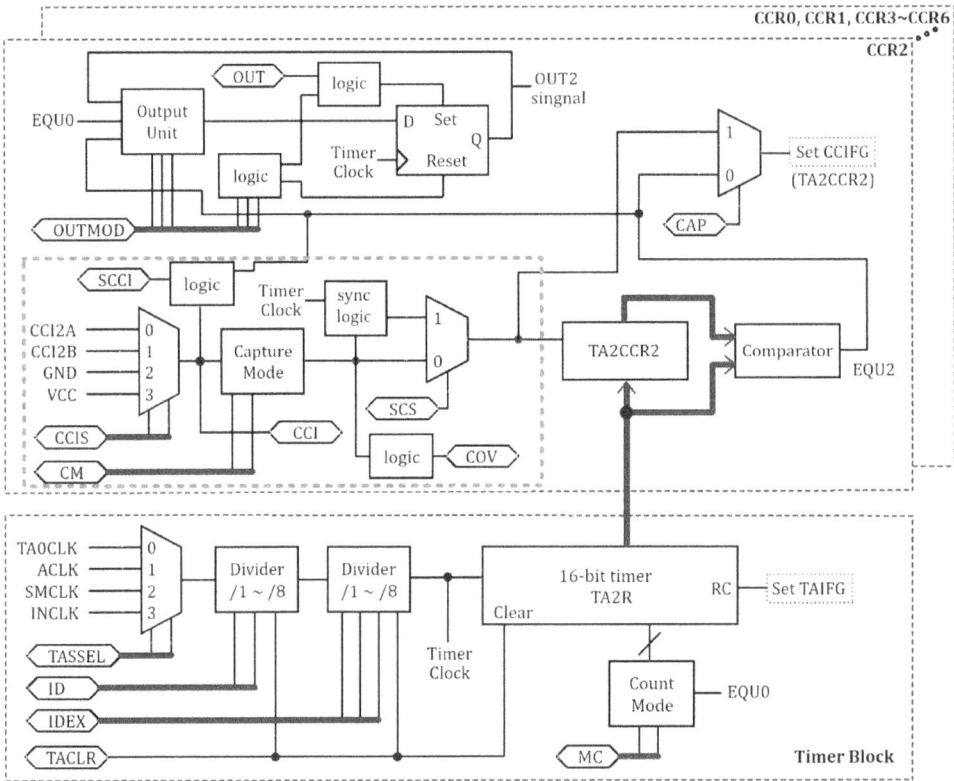

Figure 20.1. Simplified Timer_A2 block diagram showing the CCR2 block [6].

The capture mode can be selected by setting *CAP* bit. The inputs relevant to the capture mode are *CCI2A* and *CCI2B*. They can be selected by the configuration of *CCIS* bits. The *CCI1A* and *CCI2B* are connected to internally with other components or external pins. The connection to the pins is device-specific information. In this case, *TA2CCI2A* and *TA2CCI2B* are connected to P5.7.

The input signals can be captured on a rising or falling edge, or both edges. A capture mode can be configured by *CM* bits. In this setting, we use a Timer_A2 *CCR2*. In this case, the captured timer value will be stored in the *TA2CCR2* register. The capture signal can be synchronized with the capture source by setting *SCS* bit.

A capture mode test program is shown in Program 20.1. This is a loop back test program. It needs to use one jumper wire to connect P3.5 and P5.7. The P3.5 will be used to generate test signals, and the P5.7 will be used to capture the edges of the digital signals. In the test program, the direction of the P3.5 is configured as output. The direction of the P5.7 is configured as input. *P5SEL1* and *P5SEL0* are configured to be operated in capture mode.

Previously, we have used the timer in *up mode*. In order to increase the range of the upper limit of the counter, we will configure the timer to use in *continuous mode* instead in this example. This is configured by *MC* bits. This was described in the code that uses *TIMER_A_CTL_MC_2*. Given this configuration, the Timer_A2 can be operated to count up to 0xFFFF. The timer rolls off to zero when it reaches at 0xFFFF. This is a pattern of operation, and it will keep repeating.

TA2CCR2 register is configured to enable the capture mode to capture the signals on falling edges as it is described using *TIMER_A_CCTLN_CM_2*. The interrupt is configured and the *TA2_N_IRQHandler* subroutine is the relevant ISR. In this ISR, it checks whether CCIFG is set or not. Then, the TA2CCR2 will be stored in the *tcap* variable.

```
#include "msp.h"
volatile unsigned int tcap=0   // variable
int main(void) {
   WDT_A->CTL = WDT_A_CTL_PW | WDT_A_CTL_HOLD;   // hold the watchdog timer
   P3->DIR |= BIT5;   // output direction
   P5->DIR &= ~BIT7;   // input direction for P5.7
   P5->SEL0 |= BIT7;   // TA2.2 function for P5.7
   P5->SEL1 &= ~BIT7;   // TA2.2 function for P5.7
   TIMER_A2->CTL = TIMER_A_CTL_TASSEL_2 | TIMER_A_CTL_MC_2 |
TIMER_A_CTL_CLR;   // TA2CTL setup
   TIMER_A2->CCTL[2] = TIMER_A_CCTLN_CM_2 | TIMER_A_CCTLN_CCIS_0 |
TIMER_A_CCTLN_CCIE | TIMER_A_CCTLN_CAP | TIMER_A_CCTLN_SCS;
                                                // TA2CCTL[2] setup
   NVIC->ISER[0] = 1 << ((TA2_N_IRQn) & 31);   // NVIC setup
   _enable_irq();   // enable global interrupt
   while (1) {
       // begin capture test code
       P3->OUT &= ~BIT5;   // clear P3.5
```

```
      _delay_cycles(2000); // delay
      TIMER_A2->CTL |= TIMER_A_CTL_CLR; // clear TA2CCR
      _delay_cycles(1000); // delay
      P3->OUT |= BIT5; // set P3.5
      _delay_cycles(1000); // delay
      P3->OUT &= ~BIT5; // clear P3.5
      _delay_cycles(1000); // delay
          // end: capture test code
      while(1) {
        _delay_cycles(1000); // delay
      }
    }
  }

  void TA2_N_IRQHandler(void) {
    if((TIMER_A2->CCTL[2] & TIMER_A_CCTLN_CCIFG)!=0) { // check CCIFG flag
      tcap = TIMER_A2->CCR[2]; // store TA2CCR2 in tcap
      TIMER_A2->CCTL[2] &= ~TIMER_A_CCTLN_CCIFG; // clear CCIFG flag
    }
  }
```

Program 20.1. Capture mode test program.

In the while loop, a custom capture test behavior is defined. It generates ON or OFF signals through P3.5. These signals are the input signals for P5.7 since they are connected through a jumper cable.

The input signals are captured, and the proper signal edges can trigger the ISR to update *tcap* variable. In this given capture test behavior, the value of *tcap* will be about 2000 plus additional small values, when the program reaches at the infinite loop. After the TA2CCR is cleared, there is one falling edge in the capture test code block, and the tcap value is the sum of the time needed for the two delay cycle subroutine calls. In other words, the value is associated with the actual clock cycles for _*delay cycles()* calls and small extra cycles that were needed to process internally including interrupt service routines.

This loop back program can be used to help users to understand the behavior of the capture mode. Moreover, this program can be modified for other applications. In the following section, we will learn about an ultrasonic sensor example that is written based on this test program.

Ultrasonic Sensor
Ultrasound technology uses sound waves that are higher than upper limit of human hearing. Ultrasonic waves can be generated by a transducer. Ultrasonic device can be used as a ranging sensor. As an example, a low-cost ultrasonic ranging sensor,

HC-SR04, is selected. The measurement range of the ultrasonic sensor is 2 cm to 400 cm. The frequency of the waves is about 40 kHz.

A timing diagram of an HC-SR04 ultrasonic sensor is shown in Figure 20.2. The ultrasonic sensor receives a 10-µs pulse through a *trig* pin. Then, the senor transmits the 8-cycle sonic burst. These signals will travel, and they might be returned to the sensor if they were bounced back by an obstacle. The ultrasonic sensor can respond to the returned waves, and it can generate corresponding digital output signals. The travel distance is related to the time measurement from transmitting the waves until receiving the returned waves. The distance can be converted from the time measurement using the speed of sound. The speed of sound in air is about 340 m/s. In order to obtain the distance, the travel time can be divided by roughly 2.

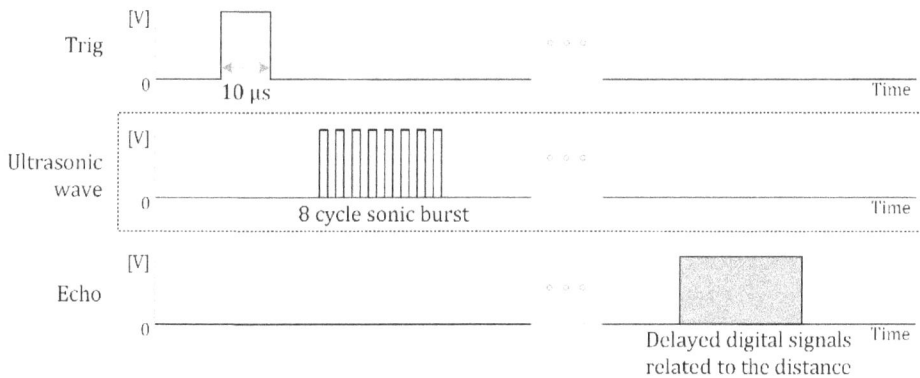

Figure 20.2. Timing diagram of an HC-SR04 ultrasonic sensor.

The HC-SR04 sensor can be connected to an MSP432P401R MCU, and the connection diagram is as shown in Figure 20.3. The operating voltage of an HC-SR04 sensor is +5 V. In order to interface with an MSP432P401R MCU safely, a bi-directional logic level converter can be used as we have studied in the previous chapter. There are several bi-directional logic level converters available. One of them is a Sparkfun® bi-directional logic level converter module [27]. In the diagram, the P3.5 and P5.7 pins are safely connected to *trig* and *echo* pins of the ultrasonic sensor using a bi-directional logic level converter module. A BH EDU board includes bi-directional logic level converter circuits, and users do not need an additional logic level converter module.

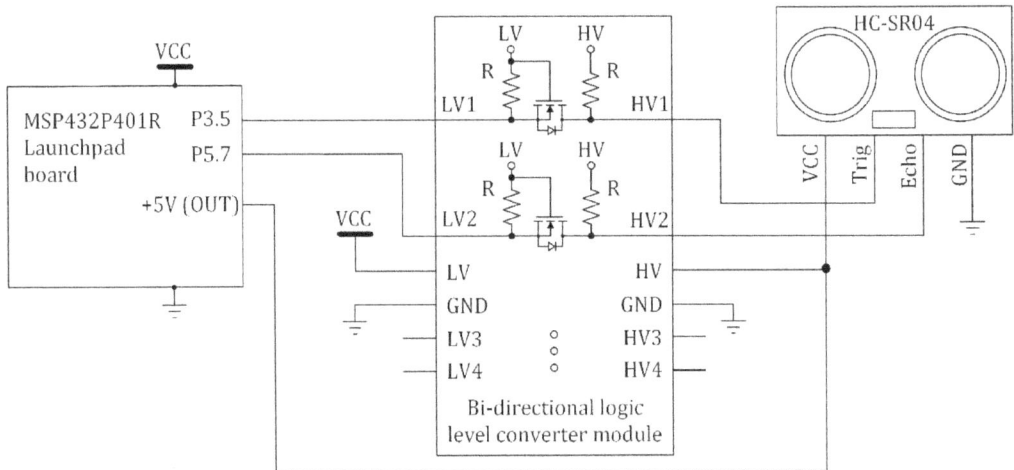

Figure 20.3. Connection diagram of an HC-SR04 ultrasonic sensor.

Let us examine +5V pins on an MSP432P401R Launchpad. The power for these 5V pins directly is from the USB port. Since the operating current of the ultrasonic sensor is about 15 mA, it may be reasonable to use the +5V power from the Launchpad. It is worth of mentioning that it is not a good idea to draw high current from these pins as they are directly connected the users' USB port. For instance, you may not want to attempt to drive a motor using these +5V pins on the Launchpad. It would draw excessive current from your laptop or a PC, and it could possibly damage the USB port.

An HC-SR04 example program is shown in Program 20.2. This is a modified program from the *capture mode test program* in the previous section. The set-up process is similar. However, additionally, the *TAIE* interrupt is enabled, and the *TAIFG* flag is processed in the ISR routine. If the returned signal is captured before the timer reaches at the maximum, the value of the timer counter stored in *tcap* will be displayed on a console. If the returned signal is captured after the timer rolls off to zero, "OVF" characters will be displayed on the console. This is a custom overflow process to validate the measurement. In the while loop, P3.5 is set or cleared with a certain time delay. This is for the generation of the trigger pulse. Thus, the program repeatedly sends and receives ultrasonic signals to measure the distance, and the captured timer values will be printed on a console.

```
#include "msp.h"
#include <stdio.h>
volatile unsigned int tcap=0, tcap_flag=0, tcap_cov=0; // variables
int main(void) {
    WDT_A->CTL = WDT_A_CTL_PW | WDT_A_CTL_HOLD; // hold the watchdog timer
    P1->DIR |= 0x01; // output direction for an LED
    P3->DIR |= BIT5; // output direction
    P5->DIR &= ~BIT7; // input direction for P5.7
```

```c
    P5->SEL0 |= BIT7;   // TA2.2 function for P5.7
    P5->SEL1 &= ~BIT7;  // TA2.2 function for P5.7
    TIMER_A2->CTL = TIMER_A_CTL_TASSEL_2 | TIMER_A_CTL_MC_2 |
TIMER_A_CTL_CLR;  // TA2CTL setup
    TIMER_A2->CCTL[2] = TIMER_A_CCTLN_CM_2 | TIMER_A_CCTLN_CCIS_0 |
TIMER_A_CCTLN_CCIE | TIMER_A_CCTLN_CAP | TIMER_A_CCTLN_SCS;
                                    // TA2CCTL[2] setup

    TIMER_A2->CTL |= TIMER_A_CTL_IE;  // enable TAIE interrupt
    NVIC->ISER[0] = 1 << ((TA2_N_IRQn) & 31);  // NVIC setup
    _enable_irq();  // enable global interrupt
    while (1) {
        tcap_flag=0;  // clear variable
        tcap_cov=0;  // clear variable
        TIMER_A2->CTL |= TIMER_A_CTL_CLR;  // clear TA2CCR
        P3->OUT |= BIT5;  // set P3.5
        _delay_cycles(30);  // delay for trigger signal
        P3->OUT &= ~BIT5;  // clear P3.5
        _delay_cycles(100);  // delay
        while (tcap_flag==0);  // wait until tcap_flag is set
        if (tcap_cov==0) printf("%d\n", tcap);  // print tcap on a console
        else printf("OVF\n");  // print 'OVF' on a console
        P1OUT ^= 0x01;  // toggle
        _delay_cycles(50000);  // delay
    }
}

void TA2_N_IRQHandler(void) {
    if((TIMER_A2->CTL & TIMER_A_CTL_IFG)!=0) {  // check TAIFG flag
        tcap_cov=1;  // set tcap overflow flag
        tcap_flag=1;  // set tcap flag
        TIMER_A2->CTL &= ~TIMER_A_CTL_IFG;  // clear TAIFG flag
    }
    if((TIMER_A2->CCTL[2] & TIMER_A_CCTLN_CCIFG)!=0) {  // check CCIFG flag
        tcap=TIMER_A2->CCR[2];  // store TA2CCR2 in tcap
        tcap_flag=1;  // set tcap flag
        TIMER_A2->CCTL[2] &= ~TIMER_A_CCTLN_CCIFG;  // clear CCIFG flag
    }
}
```

Program 20.2. HC-SR04 example program.

This ultrasonic test program is simply one of the examples written for an educational purpose. This test program is not optimized. It also does not guarantee the functionality of the ultrasonic sensor. Readers can modify and write your own code to improve the behavior and the quality of the ultrasonic distance measurement.

IR Communication

Infrared (IR) communication is an inexpensive wireless communication technology that has been used in many electronics systems such as IR remote controls. The wavelengths of the IR light are longer than the ones of the visible light. For this reason, it is generally invisibly to human eyes.

There are many applications using IR lights. One of applications is a short-range wireless communication. A simplified IR communication block diagram is shown in Figure 20.4. On the left side of the figure, a transmitter circuit block can be found. It controls the IR LED to turn ON or OFF. An amplitude shift keying (ASK) modulation is to send two different frequencies depending on whether the logic level is 0 or 1. For instance, it can generate a signal pattern at a certain carrier frequency for the logic 1. For the IR communication, the carrier frequency can be found is in the range between 30 kHz to 60 kHz.

On the right side of the figure, it shows the receiver circuit block. An IR photodiode can receive the signals. Next, the signals are amplified. A bandpass filter passes the frequencies of interest, and it blocks the noise. After the demodulation, the digital output signals can be generated.

In order to test the IR communications, we can choose an IR receiver module. A TSOP38238 is an IR receiver module that includes a PIN diode and a preamplifier [28]. On the BH EDU board, this IR receiver module was used. The TSOP38238 has three pins of Vs, GND, and OUT. This is the same configuration as the IR receiver module in the figure.

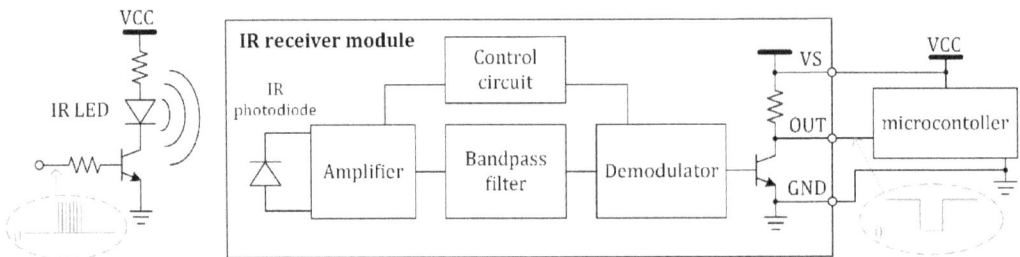

Figure 20.4. Simplified IR communication block diagram.

NEC IR Protocol

There are several IR communication protocols. One of them is a NEC® IR protocol that is commonly used in IR controlled devices. The carrier frequency is 38 kHz. The signals for logical 0 and 1 have the total transmit time of 1.125 ms and 2.25 ms, respectively. As you can see, there is a time difference between the signals for logic 0 and 1. This time difference can be detected by using a timer capture mode in an MSP432P401R MCU.

The NEC IR protocol can be summarized as follows:

(a) 9-ms leading pulse burst
(b) 4.5-ms space
(c) 8-bit address
(d) 8-bit logical inverse of the address
(e) 8-bit command
(f) 8-bit logical inverse of the command
(g) 562.5-μs pulse burst (end of message transmission)

The protocol begins with 9 ms leading pulse burst and 4.5 ms space signals. Next, the 8-bit address and its inverse can be sent. Then, the 8-bit command and its inverse can be sent. The transmission will be ended with the 562.5 μs pulse burst. The example of the NEC IR protocol is shown in Figure 20.5. The address code is 0 and the command code is 0x6A.

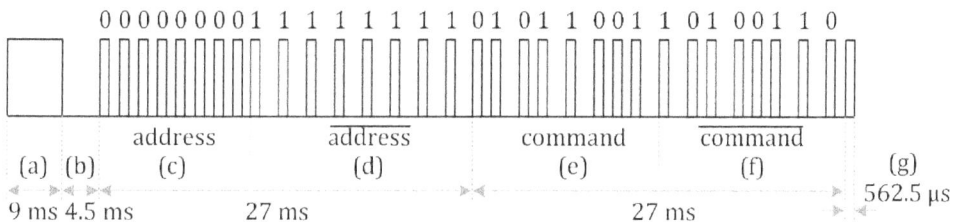

Figure 20.5. NEC® IR protocol example.

The address range can be chosen between 0 to 255. It is possible to increase the addresses range. There is an "Extended NEC IR protocol." A major difference is whether it uses a 16-bit address instead of an 8-bit address and the inversion of the address. Modern IR remote devices based on an NEC IR protocol can be found using an extended NEC IR protocol.

There are other IR protocols such as SONY®, RC5, and RC6. Many IR devices have been implemented using these IR protocols. For some of the IR devices, they choose not to use a protocol. They may send raw data, or they send the data using their own format.

There are several types of IR receiver modules. As mentioned, one of them is a TSOP38238 IR receiver. This IR receiver module can be easily connected to an MSP432P401R MCU. The BH EDU board has this IR receiver module. It has three pins. The "OUT" pin of the IR receiver can be connected to one of the pins of an MSP432P401R MCU. It can be P5.7 as we have used in the previous examples. When a user presses one of the buttons on an IR remote control, the remote transmits an IR signal pattern. The IR receiver generates output signals for an MCU to process.

Using the capture mode through Timer_A2 *CCR*, we can write a program that records the sequence of the captured timer values in an array. By analyzing this array, we can determine which button was pressed on an IR remote.

An IR remote control is an example of a simple wireless communication. An IR communication is valid within a certain angle between the transmitter and receiver. This IR communication system can be used in a mobile application such as a mobile robot. However, the robot may not be controllable if it is out of a certain angle. If this is not desired, a 2.4-GHz wireless module can be used instead. We will learn about a wireless module in the next chapter.

Chapter 21. Wireless Modules

Wireless connectivity for embedded systems has become more popular, and it changed the way of modern electronics. For instance, Apple®'s AirPods® and Amazon® Echo® Buds provide an alternative way to access the main unit remotely. Moreover, a majority of the modern IoT (Internet of Things) devices has WiFi connectivity. In this chapter, we will learn about a simple 2.4-GHz module and how to use it to create a wireless link between an MSP432P401R and a PC.

Wireless Embedded Systems

Wireless technologies in embedded systems are applied to many sensor network technologies. For instance, small sized sensor electronics devices may obtain data at multiple points and send the data wirelessly. The wirelessly transmitted data can be received by another electronics device. There are many wireless standards available for the sensor electronics. We will consider WiFi, Zigbee, and Bluetooth® technologies.

WiFi is a family of wireless networking technologies based on IEEE 802.11 standards. They are used in networking between devices and internet access. WiFi access on sensors provides the WiFi integration, and it is suitable for an IoT solution. However, typically, power consumption is an important factor and can be a concern for a battery-operated WiFi sensor device. There are low-power WiFi enabled sensors. Optimizing WiFi energy consumption is the key, and another effort is to use appropriate batteries to extend the time of the use until the next battery replacement or recharge period.

ZigBee is used for personal area networks. It is based on IEEE 802.15.4 standards. It has been used in many low power sensor devices. Digi XBEE® is a brand name. Some of the XBEE modules supports the Zigbee protocol. It is suitable for a low-power sensor solution. However, currently, Zigbee protocol may not be a common choice for some of the smart phones and tablet PCs.

Bluetooth® is a wireless standard for exchanging data between fixed and mobile devices. Typically, the supported frequencies include the ISM (Industrial, scientific, and medical) 2.4 GHz frequency band. The Bluetooth 5.2 version is released in 2020. The Bluetooth technology is widely accepted in many electronics systems including smart phones, tablet PCs, and laptops. Moreover, it is suitable for low power devices. However, the communication range of the Bluetooth devices may not be satisfactory depending on the applications. If a longer distance communication is desired, a class-1 Bluetooth device can be considered. For instance, a class-1 Bluetooth could transmit the power of 100 mW, and the range can extend to about 100 meters (328 ft).

In this chapter, we will use a simple Bluetooth module for testing. An HC-05 is a class-2 Bluetooth module, and it is based on Bluetooth v2.0+EDR.

HC-05 Bluetooth Module

There are many Bluetooth modules. One of the low-cost Bluetooth modules is HC-05. The operating voltage of this Bluetooth module is 3.6 to 6 V. In order to connect it safely to an MSP432P401R MCU, a bi-directional logic level converter can be used. The connection diagram of an HC-05 module is shown in Figure 21.1. On a BH EDU board, the logic level converter is applied. It does not need an additional converter module.

The RX and TX lines are connected through the bi-directional logic converter. As it was mentioned in the previous chapter, the 5-V power pins on an MSP432P401R Launchpad are directly from the USB port. Since the current consumption of the HC-05 module is reasonably small, in this example, we will use these 5-V pins to supply power to the HC-05 module.

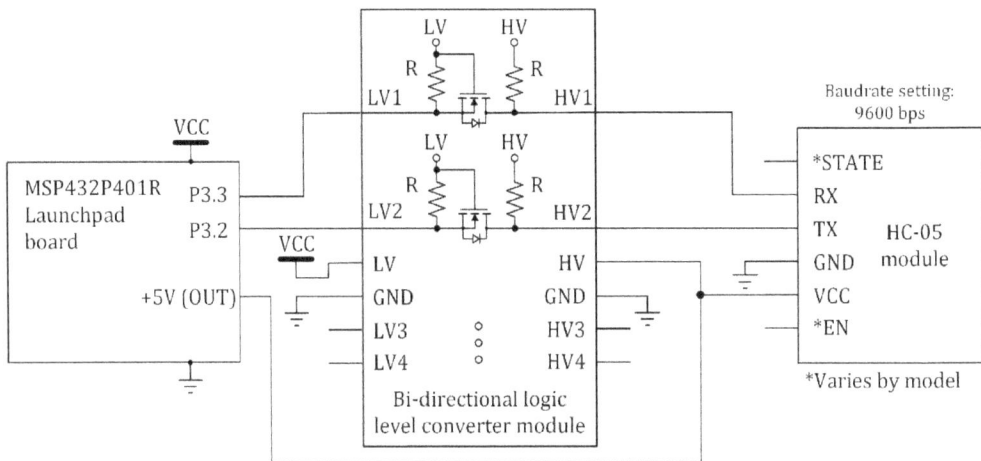

Figure 21.1. Connection diagram of an HC-05 module.

When the HC-05 module is powered, the LED on the HC-05 board may be flashing. it can be paired with a PC. If it asks to enter password, a user can try to enter the default password that is 1234 or 0000 depending on the HC-05 model.

For Windows O/S (Windows 10), after it is paired, you can find two virtual COM ports over the Bluetooth link as shown in Figure 21.2. You can select *More Bluetooth Settings*. Then, it will open a *Bluetooth Settings* window. It shows a COM port with the description of *Outgoing*. This is the COM port that will be used in opening a serial terminal for the Bluetooth test code in the following section. The Bluetooth connection status may become *paired* instead of *connected* when the Bluetooth communication channel is not used. This is not a problem. When data is sent over the Bluetooth link, it will be changed to *connected*.

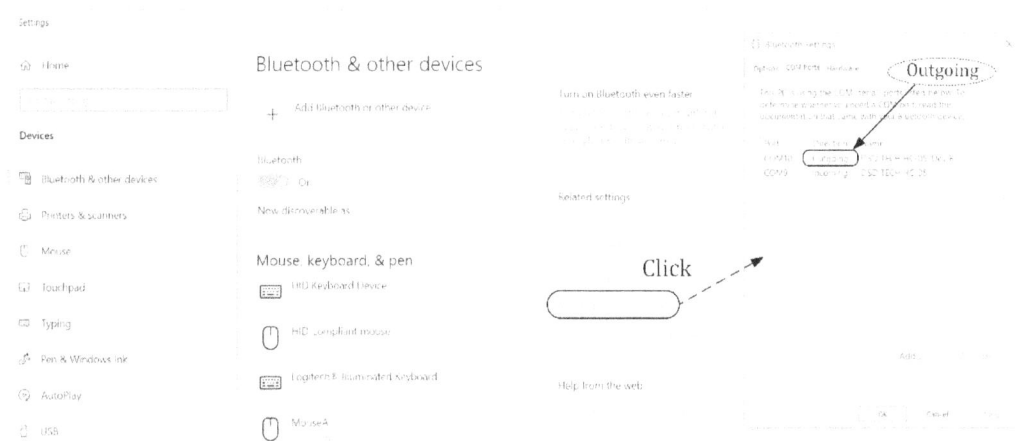

Figure 21.2. Connection diagram of an HC-05 module.

For Mac® users, they might experience some difficulties in using this HC-05 module. They can try a different Bluetooth module that supports an iOS®. Or, they can refer to the following description that would make the HC-05 module functional for the Bluetooth Test Program in this Chapter.

For macOS (Monterey), the Bluetooth module can be paired as shown in Figure 21.3. During the pairing process, a password might be asked. It is 1234 or 0000 depending on the HC-05 model. After it is connected, users can see the serial devices, and even it can be accessed by a serial terminal program. However, the communication may not be successful. In order to resolve this problem, they can use *Terminal* on Mac to access the serial device. Specifically, they can type "Terminal" in a search box, and open *Terminal as shown* Figure 21.3. Next, they can type the following command:
*ls /dev/tty.**

Figure 21.3. Connection diagram of an HC-05 module.

Then, they can find the serial device name. For instance, the serial device name can be /dev/tty.DSDTECHHC-05

This specific device name may vary by module. Next, they can type this command: *screen /dev/tty.DSDTECHHC-05 9600, cs8*

Then, the terminal may work as a serial terminal for the Bluetooth link, and this method can be used for the test program in the following section.

For more information, the serial terminal needs to be closed properly. By pressing "Ctrl + A" and "Ctrl + \", it would be asked to exit the session completely. Or, "Ctrl + D" can be pressed. It would minimize the screen. In order to restore it, "screen -r" can be used.

Bluetooth Test Program

Bluetooth test program for a HC-05 module is shown in Program 21.1. The RX and TX pins of the eUSCI_A2 in UART mode are P3.2 and P3.3. It is configured in the program. The baud rate generator is configured for 9600 bps as we have studied previously.

```
#include "msp.h"
volatile unsigned char ch;  // temporary variable
int main(void) {
    WDT_A->CTL = WDT_A_CTL_PW | WDT_A_CTL_HOLD;  // hold the watchdog timer
    P1->DIR |= BIT0;  // output direction for an LED
    P3->SEL1 &= ~(BIT2 | BIT3);  // UART function for P3.2 & P3.3
    P3->SEL0 |= BIT2 | BIT3;  // UART function for P3.2 & P3.3
    EUSCI_A2->CTLW0 = EUSCI_A_CTLW0_SWRST;  // eUSCI reset state
    EUSCI_A2->CTLW0 |= EUSCI_A_CTLW0_SWRST | EUSCI_A_CTLW0_UCSSEL_2;
                                            // eUSCI clock source, SMCLK
    EUSCI_A2-> BRW = 19;  // 9600 bps setting
    EUSCI_A2->MCTLW = (9 << EUSCI_A_MCTLW_BRF_OFS) | (85 <<
EUSCI_A_MCTLW_BRS_OFS) | EUSCI_A_MCTLW_OS16;  // 9600 bps setting
    EUSCI_A2->CTLW0 &= ~EUSCI_A_CTLW0_SWRST;  // eUSCI operation state
    EUSCI_A2->IE |= EUSCI_A_IE_RXIE;  // Set UCA2RXIE
    NVIC->ISER[0] = 1 << ((EUSCIA2_IRQn) & 31);  // NVIC setup
    __delay_cycles(1000);  // delay
    __enable_irq();  // enable global interrupt
    while(1){
        if (ch=='1') {
            P1->OUT ^= BIT0;  // toggle
            EUSCI_A2->IFG &= ~EUSCI_A_IFG_TXIFG;  // clear UCA2TXIFG flag
            EUSCI_A2->TXBUF=ch;  // store data in UCA2TXBUF
            while ((EUSCI_A2->IFG & EUSCI_A_IFG_TXIFG)==0);  // wait until UCA2TXIFG is set
            ch=0;  // clear
        }
        __delay_cycles(500000);  // delay
    }
```

```
}
void EUSCIA2_IRQHandler(void) {
  if ((EUSCI_A2->IFG & EUSCI_A_IFG_RXIFG)!=0) {  // check UCA2RXIFG flag
    ch=EUSCI_A2->RXBUF;  // read the data from UCA2RXBUF
    EUSCI_A2->IFG &=~ EUSCI_A_IFG_RXIFG;  // clear UCA2RXIFG flag
  }
}
```

Program 21.1. Bluetooth test program.

The *RXIE* interrupt is enabled. When the UART module received a byte, it will execute the interrupt service routine. It checks whether the *UCA2RXIFG* is set or not. Then, the byte data will be read and stored in the "ch" variable. Next, it clears the interrupt flag. Thus, when a user types a character in a terminal, it will be sent to the MSP432P401R MCU and it gets stored in the 'ch' variable. In the while loop, it reads the 'ch' variable. If it is '1', it can toggle the output of the pin that is connected to the LED. And, this character will be sent back to the terminal. Therefore, when a user type '1' on the serial terminal, it can turn the Red LED ON or OFF. If the communication is successful, you can see the '1' printed on the serial terminal. This program supports only one simple function. However, it can be modified to provide more and complex functions. In the next chapter, we study an educational robot application. This wireless control method can be found useful in the mobile robot applications.

Bluetooth ICs and Modules

There are many Bluetooth modules available. Designers and programmers can search and find the best one that meets the functional requirements of the given project. There are also MCUs that support Bluetooth connectivity. For instance, Microchip® provides Bluetooth low energy solutions. TI supports SimpleLink Bluetooth Low Energy solutions. The MSP432P401R MCU is one of the wired MCUs. However, there are SimpleLink wireless MCUs. You can find many MCU models with Bluetooth connectivity from the manufactures' website.

As the complexity of the system is increasing, it is a preferred to use high level driver library and Real-Time Operating Systems. If a developer wants to create fast prototype devices, an open electronics development tool can be used. This includes Arduino. For TI MCUs, Energia can be used. We will study briefly about the driver library, real-time operating system, and open electronics development platforms in Chapter 23, 24 and 25.

Chapter 22. Embedded System Integration

Embedded systems can be easily found in modern electronics products. They are used across a wide range of industries that include medical, oil/gas, process control, automotive, and communications. It is typical to find these products are integrated systems with multiple sub-systems. We have studied about various components and the programming techniques to control them using an MSP432P401R MCU. Let us discuss about development and design considerations for the successful Embedded System Integration.

System Integration

Generally, in engineering, a system integration is the process of putting sub-systems together to make one larger system. The discrete sub-systems function together as a system. A system integration typically focuses on increasing the value and functionality. Developers put all things together in order to make the system work as a single integrated system. They work together as a team to meet the project milestones.

Top-down Approach

Developers may share a big goal or idea of the system to build. Next, they can communicate with each other to come up with a plan. The project can be processed as a top-down approach. In this method, typically, it could spend an extensive research and planning phase before the next execution phase of the project such as hardware assembly or software programming.

Top-down Approach in embedded systems development is a problem-solving strategy related to many areas including hardware, software, and mechanical. During the analysis and planning phase, the system can be divided into hardware, software, and mechanical tasks.

On the software development side, a structured programming is the relevant to this approach. It performs a top-down analysis. Next, the program has been broken down it into sub-tasks to reduce the complexity of each sub-task.

Modular programming could be adopted, which is the software design technique to separate the functionality of a program into independent and interchangeable modules. Thus, sub-tasks can be divided into modules. These modules can be independently developed, and they are preferred to be reusable.

The top-down programming method is organized, and it is typically easier to maintain the program in the long run. However, it may be slow to start since it may take an extensive time in planning, and it is slow to obtain the first executable program. Moreover, as it was mentioned, the sub-tasks have to be specifically defined and could be developed separately. If the specification of the product happens to be changed after the planning phase, it might require to an extended extra effort, if it would change the major structure.

This explanation is similar to the overall top-down approach. It can solve a complex problem by breaking it down into sub-tasks. It is suitable for a traditional structured approach. However, due to the needs of the extensive planning and analysis, top-down approach may be slow in delivering the first prototype, and it is less flexible in adapting to the change of product specifications.

Bottom-up Approach

Developers share a big goal or idea of the system. Next, they can communicate with each other to come up with a plan. This process is similar to the previous top-down approach. However, it can be processed as a bottom-up approach. This means, in planning, the goal and problems are outlined. However, in this approach, it does not spend an extensive effort in breaking down the tasks and identifying the problems. After the initial planning phase, they can move on execution phase, and start building hardware assembly or writing a piece of software code.

On the software development side, a bottom-up programming is also a relevant approach. It tends to be less organized than the top-down approach. The code tends to be difficult to maintain later. However, it allows getting it started fast and it may generate the first executable program fast. Moreover, a bottom-up programming may provide a solution to a complex problem that is not clearly defined.

Traditionally, this bottom-up approach may not be highly encouraged, but a structured approach like top-down approach is more emphasized in a formal education or training setting. One of the reasons is that it could generate a *spaghetti code*. This code refers to the source code negatively that is difficult to maintain. However, this bottom-up approach may be suitable for the *experienced* developers who already hold a fair understanding of the technology and can maintain a good communication with the team.

In order words, inexperienced developers who lacks understanding of the technology may eventually generate a functional code at some point by a trial-and-error approach. But, the code may not be well-written, and the developers may fail to communicate with their team members due to the code that cannot be understood easily by other developers. This may be one of the unfavorable scenarios for the majority of product design projects.

If it is well managed, the bottom-up approach may result in providing an innovative solution to a difficult problem that was not easy to be solved in a traditional setting. Moreover, it is flexible and can be adaptable to the specification changes after the initial planning phase. This approach may be found suitable in a research project type rather than consumer electronics project types.

Blending Top-down and Bottom-up Approaches

Depending on the projects, the blended top-down and bottom-up approaches can be chosen. If it is well-structured problem to solve, a top-down approach can be a good choice. However, if the specification may need to be changed in the middle of the execution of the project, it may not be easy process for the top-down approach.

The bottom-up approach may be less structured to begin with. However, it can be flexible to adapt to the change. Moreover, the decision process in a top-down approach tends to be centralized by leaders, and the decision process in a bottom-up approach tends to be decentralized.

In software development, there is a waterfall methodology. It is a linear project management approach where the stakeholders and customers set up requirements at the early stage of the project. And, the rest of the project period is based on the execution of the project based on the requirements. Typical phases of the waterfall model are *requirements*, *design*, *implementation*, *verification*, and *maintenance*.

Agile Software Development

Waterfall project management in software development is a plan driven approach. There is another software development process. It is Agile software development. This is effective in a complex environment. Agile is based on the interactive process to receive and accept feedback and review from the customer during the product development. The process is streamlined. This means that it reduces unnecessary long meetings and documents but to have quick meetings and short documentations to move the project fast. Agile is based on time-boxed events and iterations. A time-box is an agreed maximum period of time for a person or a team for a certain goal. For instance, when the time limit is reached, it evaluates the task. The key of agile is collaboration. For instance, the specifications may be open to change according to the communication with the client even in the middle of the project execution. Agile may result in creating a better product, and it can improve the product continuously.

Design Project Management Consideration

A top-down approach is a typical choice for many companies. The changes in specifications are necessary due to the changes of the demands in the todays' electronics market. Bottom-up approach may respond to the change easier than the top-down approach. Also, the bottom-up approach can used in tacking difficult problems or creating an innovative solution. However, the lack of the organization can become a problem. Depending on the project, blended approach can be effectively used. In software development, instead of Waterfall project management, Agile software development can provide a continuously improving product.

BH EDU Robot Platform

In the previous chapters, we have studied various functions that can be applied to embedded systems. For learning purposes, readers can choose a goal of their own embedded system and start to design and build a prototype as a small educational project.

At the early stage of the development, a conceptual block diagram can be drawn, which shows the high-level description of the project. The conceptual block diagram (CBD) can serve as a roadmap for the project. Next, a functional block diagram (FBD) can be created. This FBD includes further details of the project such as wiring and connections. As the system would become more complicated, it will become challenging in making all components function properly. The FBD can be used to check to see whether there is any resource conflict or not.

Figure 22.1. BH EDU robot platform example [4].

As an example, a mobile robot can be built using a BH EDU board with an MSP432P401R Launchpad as shown in Figure 22.1. The robot base kit is assembled with the BH EDU board. The robot base kit includes the DC motors and wheel sets as well as a servo motor and manipulator set. On the BH EDU board, it has a motor driver, an accelerometer, an ultrasonic sensor, an LCD module, buttons, and a 5V regulator. This robot can be controlled wirelessly through an IR receiver or a Bluetooth module.

For learning purposes, various robot missions can be given such as solving a maze and moving objects to specified locations. As there are many components to make them operate concurrently, programming can be challenging. It may need several iterative efforts of programming, debugging, and testing.

Readers can choose other educational embedded system examples including calculators, alarm clocks, music players, fan control systems, robot arms, and remote controlled four-wheeled or tracked robots. There are many robot chassis kits and DIY kits available. However, many of them are designed for a 5-V Arduino board. Since an MSP432P401R MCU is 3.3V, the proper and safe interfaces between the board and the components are required. It is recommended that the wiring and connections need to be carefully reviewed. If it involves any components that could draw high current such as a motor driver, it should not draw the power from the Launchpad. Instead, separate regulated power through external batteries can be used to supply the power for the motor driver.

Chapter 23. Driver Library

Developers may find low-level programming methods difficult in describing complex tasks. In addition, they may want to write a program that is reusable in other platforms. In this reason, developers can choose high-level programming methods instead, and there are several high-level programming methods available. One of them is based on the hardware abstraction layer (HAL) and application programming interfaces (APIs). A HAL creates an abstract and high-level functions that can make the hardware do some tasks. APIs defines high-level interfaces that can be used in creating an application. Texas Instruments provides a Diver Library. This supports a higher-level programming method. The MSP432 Driver Library is included in the SimpleLink MSP432 Software Development Kit (SDK). It is a set of software development tools for the development of the MSP432 applications. The code written using Driver Library can be portable between other platforms. In addition, the code can be written without the in-depth understanding of the hardware. This is a middleware approach, and this is one of the recommended methods in writing a program for an MSP432P401R MCU.

Driver Library

TI MSP432 Driver Library (DriverLib) is a set of Application Programming Interfaces (APIs) [29]. It can be used to control MSP432 peripherals. In addition, it also provides a method of controlling peripherals such as the Interrupt (NVIC) and Memory Protection Unit (MPU).

The DriverLib provides higher level of programming compared to register-based C programming. The code written using this high-level software programming method can be portable between other devices. In addition, it is more readable, intuitive, and easy to program. As an example, the code that configures P1.0 as an output port can be written using DriverLib as follows:

GPIO_setAsOutputPin(GPIO_PORT_P1, GPIO_PIN0);

A copy of DriverLib is included in the device's ROM space. It is available to use. The use of DriverLib in ROM reduces the memory usage. To accessing Driver Library in ROM, add prefix *ROM_* to the API. The GPIO configuration line can be modified as follows:

ROM_GPIO_setAsOutputPin(GPIO_PORT_P1, GPIO_PIN0);

Most of DriverLib APIs can be found in ROM but, some APIs are not included in ROM due to the architectural limitation. In addition, some of the APIs in ROM may not contain bug fixes in the flash version of APIs. If prefix *MAP_* is used, the macro decides whether to use the ROM version of API or the flash version of the API. The GPIO configuration line can be modified as follows:

MAP_GPIO_setAsOutputPin(GPIO_PORT_P1, GPIO_PIN0);

The DriverLib package contains many examples. In order to access and use the DriverLib, a proper set up process such as setting up the path for the library folder is needed.

In order to access the examples and the set them up easy, you can use *Resource Explorer*. It can be found in *View* on your code composer studio and click *Resource Explorer*. Then, click *Software*. Next, select *SimpleLink MSP432P4 SDK - 3.xx.xx.xx*. Then, find the *empty* project using the sequence of selections as follows:

Examples -> Development Tools -> MSP432P401R Launchpad - Red2.x (red) -> DriverLib -> empty -> No RTOS -> CCS Compiler -> empty

Then, you can find "*import*" icon as shown in Figure 23.1 and click this icon.

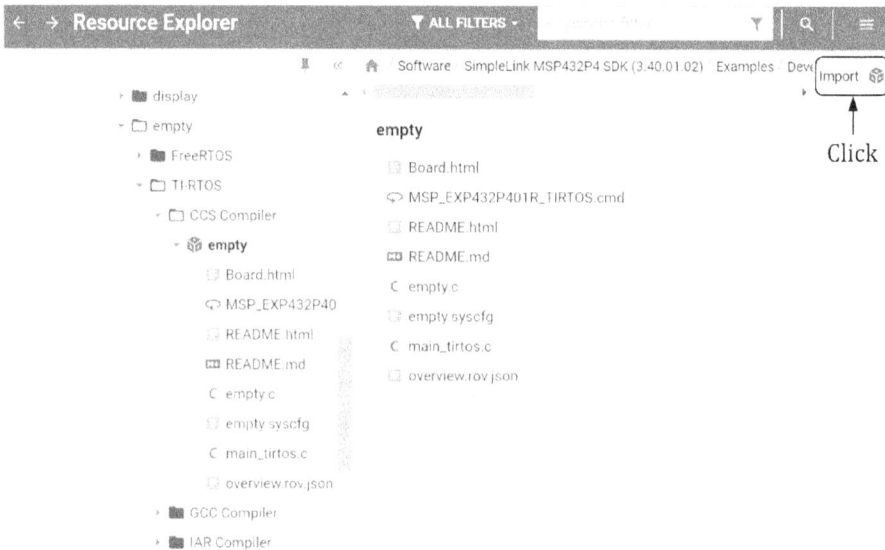

Figure 23.1. DriverLib *empty* project on TI resource explorer.

Next, you can find the *empty* project is imported in the project list . You can use this project as a default template project. You can rename the project. For the following programming examples, you can modify the *main.c* file to enter your code

SimpleLink MSP432P4 SDK

An MSP432P4 software development kit (SDK) is a software package with multiple software components including RTOS, DriverLib, and examples. As described, this

SDK can be accessed using the *Resource Explorer,* and it is an easy method to access the MSP432P4 SDK. In case, there is any difficult in accessing the MSP432P4 SDK using *Resource Explorer.* Users can choose to install the MSP432P4 SDK manually and import an example at your own risk and discretion if needed. The SimpleLink MSP432P4 SDK files may be downloaded using the web address as follows:

https://www.ti.com/tool/download/SIMPLELINK-MSP432-SDK

Users may see the list of the MSP432P4 SDK files as shown in Figure 23.2. There are installer files for Windows, macOS, and Linux operating systems. As an example, a Windows version file was download and executed the file to install the SDK.

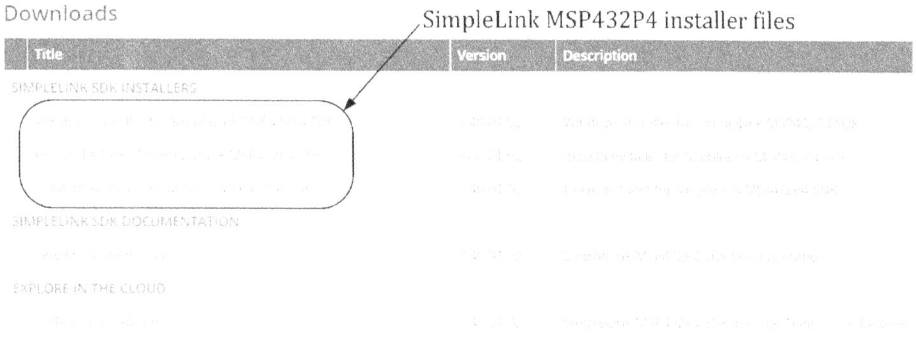

Figure 23.2. MSP432P4 SDK file download.

During the installation, it may be prompted to choose an installation folder as shown in Figure 23.3. The default folder is "C:\ti" and it can be modified if needed. Next, users can complete the SDK installation process.

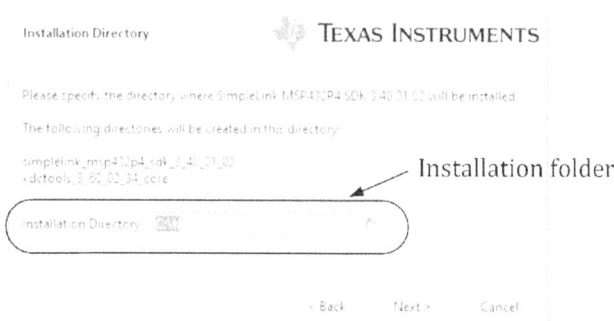

Figure 23.3. Installation directory selection.

Let's say that the MSP432P4 SDK is installed to the default folder. In order to import an example project, users can choose *import* as shown on the left side of Figure 23.4.

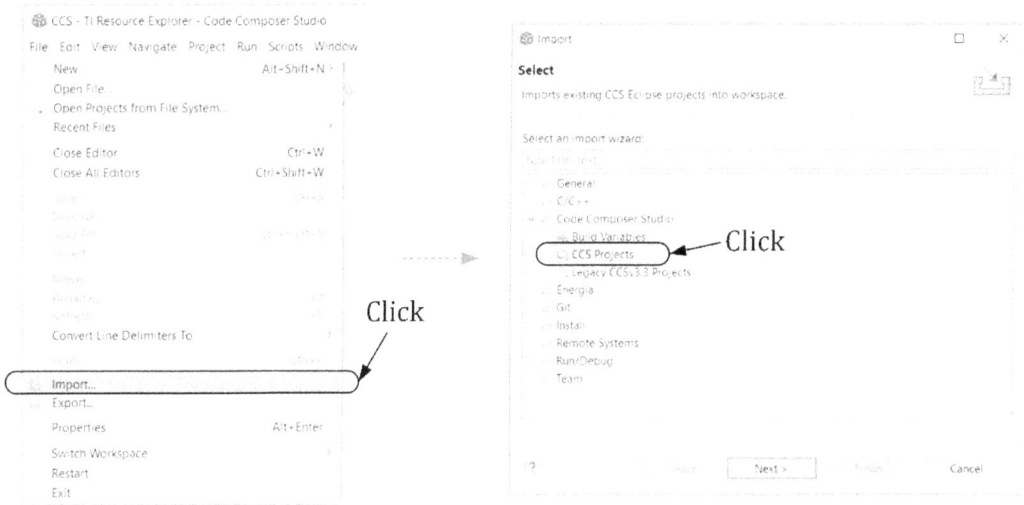

Figure 23.4. Import a CCS project.

Next, the *import* windows will be opened as shown on the right side of the figure. Users can choose the *CCS Projects*, and it will open *import CCS projects* window as shown in Figure 23.5.

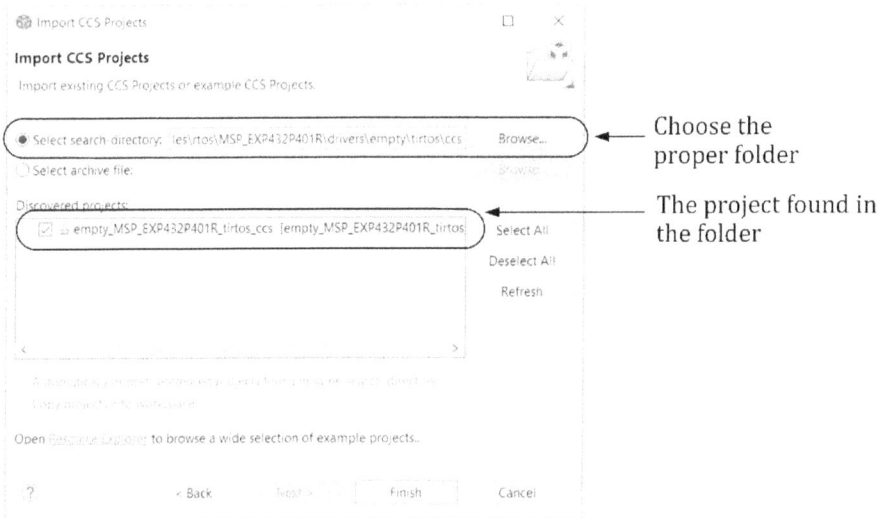

Figure 23.5. Search directory selection and the discovered project (empty project).

Assuming the Windows version of the SDK is installed to the default folder, the *empty project* can be accessed by choosing a proper folder. Although the directory could be different for many reasons, as an example, a sample search directory for the *empty project* is listed for reference, and it is followed:
C:\ti\simplelink_msp432p4_sdk_3_40_01_02\examples\rtos\MSP_EXP432P401R\drive rs\empty\tirtos\ccs

Once the import process is successfully completed, users can find the *empty project* in the project list. As described, you can use this project as a default template project for the examples in this chapter, and users can rename the project as needed.

DriverLib GPIO

A set of functions provides the control of GPIOs. Let us consider some of selected functions in this section. They are introduced in the following paragraph, and they are self-explanatory from the names of the functions.

The GPIO pin can be configured as an input or output pin with *GPIO_setAsOutputPin*, *GPIO_setAsInputPin*, *GPIO_setAsInputPinWithPullDownResistor*, or *GPIO_setAsInputPinWithPullUpResistor*.

The GPIO pin can be configured to operate in the Peripheral Module using *GPIO_setAsPeripheralModuleFunctionOutputPin* or *GPIO_setAsPeripheralModuleFunctionInputPin*.

The port interrupt on the selected pin can be configured using *GPIO_enableInterrupt*.

The interrupt flag on the selected pin can be cleared using *GPIO_clearInterruptFlag*.

The interrupt status of the selected pin can be obtained using *GPIO_getEnabledInterruptStatus*.

There are functions that can generate output on the selected pin. They are GPIO_setOutputHighOnPin, GPIO_setOutputLowOnPin, and *GPIO_toggleOutputOnPin*.

Using some of these GPIO functions, a DriverLib GPIO example is written and shown in Program 23.1. Some of APIs have been used in this example. This program shows the initiation process. In the main loop, it toggles P1.0. In the interrupt service routine, the interrupt status can be read, and the program checks whether the PIN1 is set or not. Then, it will toggle the P2.0 pin. This program uses two Red LEDs connected to P1.0 and P2.0. A port interrupt is configured for P1.1. The left push button is connected to the P1.1. One of the LED will keep blinking, and the other LED will toggle as the button is pressed by a user.

```
#include <ti/devices/msp432p4xx/driverlib/driverlib.h>  // DriverLib
int main(void) {
    MAP_WDT_A_holdTimer();  // hold the watchdog timer
    MAP_GPIO_setAsOutputPin(GPIO_PORT_P1, GPIO_PIN0);  // P1.0 (output)
    MAP_GPIO_setAsOutputPin(GPIO_PORT_P2, GPIO_PIN0);  // P2.0 (output)
    MAP_GPIO_setAsInputPinWithPullUpResistor(GPIO_PORT_P1, GPIO_PIN1);
                                    // P1.1 (input, pull up resistor)
```

```
    MAP_GPIO_clearInterruptFlag(GPIO_PORT_P1, GPIO_PIN1);
                                                    // clear interrupt flag (P1.1)
    MAP_GPIO_enableInterrupt(GPIO_PORT_P1, GPIO_PIN1);  // enable interrupt (P1.1)
    MAP_Interrupt_enableInterrupt(INT_PORT1);  // enable port1 interrupt
    MAP_Interrupt_enableMaster();  // enable master interrupt
    while (1) {
      MAP_GPIO_toggleOutputOnPin(GPIO_PORT_P1, GPIO_PIN0);  // toggle (P1.0)
      __delay_cycles(500000);  // delay
    }
  }

  void PORT1_IRQHandler(void) {
    uint32_t status;
    status = MAP_GPIO_getEnabledInterruptStatus(GPIO_PORT_P1);
                                                    // read port1 interrupt status
    if(status & GPIO_PIN1) {  // check PIN1
      MAP_GPIO_toggleOutputOnPin(GPIO_PORT_P2, GPIO_PIN0);  // toggle (P2.0)
    }
    MAP_GPIO_clearInterruptFlag(GPIO_PORT_P1, GPIO_PIN1);  // clear interrupt flag
  }
```

Program 23.1. DriverLib GPIO example.

DriverLib UART

DriverLib package includes functions for a UART module. The data structure for the UART configuration is defined. It is a *struct* data type and the name is *_eUSCI_eUSCI_UART_Config*. It contains the UART configuration data.

A UART module can be initialized using *UART_initModule*.

The UART block can be enabled by *UART_enableModule*.

The UART interrupt can be configured using *UART_enableInterrupt*.

The UART interrupt status can be obtained by *UART_getEnabledInterruptStatus*.

The data can be transmitted or received using *UART_transmitData* or *UART_receiveData*.

A DriverLib UART example is written and shown in Program 23.2. Some of these UART functions have used in this program. This is a UART echo program, and the baud rate is selected as 9600 bps. "*uartConfig*" variable contains the UART configuration data. P1.2 and P1.3 are configured to operate in UART mode.

The RX UART interrupt is configured. When data is received, the interrupt service routine will be executed. In the ISR, it checks the interrupt flag. Then, it will read the data and send it back over the UART channel.

```c
#include <ti/devices/msp432p4xx/driverlib/driverlib.h>  // DriverLib
#include <stdint.h>
#include <stdbool.h>

// UART config, 9600 baud rate
const eUSCI_UART_ConfigV1 uartConfig = {
    EUSCI_A_UART_CLOCKSOURCE_SMCLK,  // SMCLK
    19,  // UCBRx
    9,   // UCxBRF
    85,  // UCxBRS
    EUSCI_A_UART_NO_PARITY,  // no parity
    EUSCI_A_UART_LSB_FIRST,  // LSB first
    EUSCI_A_UART_ONE_STOP_BIT,  // one stop bit
    EUSCI_A_UART_MODE,  // UART mode
    EUSCI_A_UART_OVERSAMPLING_BAUDRATE_GENERATION,  // oversampling
    EUSCI_A_UART_8_BIT_LEN  // 8 bit data
};

int main(void) {
    MAP_WDT_A_holdTimer();  // hold the watchdog timer
    MAP_GPIO_setAsOutputPin(GPIO_PORT_P1, GPIO_PIN0);  // P1.0 (output)
    MAP_GPIO_setAsPeripheralModuleFunctionInputPin(GPIO_PORT_P1, (GPIO_PIN2 |
GPIO_PIN3), GPIO_PRIMARY_MODULE_FUNCTION);  // P1.2 & P1.3 in UART mode
    MAP_UART_initModule(EUSCI_A0_BASE, &uartConfig);
                                        // configure UART Module (eUSCI_A0)
    MAP_UART_enableModule(EUSCI_A0_BASE);  // enable UART module
    MAP_UART_enableInterrupt(EUSCI_A0_BASE, EUSCI_A_UART_RECEIVE_INTERRUPT);
                                        // enable ISR (RX)
    MAP_Interrupt_enableInterrupt(INT_EUSCIA0);  // enable eUSCI_A0 interrupt
    MAP_Interrupt_enableMaster();  // enable master interrupt
    while(1) {
        MAP_GPIO_toggleOutputOnPin(GPIO_PORT_P1, GPIO_PIN0);  // toggle (P1.0)
        __delay_cycles(500000);  // delay
    }
}

void EUSCIA0_IRQHandler(void) {
    uint32_t status;
    status = MAP_UART_getEnabledInterruptStatus(EUSCI_A0_BASE);
                                        // read eUSCI_A0 interrupt status
    if(status & EUSCI_A_UART_RECEIVE_INTERRUPT_FLAG) {  // check UART RX flag
        MAP_UART_transmitData(EUSCI_A0_BASE,
MAP_UART_receiveData(EUSCI_A0_BASE));  // read the data and send it back
    }
}
```

Program 23.2. DriveLib UART Echo Example.

Similar to other echo program examples shown previously, users can modify this
code to provide the functions for their project.

For more information about the Driver Library, TI provides a Peripheral Driver Library User's Guide [29]. The further details can be found in this user's guide. TI also provides Driver Library examples. Developers can access these programming examples through the *Resource Explorer or* the MSP432P4 SDK.

Chapter 24. Introduction to TI RTOS

Developers can choose to use TI Driver Library to describe functions as a high-level programming method. It is a middleware approach. Another high-level approach is to use a Real Time Operating System. There are several RTOSs for MSP432 MCUs. In this chapter, we will learn about TI RTOS. TI-RTOS can accelerate the development because it can eliminate the need of creating basic software functions. TI-RTOS provides a real-time kernel.

TI RTOS

TI-RTOS is a real-time operating system. It is an embedded system development package with source files and pre-compiled libraries. TI RTOS contains the several components. Let me briefly introduce a few key components.

SYS/BIOS is a scalable real-time kernel, and it supports real-time scheduling and synchronization [30]. SYS/BIOS provides preemptive multithreading and hardware abstraction as well as real-time analysis and configuration tools. SYS/BIOS is used as the TI-RTOS kernel component in TI RTOS.

SYS/BIOS provides deterministic performance, and it enables applications to meet real-time deadlines. SYS/BIOS also provides various thread types, and it supports *hardware interrupts (Hwi)*, *software interrupts (Swi)*, *tasks*, and *idle* functions. Moreover, SYS/BIOS supports synchronization between threads including *semaphores*, *mailboxes*, *events*, *gates*, and *messaging*.

TI-RTOS includes the board support and drivers for peripherals. These drivers are written to be thread-safe for the use with the TI-RTOS Kernel. Moreover, there is a XDCtools component. It is a core component that provides tools to configure and build SYS/BIOS and other components.

GPIO Driver

TI-RTOS includes various software libraries and drivers. GPIO driver is one of them [31]. It is an API set to manage GPIO pins and ports. In this module, it has *GPIOMSP432_Config*. The GPIO pins can be defined using *GPIO_PinConfig* array elements. The application needs to call *GPIO_init()* function to initialize all the GPIO pins defined in the *GPIO_PinConfig* array elements.

TI GPIO Driver provides the GPIO APIs that are easy to use; however, they may not be the same APIs in TI Driver Library. However, there is a similarity between TI-RTOS GPIO APIs and TI Driver Library APIs.

In order to use the GPIO module in TI-RTOS, the proper GPIO header needs to be included as follows: #include <ti/drivers/GPIO.h>

Moreover, the proper API names need to be used. Selected GPIO APIs and their description will be followed.

GPIO pins can be initialized as it is pre-defined using *GPIO_init()*.

The specified GPIO pin can be configured using *GPIO_setConfig()*.

The status of the specified GPIO input pin can be read using *GPIO_read()*.

The state of the specified GPIO output pin can be set or cleared using *GPIO_write()*.

The state of the specified GPIO output pin can be toggled using *GPIO_toggle()*.

A call back function to the specified GPIO pin can be configured using *GPIO_setCallback()*.

An interrupt on the specified GPIO pin can be enabled or disabled using *GPIO_enableInt()* or *GPIO_disableInt()*.

The interrupt flag for the specified GPIO pin can be cleared using *GPIO_clearInt()*.

For instance, a user-defined LED (CONFIG_GPIO_LED1) on the board can be turned ON, OFF, or toggled using code lines as follows:
GPIO_write(CONFIG_GPIO_LED1, CONFIG_GPIO_LED_ON),
GPIO_write(CONFIG_GPIO_LED1, CONFIG_GPIO_LED_OFF), or
GPIO_toggle(CONFIG_GPIO_LED1).

In order to access and use the TI RTOS, it needs a proper configuration and set up. This set-up process would be difficult if it has to be done manually from scratch. However, the RTOS project can be created easily by importing a project example.

As it was described in the previous chapter, you can access *Resource Explorer*. In order to set up a project example, you can find *View* on you code composer studio and click *Resource Explorer*. Then, click *Software*. Next, select *SimpleLink MSP432P4 SDK - 3.xx.xx.xx*. Then, you can find the *hello project* by following the sequence of selections:

Examples -> Development Tools -> MSP432P401R Launchpad - Red2.x (red)
-> TI-RTOS Kernel (SYS-BIOS) -> hello -> CCS Compiler -> hello

You can find "import" icon as shown in Figure 24.1 and click the icon. The, the *hello project* will be imported, and you can find this imported project in your project list. You can rename this project as needed.

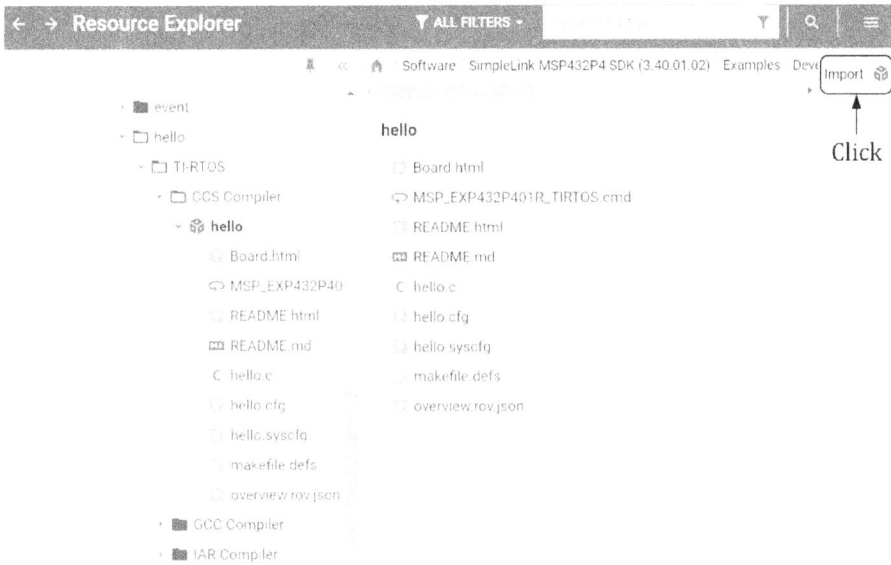

Figure 24.1. TI RTOS *empty* project example on TI resource explorer.

This project contains library, source, and configuration files. You can open "hello.c". You can find the main() routine in the file. We will learn how to set it up properly in the GPIO program example section after the following task execution state section.

As described in the previous Chapter 23, in case, there is any difficult in accessing the MSP432P4 SDK using *Resource Explorer*, users can choose to install the MSP432P4 SDK manually and import a project example at their own risk and discretion if needed. You can check out *SimpleLink MSP432P4 SDK* section in Chapter 23 for more details about the MSP432P4 SDK installation.

If users have installed the MSP432P4 SDK manually, they can select the import, and after choosing *CCS projects* in the import window, they can see the import CCS projects window open as shown in Figure 24.2. Assuming the Windows version of the SDK is installed to the default folder, the *empty* project can be accessed by choosing a proper folder.

There is a possibility that the folder would be different depending on many factors including the version of SDK, and the choice of the default folder. However, as an example, the search directory for the *hello* project is listed, and it is followed: *C:\ti\simplelink_msp432p4_sdk_3_40_01_02\examples\rtos\MSP_EXP432P401R\sysbios\hello\tirtos\ccs*

Once the import is successfully completed, users can find the *hello project* in the project list, and they can rename the project as needed.

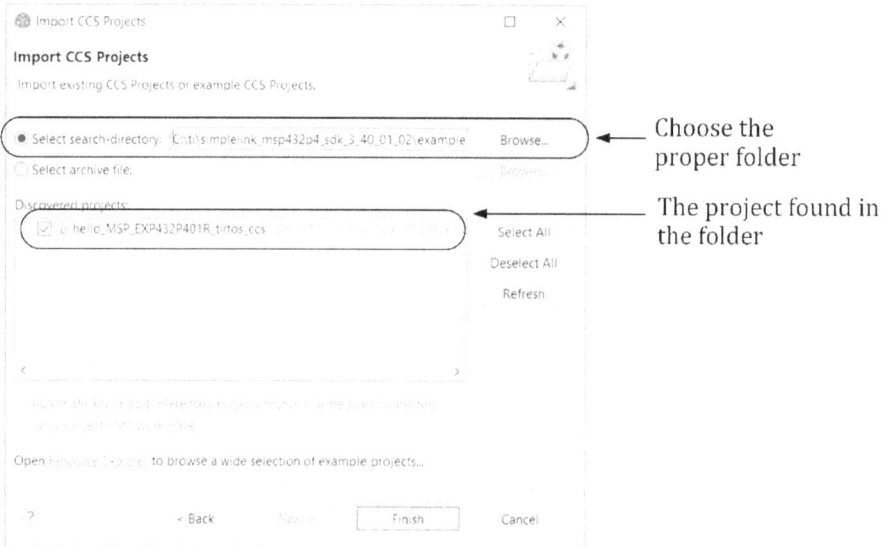

Figure 24.2. Search directory selection and the discovered project (hello project).

Task Execution States

Tasks objects are threads managed by Task module. It schedules and preempts tasks based on their priority levels and execution states. The priority level can be assigned up to 31. The priority level of 0 is reserved for the idle loop. Tasks can be created by calling *Task_create()* functions.

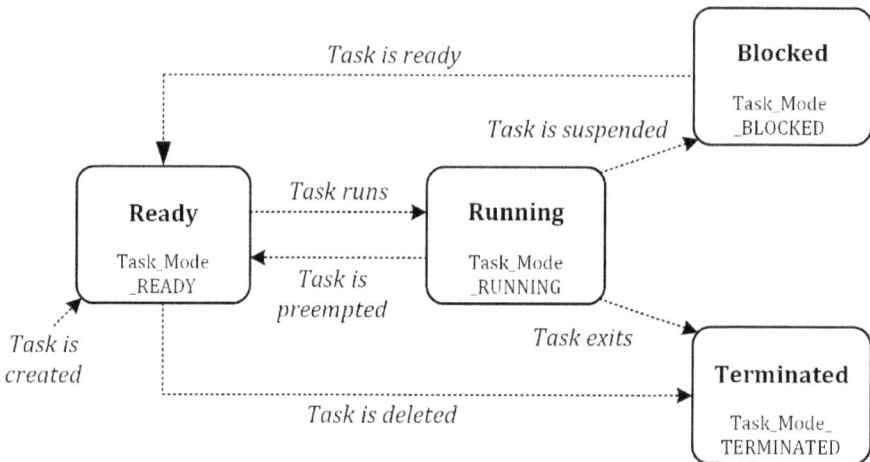

Figure 24.3. Task Execution States [30].

A task object is one of four states of execution. They are **running**, **ready**, **blocked**, and **terminated**. Task execution states are shown in Figure 24.3. They are named *Task_Mode_RUNNING*, *Task_Mode_READY*, *Task_Mode_BLOCKED*, and *Task_Mode_TERMINATED*, respectively.

The running state is the one that is actually executing using the processor time. The ready state is the one scheduled to be executed depending on the availability of the processor. The blocked state is the one that cannot be executed until a particular event. The terminated state is the one that is not executed any more.

Tasks are scheduled to be executed according to assigned priority levels. There is one task that can be in the running state. In this case, let us suppose a higher priority task is that is ready to run. Then, this task preempts, and the lower priority task that was in the running state will be in the ready state.

A task that is in a running state can be in a blocked state if the current task is suspended. Then, the task waits for a resource or a signal. For instance, the blocked state can be caused by *Task_sleep()* or *Semaphore_pend()*. A task can be terminated by calling *Task_exit()*, or automatically called when a task returns from its top-level function.

TI RTOS GPIO Example

As it was described, you can import a *hello project* example. After it is imported, you can rename the project as shown in Figure 24.4. It is renamed to "TI_RTOS_test". However, you can choose any project name. Next, you can find the "hello.c" file, and you can rename this file to "main.c". Next, you can find the "hello.syscfg" file, and you can rename this file to "main.syscfg". The purpose of this modification is to simplify the explanation of the example programs in this chapter. The screenshot after this set up process is shown in Figure 24.4 for reference. This set up process will be used for the TI RTOS examples in this chapter.

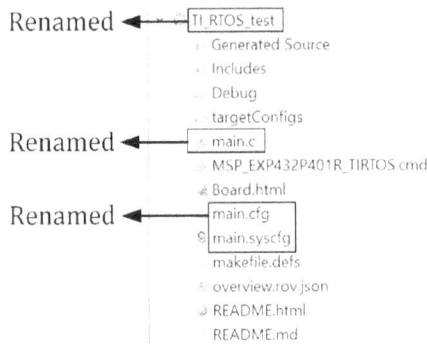

Renamed ← TI_RTOS_test
 Generated Source
 Includes
 Debug
 targetConfigs
Renamed ← main.c
 MSP_EXP432P401R_TIRTOS.cmd
 Board.html
Renamed ← main.cfg
 main.syscfg
 makefile.defs
 overview.rov.json
 README.html
 README.md

Figure 24.4. TI RTOS example project set-up

Next, you can double click "main.syscfg" file. Then you can see the screen similar to Figure 24.5. If it shows only text file, you can click right mouse button and open the file with "SysConfig editor." In this window, you can configure two LEDs and one button as shown in Figure 24.5. You can click "ADD" button on the top right corner, and enter the information listed in Table 24.1. Other than typing names, the parameters are already filled in. What you need to do is to choose proper options in the drop-down lists. For other parameters that were not listed in the table, you can leave them as default. The switch button is not going to be used in the examples in this chapter; however, it was added to the table to demonstrate how it can be configured.

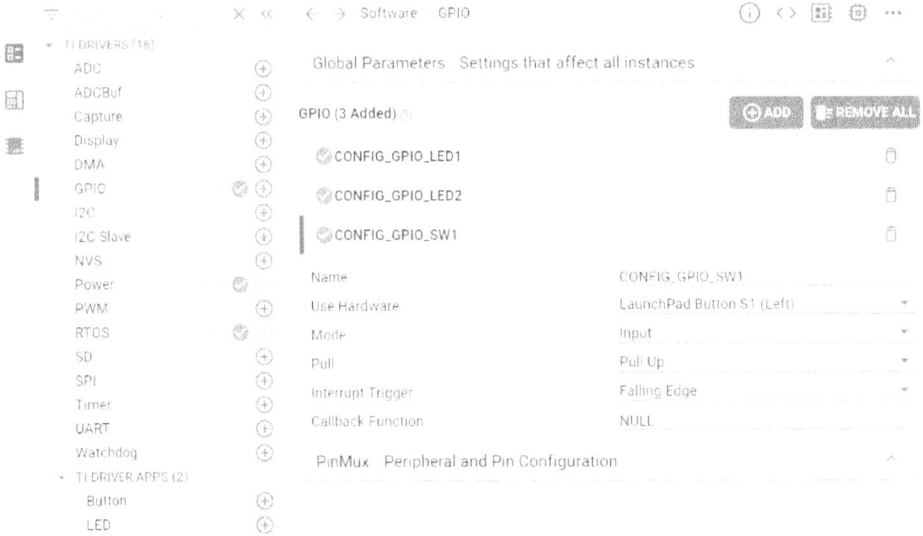

Figure 24.5. TI RTOS sysconfig – GPIO.

Parameters	LED1	LED2	Button (S1)
Name	CONFIG_GPIO_LED1	CONFIG_GPIO_LED2	CONFIG_GPIO_SW1
Use Hardware	Launchpad LED1 Red	Launchpad LED2 Red	Launchpad Button S1 (Left)
Mode	Output	Output	Input
Pull	-	-	Pull up

Table 24.1. GPIO configuration.

Next, you can type your code in "main.c". You can use the example code shown in Program 24.1. You can run this example project. If successful, you can see that two Red LEDs on your Launchpad can blink simultaneity. There are two tasks defined in this code. They can be found in the subroutines named "task1Fxn" and "task2Fxn." Each task is blinking LED1 or LED2.

```
#include <xdc/std.h>  // XDCtools
#include <xdc/runtime/System.h>  // XDCtools
#include <ti/sysbios/BIOS.h>  // SYS/BIOS
#include <ti/sysbios/knl/Task.h>  // task module
#include <ti/drivers/GPIO.h>  // GPIO driver
#include "ti_drivers_config.h"  // user driver configuration
#define TASKSTACKSIZE   1024
```

```
Task_Struct task1Struct, task2Struct;  // Task_Struct
Char task1Stack[TASKSTACKSIZE], task2Stack[TASKSTACKSIZE];  // task stack

Void task1Fxn(UArg arg0) {  // task1
  while (1) {
    GPIO_write(CONFIG_GPIO_LED1, CONFIG_GPIO_LED_ON);  // LED1, high
    Task_sleep((UInt)arg0);  // task sleep
    GPIO_write(CONFIG_GPIO_LED1, CONFIG_GPIO_LED_OFF);  // LED1, low
    Task_sleep((UInt)arg0);  // task sleep
  }
}

Void task2Fxn(UArg arg0) {  // task2
  while (1) {
    GPIO_write(CONFIG_GPIO_LED2, CONFIG_GPIO_LED_ON);  // LED2_R, high
    Task_sleep((UInt)arg0);  // task sleep
    GPIO_write(CONFIG_GPIO_LED2, CONFIG_GPIO_LED_OFF);  // LED2_R, low
    Task_sleep((UInt)arg0);  // task sleep
  }
}

int main() {
  Task_Params task1Params, task2Params;  // Task_Params
  Board_init();  // board init
  GPIO_init();  // GPIO init
  GPIO_write(CONFIG_GPIO_LED1, CONFIG_GPIO_LED_OFF);  // LED1, low
  GPIO_write(CONFIG_GPIO_LED2, CONFIG_GPIO_LED_OFF);  // LED2_R, low
  Task_Params_init(&task1Params);  // task1Params init

  task1Params.arg0 = 100;  // arg0, 100
  task1Params.stackSize = TASKSTACKSIZE;
  task1Params.stack = &task1Stack;
  task1Params.priority = 1;  // priority, 1
  Task_construct(&task1Struct, (Task_FuncPtr)task1Fxn, &task1Params, NULL);
                                                    // task1 creation
  Task_Params_init(&task2Params);  // task2Params init
  task2Params.arg0 = 100;  // arg0, 100
  task2Params.stackSize = TASKSTACKSIZE;
  task2Params.stack = &task2Stack;
  task2Params.priority = 1;  // priority, 1
  Task_construct(&task2Struct, (Task_FuncPtr)task2Fxn, &task2Params, NULL);
                                                    // task2 creation
  BIOS_start();  // start BIOS
  return(0);
}
```
Program 24.1. TI-RTOS GPIO example.

In the *main()* loop, it includes hardware initializations. Next it has task definitions.
The values of task1Params.arg0 and task2Params.arg0 are used in *Task_sleep*
functions in each task. These arguments were passed to each task, and they
determine the duration of a blink. For the priority, both of the tasks have the same

priorities. Next, the BIOS_start() code line can be found, it will start the TI RTOS. When it is running successfully, two LEDs will be turning ON and OFF simultaneously.

Synchronization Modules

TI RTOS supports several synchronization modules. They are *Semaphores*, *Event Module*, *Gates*, *Mailboxes*, and *Queues*. These modules can be used to coordinate the access of shared resources. Multiple tasks can be running concurrently. If a resource is shared among the tasks. In order to avoid a conflict, the access of the shared resource can be controlled properly by the use of the synchronization modules.

Semaphores can be used for inter-task synchronization and communication. Semaphore objects in TI RTOS can be either counting or binary semaphores. Counting semaphores keep a count of the number related to the availability of the corresponding resource. When the counter is great than zero, it can be considered that the resource is available. Semaphores can be configured either simple FIFO (First-In, First-Out) or priority-aware semaphores. The default setting for semaphores in TI RTOS is the simple counting semaphore. On the other hand, binary semaphores can represent either available or unavailable. The value of the binary semaphore cannot exceed more than 1.

The semaphore objects can be created or deleted using *Semaphore_create()* and *Semaphore_delete()*. The semaphore count needs to be initialized properly when it is being created. Typically, it is initialized as the number of resources. The task waits for a semaphore at the function of *Semaphore_pend()*. It waits for the signal. If the number of the count is great than zero, simply, the number of the count is decremented and returns. However, if the number of the count is zero, the semaphore keeps waiting for the signal. The signal can be generated by *Semaphore_post()* because it increments the number of counts and returns.

TI RTOS Semaphore Example

You can repeat the same set up as in the previous TI RTOS GPIO example. Or, simply you can reuse the project by updating your "main.c" file for the example program in this section.

The semaphore example program is shown in Program 24.2. In this example, a semaphore is used to synchronize two tasks. The task1 is to turn on both LEDs, and the task2 is to turn off both LEDs.

By using *semaphore_pend()*, the task1 waits a signal. When it is signaled, both of the LEDs will be turned on for a certain duration. During processing this LED code block in the task1, the other task, task2, cannot enter the code block in the task2 but it will wait for a signal at *semaphore_pend()*. Once the task1 sends a signal, the task2 can enter the code that will turn off the LEDs for a certain duration. Similarly, the task1 cannot enter into the code block in the task1, but it will wait for a signal. Once the code block in the task2 is processed, the task2 will send a signal and the code block in the task1 can be executed. This behavior of the task1 and the task2 keeps repeating. This result in blinking two LEDs simultaneously.

This is a simple visual demonstration of how shared resources can be accessed one at a time. Both of the LEDs are shared between two tasks, and they are accessed properly using the semaphores. While one of the tasks is accessing the LEDs, the other task needs to wait for a signal. This concept can be applied and extended to many cases where the data or resources are shared in concurrent processing.

```
#include <xdc/std.h>   // XDCtools
#include <xdc/runtime/System.h>   // XDCtools
#include <ti/sysbios/BIOS.h>   // SYS/BIOS
#include <ti/sysbios/knl/Task.h>   // task module
#include <ti/sysbios/knl/Semaphore.h>   // semaphore module
#include <ti/drivers/GPIO.h>   // GPIO driver
#include "ti_drivers_config.h"   // user driver configuration
#define TASKSTACKSIZE   1024
Task_Struct task1Struct, task2Struct;   // task_Struct
Char task1Stack[TASKSTACKSIZE], task2Stack[TASKSTACKSIZE];   // task stack
Semaphore_Struct semStruct;
Semaphore_Handle semHandle;

Void task1Fxn(UArg arg0) {   // task 1
  while (1) {
    Semaphore_pend(semHandle, BIOS_WAIT_FOREVER);   // pend on a semaphore
    GPIO_write(CONFIG_GPIO_LED1, CONFIG_GPIO_LED_ON);   // LED1, high
    GPIO_write(CONFIG_GPIO_LED2, CONFIG_GPIO_LED_ON);   // LED2_R, high
    Task_sleep((UInt)arg0);   // task sleep
    Semaphore_post(semHandle);   //post a semaphore
  }
}

Void task2Fxn(UArg arg0) {   // task2
  while (1) {
    Semaphore_pend(semHandle, BIOS_WAIT_FOREVER);   // pend on a semaphore
    GPIO_write(CONFIG_GPIO_LED1, CONFIG_GPIO_LED_OFF);   // LED1, low
    GPIO_write(CONFIG_GPIO_LED2, CONFIG_GPIO_LED_OFF);   // LED2_R, low
    Task_sleep((UInt)arg0);   // task sleep
    Semaphore_post(semHandle);   // post a semaphore
  }
}

int main() {
  Task_Params task1Params, task2Params;   // Task_Parms
  Semaphore_Params semParams;   // Semaphore_Parms
```

```
Board_init();  // board init.
GPIO_init();  // GPIO init.
GPIO_write(CONFIG_GPIO_LED1, CONFIG_GPIO_LED_OFF);  // LED1, low
GPIO_write(CONFIG_GPIO_LED2, CONFIG_GPIO_LED_OFF);  // LED2_R, low

Task_Params_init(&task1Params);  // task1Params init.
task1Params.arg0 = 100;  // arg0, 100
task1Params.stackSize = TASKSTACKSIZE;
task1Params.stack = &task1Stack;
task1Params.priority = 1;  // priority, 1
Task_construct(&task1Struct, (Task_FuncPtr)task1Fxn, &task1Params, NULL);
                                                     // task1 creation

Task_Params_init(&task2Params);  // task2Params init.
task2Params.arg0 = 100;  // arg0, 100
task2Params.stackSize = TASKSTACKSIZE;
task2Params.stack = &task2Stack;
task2Params.priority = 1;  // priority, 1
Task_construct(&task2Struct, (Task_FuncPtr)task2Fxn, &task2Params, NULL);
                                                     // task2 creation

Semaphore_Params_init(&semParams);  // semParams init.
Semaphore_construct(&semStruct, 1, &semParams);
                              // construct a semaphore, initial count 1
semHandle = Semaphore_handle(&semStruct);  // instance handle

BIOS_start();  // start BIOS
return(0);
}
```

Program 24.2. TI-RTOS Semaphore example.

UART Driver

The UART driver supports UART module APIs to access UART peripherals. In order to use the UART module in TI-RTOS, the UART header needs to be included as follows:

        #include <ti/drivers/UART.h>

A UART module can be initialized using *UART_init()*.

A UART_Params struct can be initialized using *UART_Params_init ()*.

A UART instance can be opened using *UART_open()*.

A UART instance can be closed using *UART_close()*.

A buffer of characters can be written and sent over UART using *UART_write()*.

A buffer of characters can be read over UART using *UART_read()*.

The UART needs to be properly initialized before opening a UART instance. First, a UART_Params structure needs to be created and properly initialized. Next, we need to fill in proper parameters. Then, the UART instance can be properly opened.

TI RTOS UART and Semaphore Example

You can repeat the same set-up process as shown in the previous TI RTOS semaphore example. Or, simply you can reuse the semaphore example project by updating your "main.c" file.

In addition to the LED and button configuration, you need to a UART module configuration for the example program in this section. You can click "ADD" button at the top right corner, and enter the information shown in the figure. Next, you can add a UART module as shown in Figure 24.6.

Figure 24.6. TI RTOS sysconfig - UART.

TI-RTOS UART and semaphore example is shown in Program 24.3. In this program, the *task1* is the same as we have used in the previous semaphore example. However, the *task2* has additional functions of sending data over UART. When it is running successful, certain code blocks in each task1 and task2 will be mutually executed, and it will blink two LEDs simultaneously. In the task2, data will be sent over UART. Users can see the numbers that will be displayed on a serial terminal, and the number will be incremented up to 9, then it will roll off to zero. This counting pattern and displaying on a serial terminal will keep repeating.

In this RTOS example case, it has only two tasks. However, developers can add more tasks as they need to add more functions. For instance, a *"task1"* can process buttons. A *"task2"* can read the ADC values from sensors. A *"task3"* can process control status of the device. A "*task4*" can display the data on the device. A "*task5*" can send the data over UART that is connected a wireless module. This task configuration can be one of the implementations of simple wireless embedded systems, and this is also similar to the RTOS example that we have studied previously in Chapter 12.

```
#include <xdc/std.h> // XDCtools
#include <xdc/runtime/System.h> // XDCtools
#include <ti/sysbios/BIOS.h> // SYS/BIOS
#include <ti/sysbios/knl/Task.h> // task module
#include <ti/sysbios/knl/Semaphore.h> // semaphore module
#include <ti/drivers/GPIO.h> // GPIO driver
#include <ti/drivers/UART.h> // UART driver
#include "ti_drivers_config.h" // user driver configuration
#define TASKSTACKSIZE  1024
Task_Struct task1Struct, task2Struct; // task_Struct
Char task1Stack[TASKSTACKSIZE], task2Stack[TASKSTACKSIZE]; // task stack
Semaphore_Struct semStruct;
Semaphore_Handle semHandle;

Void task1Fxn(UArg arg0) { // task1
  while (1) {
    Semaphore_pend(semHandle, BIOS_WAIT_FOREVER); // pend on a semaphore
    GPIO_write(CONFIG_GPIO_LED1, CONFIG_GPIO_LED_ON); // LED1, high
    GPIO_write(CONFIG_GPIO_LED2, CONFIG_GPIO_LED_ON); // LED2_R, high
    Task_sleep((UInt)arg0); // task sleep
    Semaphore_post(semHandle); //post a semaphore
  }
}

Void task2Fxn(UArg arg0) { // task2
  unsigned char ch, cnt; // variables
  UART_Handle uart;
  UART_Params uartParams;
  UART_Params_init(&uartParams); // uartParams init.
  uartParams.writeDataMode = UART_DATA_BINARY;
  uartParams.readDataMode = UART_DATA_BINARY;
  uartParams.readReturnMode = UART_RETURN_FULL;
  uartParams.readEcho = UART_ECHO_OFF;
  uartParams.baudRate = 9600;
  uart = UART_open(CONFIG_UART_0, &uartParams); // open UART_0
  if (uart == NULL) while (1); // trap if UART_open is failed
  while (1) {
    Semaphore_pend(semHandle, BIOS_WAIT_FOREVER); // pend on a semaphore
    GPIO_write(CONFIG_GPIO_LED1, CONFIG_GPIO_LED_OFF); // LED1, low
    GPIO_write(CONFIG_GPIO_LED2, CONFIG_GPIO_LED_OFF); // LED2_R, low
    ch='0'+cnt++; // count
    UART_write(uart, &ch, 1); // send data over UART
    if (cnt>9) { // check the range
      cnt=0;
```

```
      UART_write(uart, "\r\n", 2); // newline
    }
    Task_sleep((UInt)arg0); // task sleep
    Semaphore_post(semHandle); // post a semaphore
  }
}

int main() {
  Task_Params task1Params, task2Params; // Task_Parms
  Semaphore_Params semParams; // Semaphore_Parms

  Board_init(); // board init.
  GPIO_init(); // GPIO init.
  GPIO_write(CONFIG_GPIO_LED1, CONFIG_GPIO_LED_OFF); // LED1, low
  GPIO_write(CONFIG_GPIO_LED2, CONFIG_GPIO_LED_OFF); // LED2_R, low
  UART_init(); // UART init.

  Task_Params_init(&task1Params); // task1Params init.
  task1Params.arg0 = 100; // arg0, 100
  task1Params.stackSize = TASKSTACKSIZE;
  task1Params.stack = &task1Stack;
  task1Params.priority = 1; // priority, 1
  Task_construct(&task1Struct, (Task_FuncPtr)task1Fxn, &task1Params, NULL);
                                               // task1 creation

  Task_Params_init(&task2Params); // task2Params init.
  task2Params.arg0 = 100; // arg0, 100
  task2Params.stackSize = TASKSTACKSIZE;
  task2Params.stack = &task2Stack;
  task2Params.priority = 1; // priority, 1
  Task_construct(&task2Struct, (Task_FuncPtr)task2Fxn, &task2Params, NULL);
                                               // task2 creation

  Semaphore_Params_init(&semParams); // semParams init.
  Semaphore_construct(&semStruct, 1, &semParams);
                              // construct a semaphore, initial count 1

  semHandle = Semaphore_handle(&semStruct); // instance handle

  BIOS_start(); // start BIOS
  return(0);
}
```

Program 24.3. TI-RTOS UART and semaphore example.

TI provides a broad range of wireless connectivity such as Bluetooth, WiFi, Zigbee, and so forth. There are many options for programmers to choose to use these wireless technologies. One of the choices is to use a TI RTOS and relevant wireless library. The development of the wireless protocol stack from scratch is not trivial. However, TI RTOS provides a wireless protocol stack that is well integrated with Code Composer Studio. Moreover, the code that is written in the TI RTOS environment can be reusable in other SimpleLink devices.

Chapter 25. Open Source Electronics Development Platform

Open-source hardware had started in the late 1990s. It has been started much later than open-source software. Hardware designs have not been considered to be shared outside of a company. This may be the case for many companies even these days. However, in some areas of electronics system development, hardware designs are not relativity complex, but they use many existing common components and circuits such as basic functional microprocessor or microcontroller circuits. Given such a development platform with these common components, developers can add their own designs on top of it. Thus, they are capable of creating new prototype electronics in a short time. Besides, they share their designs in an internet community for improvement. Other developers may contribute to the current designs to make it work better. Or, they can even create new derivative prototype electronics. Currently, this mode of open and fast paced development operations has been widely accepted in many educational institutions and organizations. One of these open source electronics development platforms is Arduino®. An MSP432P401R MCUs can be programmed like Arduino using Energia. In this chapter, we will learn about open source electronics development platform and Energia programming for an MSP432P401R MCU

Arduino

The Arduino project started in 2005. Arduino is an open-source computing platform with a simple I/O board and a simple development environment [23]. Arduino hardware design files are open and released under a Creative Commons Attribution Share-Alike license. This means it allows personal and commercial derivative works. However, the condition is to credit Arduino and to release their designs under the same license. Arduino software is also open and released under GPL (Java environment) and LGPL (C/C++ microcontroller libraries). This license allows manufacture and the software distribution by anyone. Arduino has been widely used by open source communities, hobbyists, and educators.

The programming language for Arduino boards is C/C++. Arduino provides an integrated development environment (IDE) that is easy to use. Many Arduino boards are based on Atmel® 8-bit AVR® microcontroller models including ATmega328, ATmega8, ATmega168, ATmega1280, or ATmega2560. Arduino Due is based on Arm Cortex M3 (Atmel SAM3X8E). Recent small Arduino boards are based on Arm Cortex M0+. In addition, there are many Arduino-compatible and Arduino-derived boards.

A *sketch* is a program that Arduino uses. It contains two functions which are setup() and loop(). The code in the "setup" function will be executed once, and the code in the "loop" function will be executed repeatedly.

Enerigia

Energia is an open-source electronics platform started in 2012 [32]. It is a modified version of Arduino for some selected TI Launchpads. It made possible for the selected TI Launchpads to use Energia sketch. Energia can be downloaded using the link as follows:

> https://energia.nu

Energia IDE is similar to Arduino IDE. But, Energia IDE theme is Red. In order to use an MSP432P401R Launchpad, the board package needs to be installed. "Boards Manager" can be selected using the sequence of selections as follows:

> Tools -> Board: "xxxx" -> Boards Manager

Next, *boards manager* window will be opened. In the search box, you can type, "MSP432" Then, you can see the narrowed choices. Next, select and install "Energia MSP432 EMT RED boards" In order to use the MSP432P401R Launchpad, select the correct board and port as shown in Figure 25.1

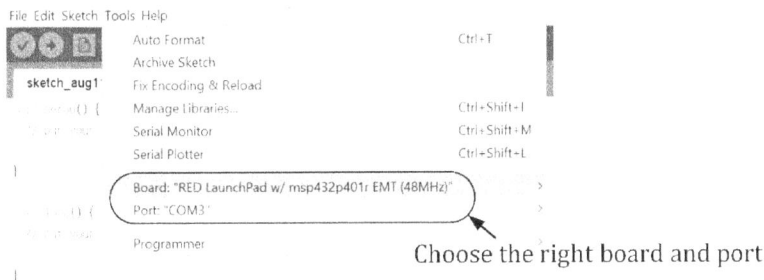

Figure 25.1. Selection of the board and port.

You can start learning Energia from example programs. The examples programs can be found in the Energia IDE by selecting "Examples" (Files -> Examples).

Eneriga Sketch in Code Composer Studio

Energia sketch can be used in Code Composer Studio. You can find *View* in you code composer studio and click *Resource Explorer*. Then, click *Software*. Next, you can find and select Energia MSP432 EMT RED boards (x.xx.x) as follows:

> Software -> Energia -> Energia MSP432 EMT RED boards (x.xx.x)

Then, you can click "install" icon on the top right and install the Energia core. Next, "Energia Sketch" can be selected by using the selections as follows:

File -> New -> Other... -> Energia

Then, select "Energia Sketch" and click "Next" as shown in Figure 25.2. You may prompt to enter the Energia install location, and you may need to select a folder where you have installed the Energia. Next, you can see the Energia sketch functions of setup() and loop() in your Code Composer Studio.

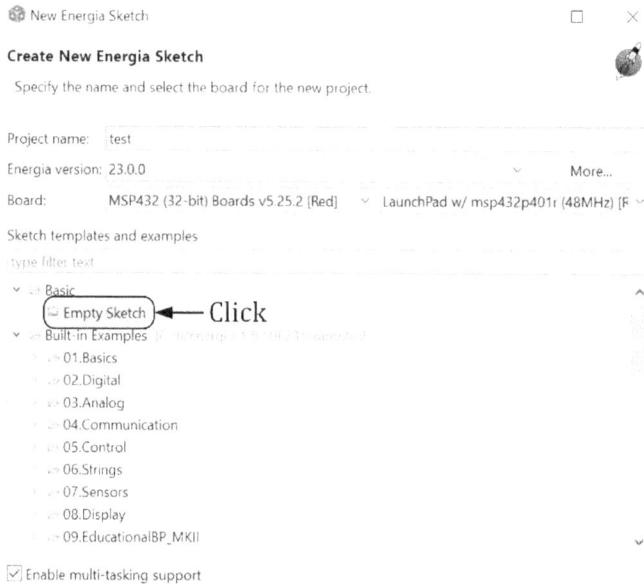

Figure 25.2. Energia Empty Sketch selection.

Eneriga GPIO and UART Example

An Enegia GPIO and UART example is shown in Program 25.1. The buttons and LEDs are defined. In the setup() function, the pins are configured, and the UART is initialized. While the code in the setup() function is executed once, the code in the loop() function will be executed repeatedly. In the loop() function, it blinks a Red LED. Moreover, it reads the status of the two buttons, and it controls the color of the RGB LED to be Red or Blue. When the button is pressed, it will send a character array over UART to display whether the button1 or button2 is pressed on the serial terminal.

```
const int button1 = PUSH1;  // push button (left)
const int button2 = PUSH2;  // push button (right)
const int led1 = YELLOW_LED;  // Red led (LED1)
const int led2 = RED_LED;  // RGB Red (LED2)
const int led3 = BLUE_LED;  // RGD Blue (LED2)
```

```
void setup() {
  pinMode(led1, OUTPUT);  // output direction
  pinMode(led2, OUTPUT);  // output direction
  pinMode(button1, INPUT_PULLUP);  // input direction, pull-up resistor
  pinMode(button2, INPUT_PULLUP);  // input direction, pull-up resistor
  Serial.begin(9600);  // UART init.
  delay(100);  // delay
  Serial.println("Connected");  // send data over UART
}

void loop() {
  int buttonState;  // variable
  buttonState = digitalRead(button1);  // read button1
  if (buttonState == LOW) {  // check button state
    digitalWrite(led2, HIGH);  // turn on led2
    Serial.println("Button1 pressed");  // send data over UART
  } else digitalWrite(led2, LOW);  // turn off led2

  buttonState = digitalRead(button2);  // read button2
  if (buttonState == LOW) {  // check button state
    digitalWrite(led3, HIGH);  // turn on led3
    Serial.println("Button2 pressed");  // send data over UART
  } else digitalWrite(led3, LOW);  // turn off led3

  digitalWrite(led1, !digitalRead(led1));  // toggle
  delay(100);  // delay
}
```

Program 25.1. Energia GPIO and UART Example.

This Energia sketch is easier to understand and can be written in a short time. Arduino or Energia can be effectively used in a rapid prototyping project or a quick verification of the functions. If a developer wants to create a commercial product using Energia, it is recommended to check the license information thoroughly carefully, which can be found in the Energia and Arduino websites.

Chapter 26. Power Management Considerations

There are many battery-powered embedded systems. In these applications, the energy consumption is an important factor. In order to increase the length of the operations, it needs various power management efforts. Even for the application that are not dependent on batteries, it is common to design electronics to consume lower energy for green electronics. In this chapter, we will learn about the power management and lower power modes for an MSP432P432P401 MCU.

MSP432P4 Power management

There are various efforts and methods in power management. Typically, it is associated with reducing or minimizing the overall energy consumption.

First, the supply voltage can be lowered to reduce the power consumption. IC manufacturers provide the minimum and maximum supply voltage specification in the datasheet. For instance, the supply voltage level of the MSP432P401R IC can be lowered to 2.2 V. To generate the internal core voltage, there are two internal voltage regulator configurations for the MSP432P401R IC. They are LDO (Low-dropout regulator) and DC-DC regulators. For the LDO regulator, the supply voltage can be even lower, but it needs to be higher than 1.62 V. For the DC-DC regulator, the supply voltage can be also lower but, it needs to be higher than 2.0 V. However, in order to enable SVSMH (Supply Voltage Supervisor/Monitor High Side), the supply voltage needs to be higher than 1.71 V. For reference, the maximum supply voltage is 3.7 V.

The internal LDO regulator is the default setting. But, instead, MSP432P401R system can be configured to use the DC-DC regulator for high operating frequency applications to achieve better efficiency. For the DC-DC regulator, the MSP432P401R system needs an additional external inductor. In this DC-DC regulator setting, some of the low power modes are not available. To simplify the explanations, it is assumed to use a default LDO regulator configuration for the rest of the discussion in this chapter.

Second, the current consumption in a microcontroller system is closely related to the operating frequency. The operating frequency can be lowered to reduce the power consumption of the system. The operating frequency of the MSP432P401R IC can be up to 48 MHz, and it can be lowered to a few hundred kHz. For instance, it can be lowered to 128 kHz. This would be effective in saving power for some embedded applications. However, in some real-time applications, there is a limitation of lowering the operating frequency because the CPU needs to be kept reasonably fast.

Third, in many embedded systems, the CPU resources are not constantly used, and a system may be in an idle or stand-by status for an extended period of time. This system can save power by entering a low power state such as sleep mode instead. The effort of lowering the operating time in active mode but increasing the time in sleep mode can reduce the power consumption.

Lastly, an embedded system may have dependencies in processing tasks in both hardware and software sides. Some dependencies may have caused an increased time in active mode. There is a potential in reducing the time of active mode by managing the dependencies effectively. However, this task may not be necessarily straightforward depending on the degree of the interdependencies and the complexity of the system.

MSP432P401R Power Modes

The MSP432P401R power modes are shown in Figure 26.1. These modes are available for the internal LDO regulator setting. When the CPU is started up, the MSP432P401R will be in active mode. There are six active modes depending on the core voltages and regular types. In Active Modes (AM), the CPU can execute a program.

Let us examine Low power modes. The Low Power Mode (LPM0) can halt the CPU execution and the CPU can be in sleep mode. To reduce more power, three are other lower power modes such as Lower Power Mode 3 (LPM3) and Lower Power Mode 4 (LPM4). Moreover, the MSP432P401R IC provides more low power modes such as Lower Power Mode 3.5 (LPM3.5) and Lower Power Mode 4.5 (LPM4.5). The summary of power modes for an MSP432P401R IC is shown in Table 26.1.

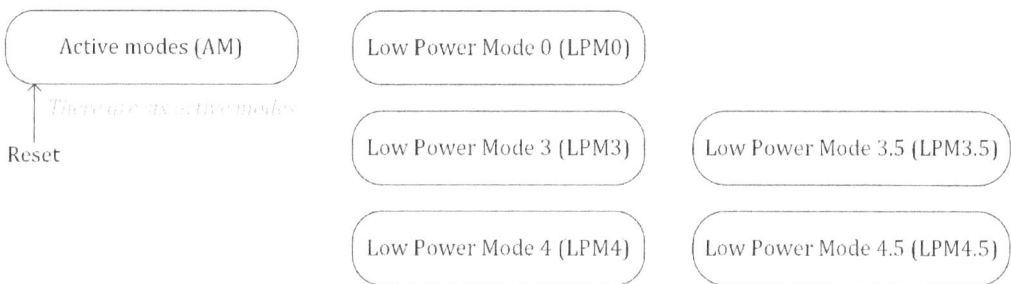

Figure 26.1. Simplified diagram of MSP432P401R Power Modes.

For, Lower Power Mode 3 (LPM3), the MSP432P4 IC can be controlled to disable all peripherals except RTC and WDT modules. LPM3 can save more power than LPM0. For Lower Power Mode 4 (LPM4), the MSP432P4 IC can be controlled to disable all peripherals. An Arm Cortex-M4 core supports two sleep modes of *sleep* and *deep sleep* mode. For LPM3 and LPM4, an Arm Cortex-M4 core gets to be operated is in deep sleep mode. An Arm Cortex-M4 core supports a shutdown mode. For Lower Power Mode 3.5 (LPM3.5) and Lower Power Mode 4.5 (LPM4.5), an Arm Cortex-M4 core will operate in shutdown mode. For LPM4.5, the MSP432P4 IC can be controlled to disable all peripherals but, for LPM3.5, RTC and WDT modules can stay as enabled.

Parameters	Power Mode	Description
Active Modes (AM)	Active	CPU execution. There are six active modes depending on core voltages and regulator types.
Low Power Mode 0 (LPM0)	Low Power	Processor execution: halted. Arm: Sleep mode.
Low Power Mode 3 (LPM3)	Low Power	Processor execution: halted. All peripherals are disabled except for RTC and WDT modules. Arm: Deep sleep mode.
Low Power Mode 3.5 (LPM4)	Low Power	Processor execution: halted. All peripherals are disabled. Arm: Deep sleep mode.
Low Power Mode 5 (LPM3.5)	Low Power	Processor execution: halted. All peripherals are disabled except for RTC and WDT modules. Peripheral register data is not retained. SRAM data retention: limited. Arm: Shutdown mode.
Low Power Mode 4.5 (LPM4.5)	Low Power	Processor execution: halted. All peripherals are disabled. Neither peripheral register data nor SRAM data is retained. Arm: Shutdown mode.

Table 26.1. Summary of MSP432P401R Power Modes.

Low Power Mode Example

The low power mode example in register C/C++ programming is shown in Program 26.1. This is a simple program that can turn on and off an LED for a certain amount of time when the button is pressed. The MSP401P401R MCU enters a low power mode 3, while it waits for a button press. The code line that can put the MSP432P4 MCU to sleep using _low_power_mode_3(). This is an intrinsic function, and it sets the *SLEEPDEEP* bit in the *SCR* (System Control Register) register. When this code line is executed, the system goes into LPM3 sleep mode.

The Port 1 interrupt is configured. The system can wake up when the Port 1 interrupt is triggered. In the Port 1 ISR, it checks whether the button is pressed. If it is the case, the LED1 will be turned on. The code line of *SCB->SCR &= ~SCB_SCR_SLEEPONEXIT_Msk* in the Port 1 ISR is to exit the lower power mode, when the program exits the ISR. This is an optional code line because the behavior is to exit the low power mode once this Port 1 ISR is triggered. The following code line is _DSB(). Data Synchronization Barrier (DSB) can block execution of any further instructions to ensure this code is executed before exiting ISR. It is worth of mention that the system can enter a sleep mode on exiting the ISR by setting the *SLEEPDEEP* bit in the *SCR* (System Control Register) register.

When the button is pressed, the MSP432P4 IC will wake up and operate in active mode, and the LED will be turned on. On exiting the ISR, the program executes the next instruction in the while loop. It delays the program for a certain period of time, and the LED will be turned off. Then, the MSP432P4 IC will enters the sleep mode again. This pattern keeps repeating as the button gets pressed.

```
#include "msp.h"
void main(void) {
    WDT_A->CTL = WDT_A_CTL_PW | WDT_A_CTL_HOLD;  // hold the watchdog timer
    P1->DIR |= BIT0;  // output direction for P1.0
    P1->DIR &= ~BIT1;  // input direction for P1.1
    P1->REN |= BIT1;  // enable internal resistor
    P1->OUT |= BIT1;  // pull-up resistor
    P1->IES |= BIT1;  // interrupt on high-to-low transition
    P1->IFG &= ~BIT1;  // clear interrupt flag
    P1->IE |= BIT1;  // enable interrupt for P1.1
    _enable_irq();  // enable global interrupt
    NVIC->ISER[1] = 1 << ((PORT1_IRQn) & 31);  // NVIC setup
    while(1) {
        _delay_cycles(500000);  // delay
        P1->OUT &= ~BIT0;  // turn off LED1
        _low_power_mode_3();  // enter low power mode (LPM3)
    }

}

void PORT1_IRQHandler(void) {
    if(P1->IFG & BIT1) {
        P1->OUT |= BIT0;  // turn on LED1
        SCB->SCR &= ~SCB_SCR_SLEEPONEXIT_Msk;  // disable SLEEPONEXIT
        _DSB();  // ensures SLEEPONEXIT is cleared
    }
    P1->IFG &= ~BIT1;  // clear interrupt flag
}
```

Program 26.1. Low Power Mode Example

DriverLib - Low Power Mode Example
The low power mode example using DriverLib is shown in Program 26.2. The function of the program is similar to the previous low power mode example program. The code line that can enter the low power mode is *MAP_PCM_gotoLPM3()*. In the Port 1 ISR, the code lines of SCB->SCR and _DSB() are used. As described, these lines are optional because the MSP432P4 exits the low power mode after this Port 1 ISR.

As the button pressed, the LED will be turned on and off. While the LED is turned on, the MSP432P4 IC is in active mode. While the LED is turned off, the MSP432P4 is in sleep mode. This program has a code line to delay the time. This is an example pattern of the execution as an embedded system to perform necessary functions for a short amount of time and to enter a sleep mode.

```
#include <ti/devices/msp432p4xx/driverlib/driverlib.h>   // DriverLib
#include <stdint.h>
#include <stdbool.h>
int main(void) {
  MAP_WDT_A_holdTimer();   // hold the watchdog timer
  MAP_GPIO_setAsOutputPin(GPIO_PORT_P1, GPIO_PIN0);   // P1.0 (output)
  MAP_GPIO_setAsInputPinWithPullUpResistor(GPIO_PORT_P1, GPIO_PIN1);
                                            // P1.1 (input, pull-up resistor)
  MAP_GPIO_clearInterruptFlag(GPIO_PORT_P1, GPIO_PIN1);
                                            // clear interrupt flag (P1.1)
  MAP_GPIO_enableInterrupt(GPIO_PORT_P1, GPIO_PIN1);   // enable interrupt (P1.1)
  MAP_Interrupt_enableInterrupt(INT_PORT1);   // enable port1 interrupt
  MAP_Interrupt_enableMaster();   // enable master interrupt
  while (1) {
    _delay_cycles(500000);   // delay
    MAP_GPIO_setOutputLowOnPin (GPIO_PORT_P1, GPIO_PIN0);   // toggle (P1.0)
    MAP_PCM_gotoLPM3();   // enter low power mode (LPM3)
  }
}

void PORT1_IRQHandler(void) {
  uint32_t status;
  status = MAP_GPIO_getEnabledInterruptStatus(GPIO_PORT_P1);
                                            // read port1 interrupt status
  if(status & GPIO_PIN1) {   // check whether the PIN1 is set
    MAP_GPIO_setOutputHighOnPin(GPIO_PORT_P1, GPIO_PIN0);   // toggle (P2.0)
    SCB->SCR &= ~SCB_SCR_SLEEPONEXIT_Msk;   // disable SLEEPONEXIT
    _DSB();   // ensures SLEEPONEXIT is cleared
  }
  MAP_GPIO_clearInterruptFlag(GPIO_PORT_P1, status);   // clear port1 interrupt flag
}
```

Program 26.2. DriverLib - Low Power Mode Example.

Users may need test equipment to measure the power consumption of the device for the development. However, MSP432P401R Launchpad supports the EnergyTrace™ Technology. The EnergyTrace Technology is useful in performing analysis of the energy consumption. Code Composer Studio supports the EnergyTrace mode and provides an EnergyTrace Window. The energy measurement can be performed, and the data can be viewed using the EnergyTrace Window.

Chapter 27. Embedded System Security

The Internet of things (IoTs) are the systems and devices that are connected to the internet. Many of these devices and systems are commonly found in modern embedded systems. Even devices and systems that were not traditionally connected to the internet are now connected to the internet. At the same time, embedded system security becomes more important as there are more IoT devices in our everyday lives. There are many aspects in the embedded system security. However, in this chapter, we will consider one specific hardware component that may cause security issue in embedded systems.

JTAG/Boundary Scan

Boundary scan provides a method of testing interconnections of sub-blocks inside ICs. It can test multiple cells inside of ICs or PCBs. Those multiple test cells can be internally connected to each other. To access the test cells, external interface or external pins are needed. Boundary scan is a test method for the components inside of an integrated circuit. Boundary scan is also widely used in debugging, analyzing, and monitoring circuit states, voltages, and memory devices inside ICs.

The Joint Test Action Group (JTAG) was formed in 1985, and the boundary scan architecture was approved in 1990 as IEEE Std. 1149.1. There have been enhancements, and the latest update was done in 2013. This technology has been widely adopted by electronic device companies. JTAG is an industry standard that can be used in verifying designs and testing after the fabrication. JTAG is named after the Joint Test Action Group. In some settings, the boundary scan can be called simply JTAG. This technology is relevant because it has been used for debugging, programming, and testing for most of the modern microprocessors and microcontrollers. Readers may already have used this technology while they write a program and load it on their MSP432P401R MCU. They have seen the program could be interrupted, and various internal registers could be read and displayed in Code Composer Studio. This is very effective and useful tool for the programmer to develop and debug embedded systems.

JTAG uses several pins for communication. "TDI" is used for *Test Data In*. "TDO" is for *Test Data Out*. "TCK" is for *Test Clock*. "TMS" is used for *Test Mode Select*. These TDI, TDO, TCK, TMS pins are typically used for the JTAG connection. Optionally, "TRST" pin is used for *Test Reset*.

On the MSP432P401R Launchpad, these pins can be found in the header block that is located between a XDS110-ET and the MSP432P401R IC. As it was discussed, the MSP432P401R Launchpad already has an on-board debugger. This setting of the attachment of the JTAG may not be a typical setting as a product, but it is useful and effective as a development tool and an educational board because users do not need to obtain a separate JTAG tool.

JTAG Security

JTAG is very useful and important. On the other hand, it can be a target for a potential attack. This vulnerability is supposed to be well known to the developers, and many of them need to be aware of this risk. For instance, let us suppose a company developed a voice-activated alarm clock that can be connected to the WiFi network. If a hacker could access JTAG connection of this device, then, the hacker could put their modified firmware that could hijack the data packet or to access the internet. In this case, this IoT alarm clock has been compromised, and it has been turned into a spy device. A bigger problem may arise if the hacker could access bigger critical systems such as industrial robots, plants, or traffic control systems. It could jeopardize someone's physical safety due to the malfunction caused by the hacker. Although JTAG is a very useful and important in the embedded system development, if not properly handled, it could open a back door in a hardware level, and it could allow unwanted person to access the entire firmware, data, and the operating system. In a worst case, it could serve as a hidden gateway that opens unwanted access to a supposedly secured system.

There are several efforts in securing JTAG. In some cases, the JTAG header pins are not populated on the PCB board, and markings on the board are hidden purposefully from the users. However, even in this case, JTAG may be still accessible by populating the JTAG header pins. It is a matter of simply figuring out the connection of the hidden pins. This would be one of the counter examples of open design projects. It could be a valid reason keeping designs confidential as a product. Surprisingly, some electronics projects' JTAG can be accessible relatively easily after some moderate effort in modifications.

For production parts, the system can be deployed to end users with disabled JTAG access. This is an IC level protection. This can be achieved by blowing off JTAG fuses. In this case, the system's JTAG is not accessible. However, it makes JTAG is unable to be accessed by the manufacturer. This means that it is hard to diagnose the problem for the devices in the field if the systems are not functioning as they are supposed to be. In addition, although this may seem an effective method, it is not the perfect solution because there is a chance that the blown-out JTAG fuses could be restored by highly advanced hackers.

Moreover, there is another method of regulating the access by secret key-based authentication mechanism. As you can imagine, there are many other complex JTAG defense methods.

An MSP432P401R MCU has security features. Debug access through JTAG or SWD (Serial Wire Debug) can be disabled by the user configuration. It supports AES encryption and decryption. Moreover, it has a software IP protection (IPP). This feature allows for incremental debug as it has IP protected zones. Furthermore, it supports the encrypted firmware update mechanism that requires a password to program new firmware.

Developers may need to consider using the security features, as the embedded system in development is getting close to be a product and getting deployed. If necessary, additional security features might need to be applied depending on the security requirements of the embedded system.

Chapter 28. Educational Embedded Linux System Platforms

MSP432P4 microcontrollers are based 32-bit Arm Cortex-M4F cores. The performance as a microcontroller is decent. It can be used in various applications. However, in some embedded systems, they require to process more complex functions. Or, simply, sometimes, they need a small computer with a monitor and input devices. In this case, they can consider implementing their systems as Embedded Linux Operating Systems. Examples of these systems are Android/Linux based smart phones and tablet PC. In these applications, microprocessor-based systems are suitable. Arm Cortex-A processors are suitable for performance-intensive systems and rich operating systems such as Linux. There are several platforms with Arm Cortex-A processors. For educational purposes, there are two popular groups of platforms, which are *Raspberry Pi®* and *BeagleBone®*.

In this chapter, Embedded Linux Systems as educational platforms will be briefly introduced to provide a perspective on embedded systems for complex tasks. However, learning embedded Linux systems in detail is not the primary goal.

A great benefit of using educational embedded Linux systems is about rich educational resources with a large community. Readers can gain and access rich development resources and information including programming examples through other developers, manufacturers, and suppliers.

Raspberry Pi

Raspberry Pi series boards are small single-board computers [33]. The Raspberry Pi was developed in the United Kingdom by the Raspberry Pi Foundation. Initially, it was created for the use in teaching basic computer science in schools and in developing countries.

Raspberry Pi 1 Model B was released in 2012. In 2015, Raspberry Pi 2 Model B was released. In 2017, Raspberry Pi Zero was released. Raspberry Pi 3 Model B was released in 2016. Raspberry Pi 3 Model B+ was released in 2018.

Moreover, Raspberry Pi 4 Model B was released in 2019. The pictures of the Raspberry Pi 3 Model B+ and Raspberry Pi 4 Model B are shown in Figure 28.1. Raspberry Pi 4 Model B is faster than Raspberry Pi 3 Model B+. However, there are other factors including power consumption to consider in choosing a platform for your application.

These devices are based on Broadcom processors with Arm Cortex-A series cores. They are small-scale general-purpose computers; however, the performance is not as good as typical general-purpose computers like desktops or laptops. The operating system such as Raspberry Pi O/S is a customized compact sized Linux System, and it contains proper drivers to use the hardware resources.

Figure 28.1. Raspberry Pi 3 Model B+ and Raspberry Pi 4 Model B.

Using a Linux operating system, developers can create their own customized applications fast and easy for IoT projects or Robot projects. One of the popular programming languages is Python.

Python programming language is generally easy to learn, although it could get complicated depending on applications. But, Python programs are generally slower than C/C++ based programs. Raspberry Pi has a large size community as well as many users. There are many shared sample projects and programs. Many of the programming examples are based on Python language. Readers can increase their knowledge through various shared projects and programming examples.

BeagleBone

The BeagleBoard® series boards are single-board computers using Texas Instruments processors with Arm Cortex-A series cores [34]. They were designed for hobbyists as educational tools.

BeagleBoard was released in 2008. It was based on a TI OMAP3530 processor. BeagleBone using a TI AM3358 processor was released in 2011. BeagleBone Black was released in 2013. PocketBeagle is released in 2017.

Moreover, BeagleBone AI was released in 2019. The pictures of the BeagleBone Black and BeagleBone AI are shown in Figure 28.2. The BeagleBone AI is faster than the BeagleBone Black. However, as it was mentioned, there are other factors including power consumption to consider in choosing a platform for your application.

Figure 28.2. BeagleBone Black and BeagleBone AI.

These devices are based TI Sitara™ processors with Arm Cortex-A series cores. *Node.js* is a JavaScript runtime environment. The BeagleBone.org foundation supports BoneScript that is based on a Node.js library. Moreover, users can install a Python package and use Python Programming Language for the development.

Educational Embedded Linux Platforms

The educational embedded Linux system development platforms can provide rich, resources, examples, and friendly environment for students, hobbyists, and engineers. Readers can learn the embedded Linux systems rapidly. These educational embedded Linux systems have impacted a wide range of students in science and engineering fields.

Embedded Linux systems can be considered easy to learn and easy to start. This is because there are many approaches that are focused on high-level programming. A custom system can be rapidly developed without the need of in-depth understanding of hardware. Moreover, the development environment is rich, and it is similar to the one that we use in a desktop or laptop computer. Therefore, for the developers' side, they could view it as simply a slow computer.

These platforms can be used as an effective learning tool. It is great for developers to create a system rapidly using high level libraries. However, at the same time, it can be controversial because, in fact, embedded Linux systems are fairly complicated, and it might need a long-term training and learning in many aspects of hardware and software to become an experienced embedded Linux system developer. Moreover, the pace of the development in embedded Linux systems is very fast. Without the continued support, embedded Linux systems that are not designed properly potentially could cause significant damages such as by the accidental creation of security hole causing data privacy and data security issues. However, for an entry level developer, there can be some technical aspects that they are easily overlooked. For some experimental development or educational environments, they could be acceptable. At any rate, it is up to developers to understand the requirements of their system, and they need to choose proper hardware and software platforms.

In summary, embedded Linux system is a desirable solution in many applications these days. It has gained more attention as the computing requirements have been increasing. This is partially relevant to increasing popularity of the machine learning, image processing, and IoT.

As an example of a system with the mixed use of an MSP432 MCU and an embedded Linux system, a sensor device for a network can be implemented using an MSP432 MCU. It can communicate with an embedded Linux system that work as a host or an IoT gateway.

What's next

We have studied various aspects of embedded systems using an MSP432P401R MCU and Composer Studio. We have studied low to high level of the programming as well as hardware concepts.

An embedded system is typically an integrated system that involves a wide range of knowledge. For embedded system developers, it is encouraged to have a good understanding of microcontrollers, modules, sensors, and mechanical systems that are used in their system.

Readers can create their own embedded systems. Examples of embedded systems can be found everywhere such as Game consoles, Mobile phone, Digital cameras, Vending Machines, Washing machines, Cooking machines, Toys, Printers, Scanners, Televisions, and Electronic instruments. The list will go on as we will see more new and innovative embedded systems.

Lastly, we have studied embedded systems based on a specific MCU for educational purposes. However, readers can continue to learn other microcontrollers and microprocessors, and they can continue to expand their knowledge.

Appendix A. Basic Digital Logic Circuits

Firmware programmers may need to understand hardware components to a certain extent. In this Appendix A, basic digital logic circuits are introduced. However, this is a simply brief introduction to the basic digital logic circuits. For readers who are not already familiar with basic logic circuits, it is recommended to take introductory level digital logic lessons. It was assumed that readers are already familiar with the basic digital circuits.

Basic Digital Logic Gates

In digital circuits, a logic level is one of the finite number of states. Typically, we use a 2-level logic, which is a binary logic. Two levels are logical high and logical low, which are related to the binary number 1 and 0, respectively. In addition, there is another state to be considered. That is a high impedance state. In this state, the signal is not clearly driven high nor low. This is similar to a floating state or an open circuit.

Some of the basic logic gates are shown in Figure A.1. An **AND** gate generates a logical high signal when both input signals are logical high. Otherwise, the output is logical low. A **NAND** gate generates the inverted output of the **AND** gate. A **buffer** generates the same logical output signals as the logical input signals. An **inverter** generates an inverted output logical signal from the input logical signal. An **OR** gate generates a logical low signal when both input signals are logical low. If any of the input signal is logical high, the output of the **OR** gate is logical high. A **NOR** gate generates an inverted output of the **OR** gate. A **XOR** gate generates a logical low signal when two input logic signals are the same. If two input logic signals are not the same, it will generate a logical high signal. A **XNOR** gate generates an inverted output of the **XOR** gate.

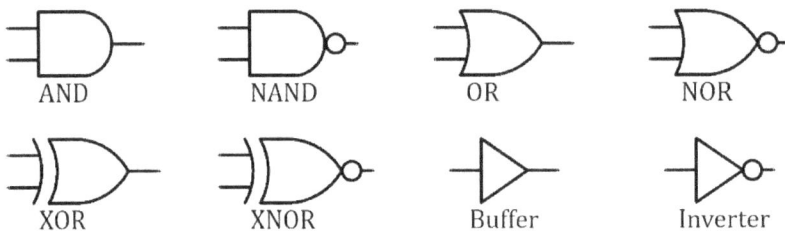

Figure A.1. Basic logic gates.

Digital Logic Gates with Negated Inputs

It is common to use an **inversion bubble** in a circuit diagram. This is also simply called a **bubble**. This bubble inverts the logic signal. It is similar to an inverter. The **bubbles** can be used at input or output of a gate. Some of the examples are shown in Figure A.2.

One of the input signals of an **AND** gate is negated. One of the input signals of an **OR** gate is negated. In addition, one of the input signals of an **XOR** gate is negated. Moreover, a **bubble** can be used in a **buffer** gate. In this case, the function is similar to an **inverter**.

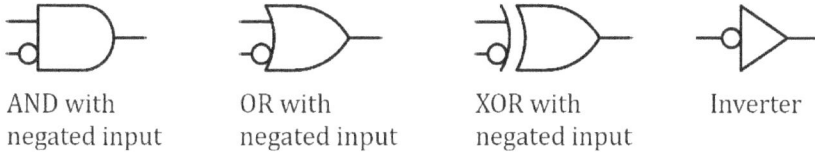

| AND with negated input | OR with negated input | XOR with negated input | Inverter |

Figure A.2. Gates with bubbles.

The truth table for the **AND** gate with a negated input is shown in Table A.1. As it can be seen, the output behavior is different than a typical **AND** gate. The truth table for the **OR** gate with a negated input is shown on the right side. As it was shown, the output behavior is not same as a typical **OR** gate.

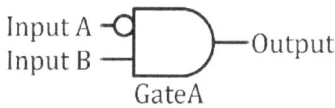

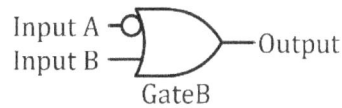

Input A	Input B	Output
Low	Low	Low
Low	High	High
High	Low	Low
High	High	Low

Input A	Input B	Output
Low	Low	High
Low	High	High
High	Low	Low
High	High	High

Table A.1. Gates with negated inputs.

Active Low Signal and Bubble Matching

This **bubble** representation is useful in dealing with active low signal connections. An example was shown in Figure A.3. The IC1 has an active low input that is $\overline{CE}$. In order to match with this bubble, a bubble can be added to a three input AND gate. Then, in this case, the logic gate became a 3-input NAND gate instead.

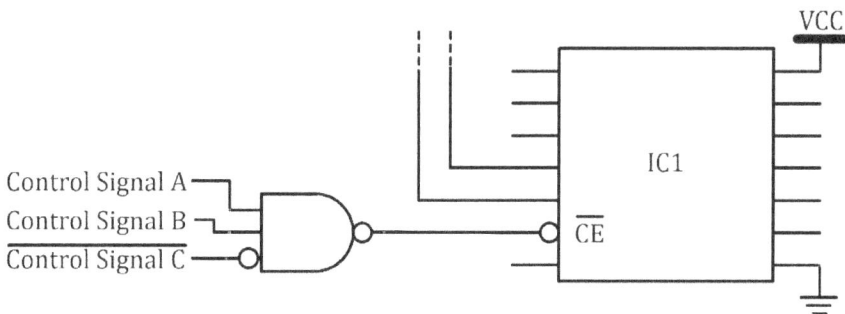

Figure A.3. Active low signal and bubble matching.

This **NAND** gate has three control input signals of A, B, and C. Since the control signal C is active low, it was matched with a **bubble** at the one of the **NAND** input pins. Therefore, the IC1 will be activated when both control signals of A and B are logical high, and the control signal of C is logical low. This is a digital circuit design technique that can assist in creating circuit schematics intuitively.

Open Collector/Drain Circuits

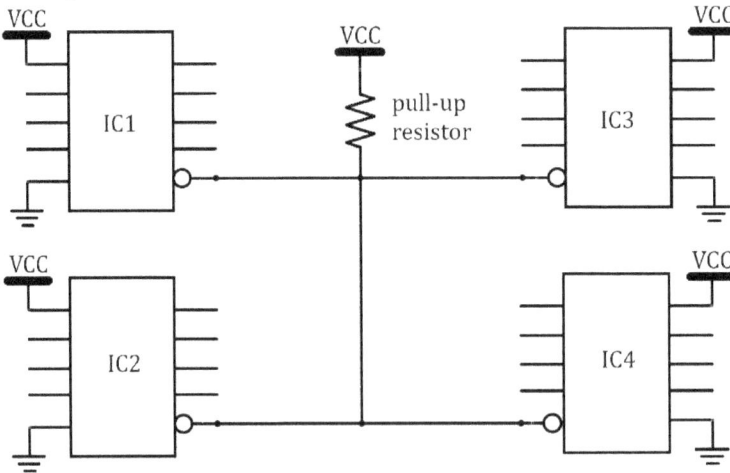

VCC VCC VCC

IC1 pull-up resistor IC3

VCC VCC

IC2 IC4

Figure A.4. Open collector type connection.

Some of the pins of ICs are open collector type outputs. The **open collector** type output may have left a collector of a BJT (Bipolar Junction Transistor) open. In this case, this open collector output pin needs to be connected to a resistor tied to VCC. This is a pull-up resistor. Figure A.4 shows the case where it needs a pull-up resistor. Some of the pins of an IC can be **open drain** type outputs. This open drain type output may be relevant to a FET (Field Effect Transistor). For this open drain type output pin, it also needs to a pull-up resistor similar to the open collector type output.

Tri-state Logic
A tri-state logic allows a high impedance state output. If a "*select*" control signal is logical high, the logical output signals will follow the logical input signals. If the "*select*" control is logical low, the output of the logic will be in a high impedance state.

A multiplexing circuit is shown in Figure A.5. In this circuit, the output will follow the input signals of A, B, C, or D as the one of them is activated. You can see the output line that are drawn as a thick line. You can see that this output line can be one bus line for a single bit, and you can imagine multiple lines for a data bus such as 16-bit or 32-bit data bus.

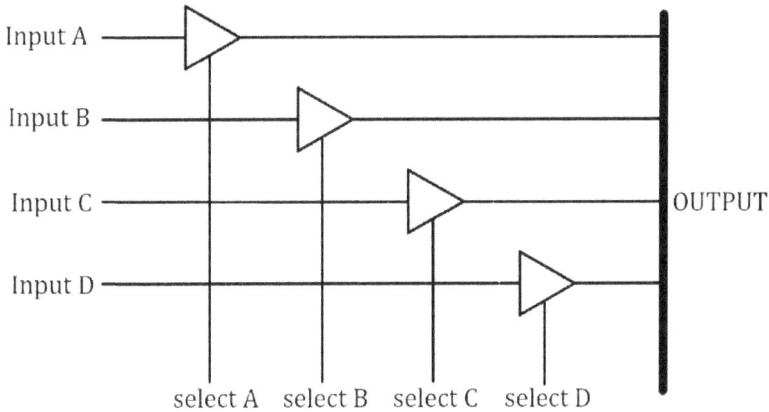

Figure A.5. Tri-state logic and multiplexing.

Propagation Delay Consideration

A propagation delay is the transition time for a digital signal to travel from a source to a destination. Practically, propagation delays need to be considered for logic gates. The propagation delay can be also affected by the load capacitance. In Figure A.6, it shows a control signal is driving many circuit components. It can be understood as a large equivalent load capacitor for the inverter to drive. In this case, the propagation delay for the inverter may suffer and it will cause a slow response.

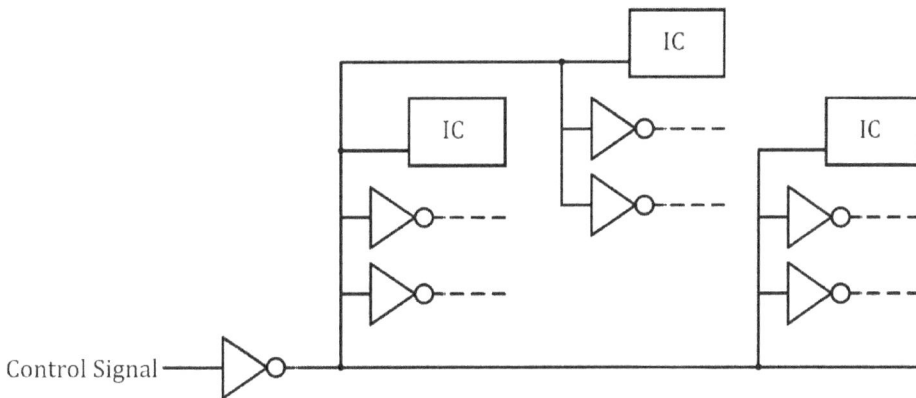

Figure A.6. Circuit with loading.

A prorogation delay can be improved by using a **buffer** as shown in Figure A.7. Using this **buffer** gate might be seen as adding more delay. However, if it is handled properly, the capacitance loading can be divided nicely using this additional buffer gate. Assuming the buffer gate is reasonably well designed, it may result in improving the response. It is worth of mentioning that a buffer needs to be designed with the consideration of many aspects. You can image this can be one line for multiple bus lines, and many components may share these bus lines. Then, for a single line, an optimally designed buffer gate or multiple inverters in series called an inverter chain may improve the performance.

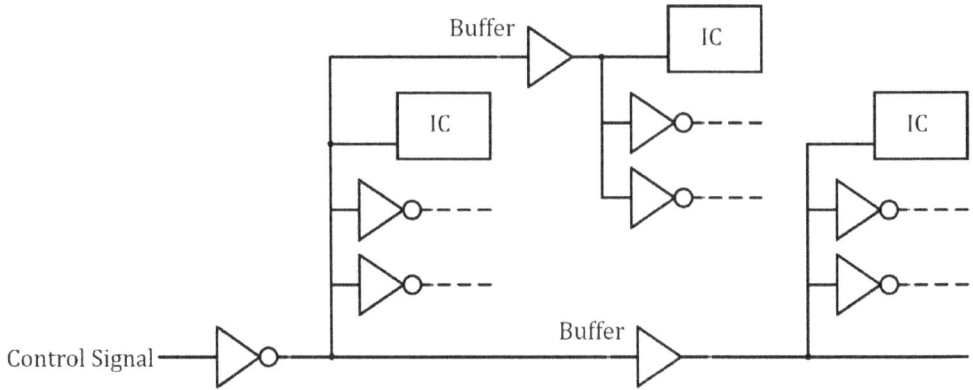

Figure A.7. Improved propagation delay.

Decoupling Capacitors

It is common to find the circuit schematics with many capacitors merged as shown at the top of Figure A.8. Because the capacitors are connected in parallel. This may be considered as equivalently one big capacitor.

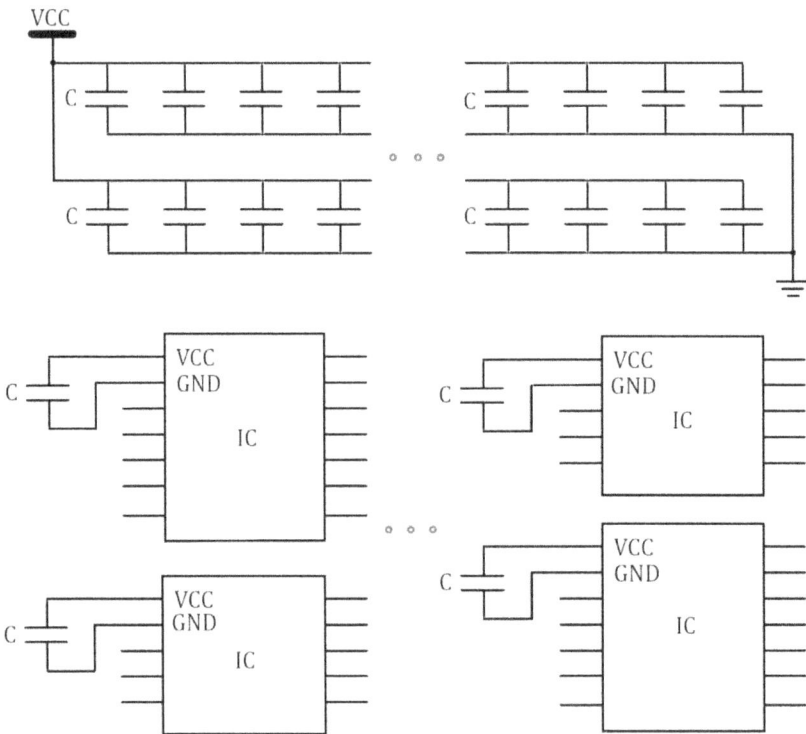

Figure A.8. Decoupling Capacitors.

However, that may not be the actual implementation. Practically, these capacitors may be distributed across the PCB (Printed Circuit Board) as shown at the bottom of the figure. Most likely, these capacitors are placed close to ICs on the PCB. These capacitors can reduce the noise across VCC and ground. While decoupling capacitors are essential and effective, in this book, most of decoupling capacitors were purposefully not placed or not drawn to simplify block diagrams.

Memory Types

Memory is one of essential elements for microcontrollers. There is a type of memory called ROM which means Read Only Memory. For instance, a certain program code does not need to change as it gets executed. And some of the numbers such as constants do not need to change while the program is running. ROM can be the memory that can contain these read only code blocks or constants.

There is other type of memory called RAM which means Random Access Memory. This is a memory space can be read or written. RAM can be used to store some of the data that may need to be updated frequently. One of the examples is stack memory. This is the memory space that can store temporary variables. As the program gets running, it could generate several arrays of data. They can be stored in the stack memory area.

There is a non-volatile memory. This is a type of memory that can hold the data even when the system would be turned off. Generally, ROM can be an example of this type. EEPROM (Electrically erasable programmable read-only memory) is a non-volatile memory. Another example is Flash memory. It keeps the data when the power is turned off.

On the other hand, there is volatile memory. This is a type of memory that losses the data when the power goes off. Generally, RAM is an example of this type. Particularly, static RAM (SRAM) and Dynamic RAM (DRAM) would be the examples of volatile memory. Internal SRAM is typically faster than DRAM in a microcontroller or microprocessor.

An SRAM IC Example

In Figure A.9, a SRAM IC example is shown. This SRAM IC has 17 address lines and 16 data lines. The memory size of this chip is $(2^{17} - 1) \times 16$ bits. Therefore, the memory size is 128k × 16 bits.

It has one active low *output enable* ($\overline{OE}$), one active low *write enable* ($\overline{WE}$), and one active low *chip enable* ($\overline{CE}$) pins.

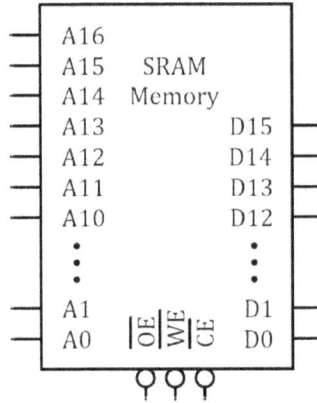

Figure A.9. A typical SRAM IC.

The example waveform is shown in Figure A.10. The address signals can be read when *CE* signal falls. During this operation, it is assumed that *WE* signal kept high properly. Then, the IC can generate the output data signals, when *OE* signal falls. Both address and data lines become high impedance states when *CE* rises. Later, in the Appendix C, we will use this SRAM IC as a component for simple embedded system examples.

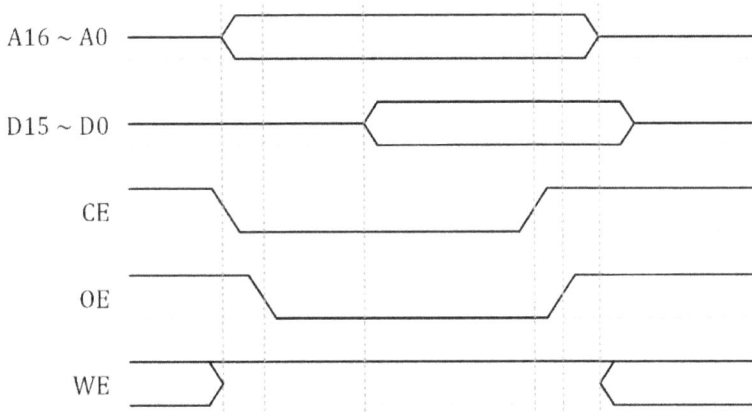

Figure A.10. Timing Diagram of an SRAM IC.

Appendix B. Basic Verilog Hardware Description Language

A hardware description language (HDL) has been used in describing the structure and behavior of electronics circuit models. An HDL can be used for text-based expressions of the electronics systems and their behaviors. The first hardware description languages were introduced in the late 1960s. Programmable logic devices (PLDs) became popular in the late 1970s.

Types of Hardware Description Language

Verilog HDL was introduced by Gateway Design Automation in 1985, and the Cadence Design Systems later acquired the rights. Later, Cadence Design Systems transferred it into the public domain under the Open Verilog International (OVI) organization. In 1987, VHDL (Very High speed integrated circuits Hardware Description Language) was developed by the request from the U.S. Department of Defense. There are other HDLs. However, these two HDLs, Verilog HDL and VHDL, are supported by IEEE, and they are dominant HDLs in the industry.

Verilog HDL

In this book, we will use Verilog HDL. There are many FPGA boards that support Verilog HDL. As of 2022, one of the major FPGA suppliers is Intel®. For those of who are familiar with Altera®, Intel acquired Altea in 2015. Another major FPGA supporter is Xilinx®. For low-cost educational FGPA boards, Intel has a Terasic® DE 10-Lite an Intel® FPGA, and Xilinx has a Basys 3 board.

Verilog HDL uses pre-defined keywords, and it is a case sensitive language. Example of keywords are **module**, **endmodule**, **input**, **output**, **wire**, **and**, **or**, **not**, and etc.,

Verilog modules are like functions in other programming languages. Verilog modules are defined using the **module** keyword and they are ended with the **endmoudle** keyword.

For comments, two slashes (//) can be used.

HDL Modeling

HDL has several abstraction levels, and HDL modeling can be described in one or any combination of these abstraction levels.

Gate-level modeling is a low-level abstraction approach. It describes the circuit through primitive gates and user defined modules, and it describes how they are connected.

Data flow level modeling is a higher level of abstraction approach than the gate level modeling. It describes the circuit through their function and continuous assignments.

Behavioral modeling is a higher level of abstraction approach than the data flow level modeling. It describes the circuit through procedural assignment statements.

Gate Level Description

Verilog HDL has primitive gates and instances. For instance, it supports **and**, **nand**, **or**, **nor**, **xor**, **xnor**, and **not**. A circuit can be described using these gates. Figure B.1 shows a simple logic example.

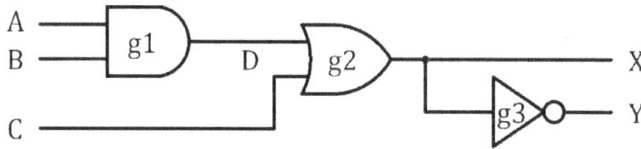

Figure B.1. Simple logic example.

This circuit has three inputs and two outputs, and it has three gates. This circuit can be described in a gate level abstraction. This circuit module was described in Program B.1. In order to describe this circuit, the **wire** keyword was used. The **wire** is a scalar net description. In this case, one wire net of D was used.

```
module LogicA(A, B, C, X, Y);
   input A, B, C;
   output X, Y;
   wire D;
   and  g1(D, A, B);
   or  g2(X, D, C);
   not  g3(Y, X);
endmodule
```

Program B.1. Gate level modeling for the simple logic example.

Dataflow Modeling

Dataflow modeling describes the circuit through its function. Verilog HDL supports several operator types as shown in Table B.1. Also, dataflow modeling uses continuous assignments. Typically, it uses the **assign** keyword. A continuous assignment is associated with assigning a value to a net.

Symbol	Operation
&	bit-wise AND
|	bit-wise OR
^	bit-wise XOR
~	bit-wise NOT
+	addition
-	subtraction
==	equality
>	greater than
<	less than

Table B.1. Selected Verilog HDL operator types.

The dataflow-modeling example is shown in Program B.2. This is the description for the simple logic example circuit shown in Figure B.1. There are two **assign** statements used in this example. Output nodes of X and Y were described.

```
module LogicB(A, B, C, X, Y);
    input A, B, C;
    output X, Y;
    assign X=(A & B) | C;
    assign Y=~X;
endmodule
```

Program B.2. Dataflow Modeling for the simple logic example

A 2-to-1 multiplexer circuit diagram is shown in Figure B.2. When the select signal is logical low, the output will follow the input signal of "B". However, when the select signal is logical high, the output will follow the input signal of "A". This circuit has two **and** gates, one **or** gate, and one **not** gate.

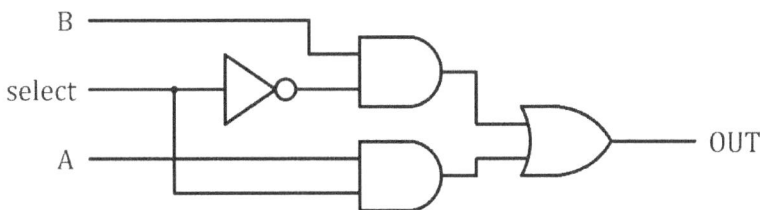

Figure B.2. 2-to-1 multiplexer circuit diagram.

The dataflow modeling of this circuit was implemented, and the description is shown in Program B.3. In this case, one **assign** keyword is used to describe this circuit.

```
module mux2to1A(A, B, select, OUT);
    input A, B, select;
    output OUT;
    assign OUT=((A & select) | (B & ~select));
endmodule
```

Program B.3 Dataflow modeling for a 2-to-1 multiplexer

Behavioral Modeling

Behavioral modeling describes the circuit at a functional and algorithmic level. It can describe sequential circuits and combinational circuits. Behavioral modeling uses **always** keywords with the procedural assignment statements. The output of procedural assignment statement is **reg** data type. The **reg** is one of the data types. It represents the variable that can store data. Figure B.3 shows a 2-to-1 multiplexer symbol, and the Program B.4 shows its behavior modeling.

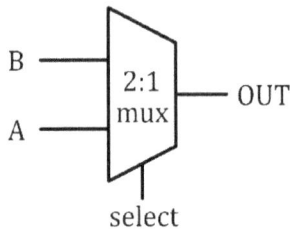

Figure B.3. 2-to-1 multiplexer symbol.

The procedural assignment statement in this example was described using an **always** block. If there is a change in any of variables of "*Select*", A, or B, it will execute the "if else" block. And, if "*Select*" is logical high, the logical output will be the same as "A". Otherwise, the logic output will be the same as "B".

```
module mux2to1B (A, B, select, OUT);
    input A, B, select;
    output OUT;
    reg OUT;
    always @(select or A or B) begin
        if (select==1) OUT=A;
        else OUT=B;
    end
endmodule
```

Program B.4. Behavior modeling for a 2-to-1 multiplexer.

Tri-state Gates

As it was previously mentioned in Appendix A, tri-sate gates are useful in describing many circuit components including multiplexers and bus lines. In Verilog HDL, tri-state gates are available. These symbols and types are shown in Figure B.4.

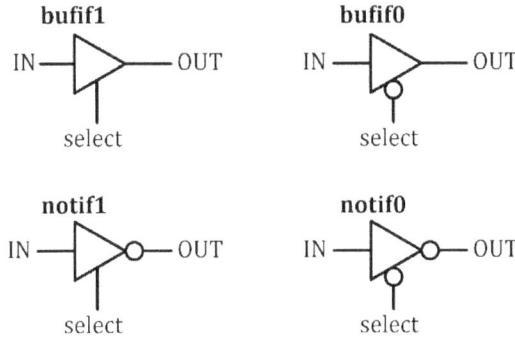

Figure B.4. Types of tri-state gates.

Tri- state gates have an input and output with a control input. The **bufif1** gate is a typical tri-sate gate. And it behaves like a normal buffer when the control is logical high. The output becomes a high-impedance state when the control is logical low. **bufif0** gate has a bubble at the control input. It will invert the control input. The **notif1** gate has a bubble at the output, which will invert the output signal. The **notif0** gate will invert both the control signal and the output.

The output nodes of tri-state gates can be connected each other to form a common output line. To define this type of the connections, the keyword **tri** needs to be used to indicate that the output has multiple drivers. Figure B.4 and Program B.5 show a 2-to-1 multiplexer symbol and the Verilog HDL description example using tri-state gates.

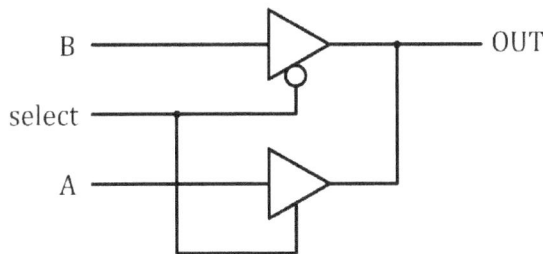

Figure B.4. Circuit diagram of a 2-to-1 multiplexer using tri-sate gates.

```
module mux2to1C (A, B, select, OUT);
    input A, B, select;
    output OUT;
    tri OUT;
    bufif1 (OUT, A, select);
    bufif0 (OUT, B, select);
endmodule
```

Program B.5. Verilog HDL modeling for the 2-to-1 multiplexer

Net Data Types

Verilog HDL net data types are summarized in Table B.2. We have used **wire** and **tri** previously. There are more net data types such as wired OR and wired AND connections. In addition, **supply0** and **supply1** can be used to describe logical low or logical high signals.

Symbol	Operation
wire, **tri**	Interconnection wire
wand, **triand**	Wired AND connection
wor, **trior**	Wired OR connection
supply0, **supply1**	Logic 0, Logic 1

Table B.2. Selected Verilog HDL net data types.

Appendix C. Memory Mapped I/O

CPU (Central Processing Unit) can perform logical and arithmetic operations. A memory mapped I/O technique has been used in exchanging data between the CPU and peripheral devices. The CPU can read and write the data accessing address space. For memory mapped I/O, a certain address of the memory area can be related to physical hardware components and peripherals. Let us examine the memory mapped I/O technique for a microcontroller or microprocessor-based system. For an education purpose, we will study the case of a simplified 16-bit CPU and its system to explain this memory mapped I/O further in this appendix.

Simplified 16-bit CPU model

A simplified 16-bit CPU model is shown in Figure C.1. This CPU has sixteen data signal pins (D0 ~ D15), twenty address line pins (A0 ~ A19), one read control ($\overline{RD}$) pin, one write control pin ($\overline{WR}$), and one clock pin.

In this simplified 16-bit CPU model, memory devices were not included. We will add memory devices as well as other devices later. In this CPU, the data lines are bidirectional, and they form a 16-bit data bus. The CPU has a 20-bit address bus. *RD* is an active low output. This "read control" indicates that the CPU needs to read data at the specified address. *WR* is an active low output port. This "write control" signal indicates that the CPU needs to store data at the specified address.

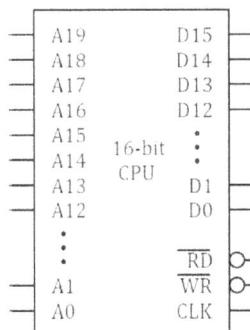

Figure C.1. A simplified 16-bit CPU [16].

16-bit CPU with memory ICs

The connections of the 16-bit CPU and memory ICs are shown in Figure C.2. A non-volatile memory IC is used for a program section. Examples of the non-volatile memory ICs are Flash memory and EEPROM ICs. An SRAM memory IC is used for a data section. The memory ICs have control pins of $\overline{OE}$, $\overline{WE}$, and $\overline{CE}$. They are "Output Enable,", "Write Enable," and "Chip Enable", respectively. They are active low input pins.

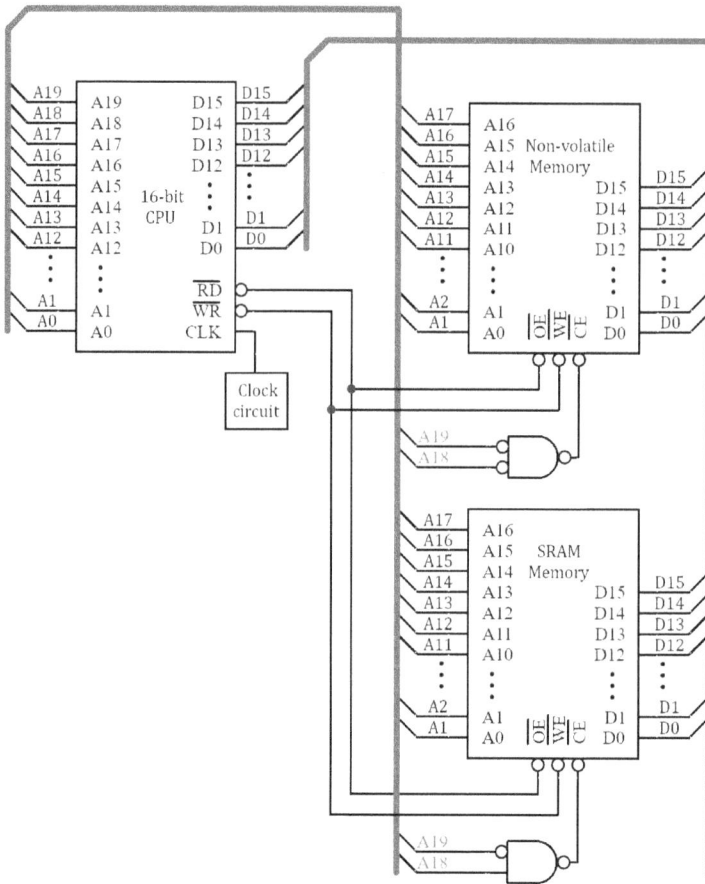

Figure C.2. 16-bit CPU and memory ICs.

The two address lines (A19 and A18) are connected to the chip enable pins, and they control the memory ICs, which can make the ICs accessible through certain address ranges. Based on this configuration in Figure C.2, the low and high addresses can be defined as shown in Table C.1. Let's say this is a basic configuration as a 16-bit system. The non-volatile memory IC may include the program routines such boot firmware, and the SRAM memory IC may be used to store temporary variables that are needed to execute the program.

	Low address	High address
Non-volatile Memory	0x00000	0x3FFFF
SRAM memory	0x40000	0x7FFFF

Table C.1. Address space (Memory ICs).

Adding more devices

More devices can be added to this basic system studied in the previous section. Now, two devices of Device A and Device B are added, and their connections are shown in Figure C.3. The Device A has 8-bit address lines. The Device B has 4-bit address lines. As of the control method, both of them can be accessible for read or write operations. Moreover, the four address lines (A19, A18, A17, and A16) can control the chip enable pins, and the devices can be accessible through certain address ranges. Given this configuration, the low and high addresses with these additional two devices are shown in Table C.2.

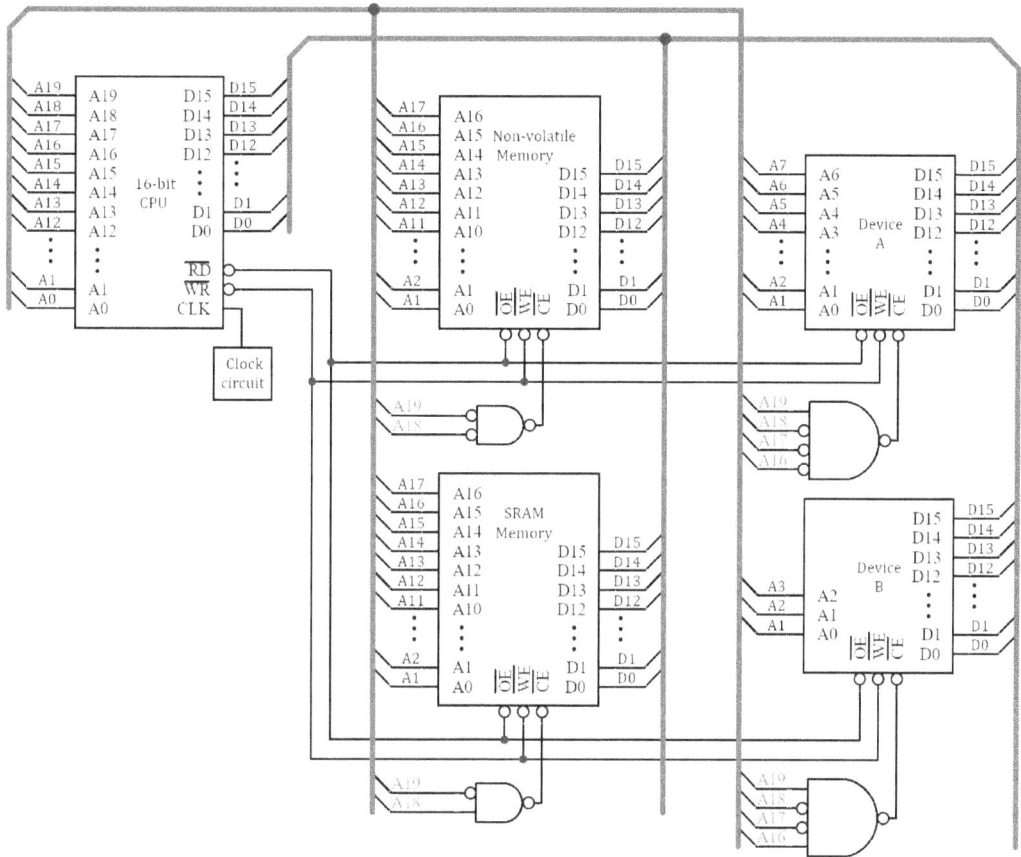

Figure C.3. 16-bit CPU, memory ICs, and two devices.

	Low address	High address
Non-volatile memory	0x00000	0x3FFFF
SRAM memory	0x40000	0x7FFFF
Device A	0x80000	0x800FF
Reserved	0x80100	0x8FFFF
Device B	0x90000	0x9000F
Reserved	0x90010	0x9FFFF

Table C.2. Address space (Memory ICs and Devices).

Let us examine this address space allocation. If the CPU performs read or write memory operations, for the address space of Flash or SRAM ICs, the CPU can read data from the memory, or write data to the memory. This is a typical operation.

However, if the CPU performs read or write operations for the address space allocated to Device A or B, this is not a typical memory operation. But, in fact, it is accessing peripheral devices. It was generalized as Device A and Device B in the figure. For instance, practically, the Device A can be a general purpose I/O, and the Device B can be a timer.

This is a simplified explanation of how the memory mapped I/O would work, and how to connect the devices to the CPU. In a modern microprocessor system, these connections are much more complex, as they have more addresses lines and more peripheral devices. In order to make it more efficient, some of the peripheral devices are controlled by a direct memory access (DMA) unit that allows accessing memory from certain external devices without interventions of the CPU.

FPGA for Control Signals

The control circuit components can be implemented using a FPGA chip. This FPGA can replace individual digital logic gates. Figure C.4 shows a FPGA implementation example. The control logic circuits were replaced by a single FPGA IC as shown in Figure C.4.

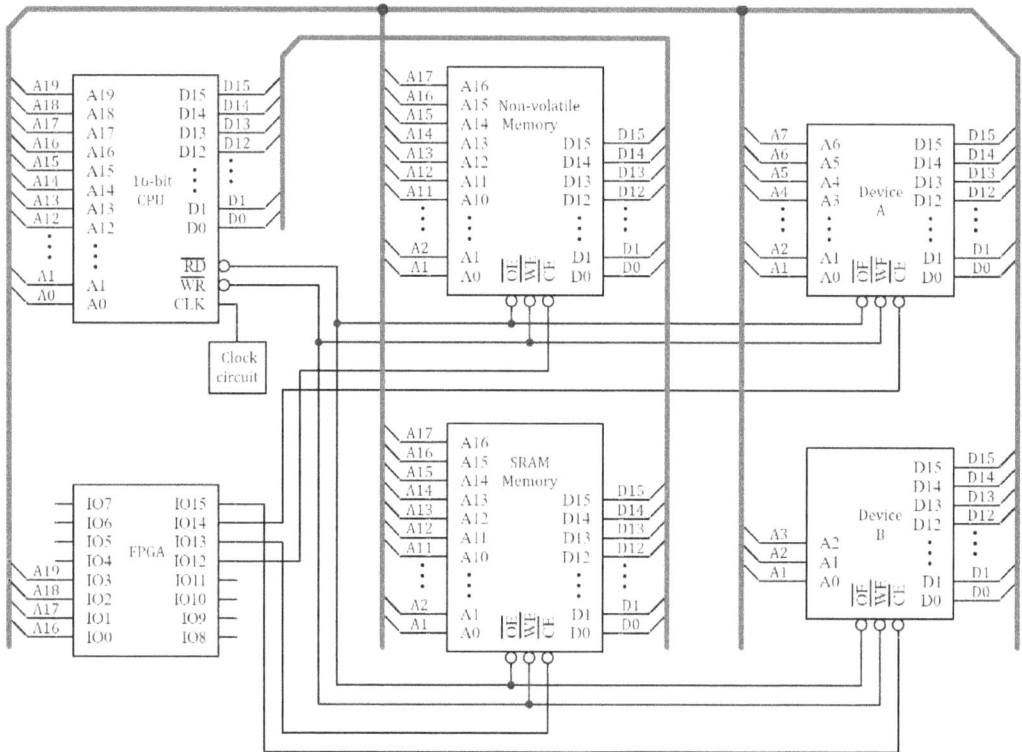

Figure C.4. FPGA implementation

This FPGA chip is a simplified version of an FPGA IC. It has a 16 IO pins (IO0 ~ IO15). IO1, IO2, IO3, and IO4 pins are connected to A19, A18, A17, and A16, respectively. IO12, IO13, IO14, and IO15 pins are connected to the chip enable pins of memory ICs and devices. Based on the configuration shown previously in Figure C.3, for the equivalent functions in Figure C.4, the logical expressions for the control signals can be derived as follows:

$$IO12 = \overline{\overline{IO3} \cdot \overline{IO2}}$$

$$IO13 = \overline{\overline{IO3} \cdot IO2}$$

$$IO14 = \overline{IO3 \cdot \overline{IO2} \cdot \overline{IO1} \cdot \overline{IO0}}$$

$$IO15 = \overline{IO3 \cdot \overline{IO2} \cdot \overline{IO1} \cdot IO0}$$

Using Verilog HDL, these logical expressions can be implemented as shown in Program C.1. This FPGA implementation method has an advantage in resolving complex hardware issues that might occur after production. Many issues can be resolved in a software level; however, sometimes, it may need hardware modifications to tackle a complex problem such as critical timing or resource conflict issues.

```
module GCA(IO3, IO2, IO1, IO0, IO15, IO14, IO13, IO12);
   input IO3, IO2, IO1, IO0;
   output IO15, IO14, IO13, IO12;
   assign IO12=~(~IO3 & ~IO2);
   assign IO13=~(~IO3 & IO2);
   assign IO14=~(IO3 & ~IO2 & ~IO1 & ~IO0);
   assign IO15=~(IO3 & ~IO2 & ~IO1 & IO0);
endmodule
```

Program C.1. Verilog HDL description for the control signals.

Appendix D. C/C++ Data Types

Table D.1 lists the sizes and the ranges of the selected data types for an MSP432P4 MCU with an Arm Cortex-M4 core [35].

Type	Size	Minimum	Maximum
signed char	8 bits	-128	127
unsigned char	8 bits	0	255
signed short	16 bits	$-32,768$	32,767
unsigned short	16 bits	0	65,535
signed int	32 bits	$\sim -2.147 \times 10^9$	$\sim 2.147 \times 10^9$
unsigned int	32 bits	0	$\sim 4.295 \times 10^9$
signed long	32 bits	$\sim -2.147 \times 10^9$	$\sim 2.147 \times 10^9$
unsigned long	32 bits	0	$\sim 4.295 \times 10^9$
float	32 bits	$* \sim 1.175 \times 10^{-38}$	$\sim 3.403 \times 10^{38}$
Double	64bits	$* \sim 2.225 \times 10^{-308}$	$\sim 1.798 \times 10^{308}$

Table D.1. Selected C/C++ data types for Arm Cortex-M4 cores (*Excluded negative cases) [35].

It is important to understand the data types and the range of the data as a developer. For instance, they can examine this test code shown in Program D.1.

```
#include "msp.h"
void main(void) {
   WDT_A->CTL = WDT_A_CTL_PW | WDT_A_CTL_HOLD;  // hold the watchdog timer
   unsigned char kp;  // data type definition
   for (kp=0; kp<255; kp++) {
      printf("%d\n", kp);
   }
   while(1);
}
```

Program D.1. Data range test

In this code, the numbers from 0 to 254 can be printed. Let us consider a case as an experimentation. We can modify the code to increase "kp" by two instead of one. Then, this *for loop* will not stop as the variable "kp" cannot be 256. Instead, the value of "kp" becomes one, and this would cause an infinite loop. Therefore, developers may need to understand the minimum and maximum of the numbers of the variable types they have been using and chosen in their program.

References

[1]   Texas Instruments, "MSP432P401R, MSP432P401M SimpleLink Mixed-Signal Microcontrollers datasheet," Revision H, 2019

[2]   Texas Instruments, "MSP430F552x, MSP430F551x Mixed-Signal Microcontrollers datasheet," Revision P, 2009

[3]   Texas Instruments, "MSP432P401R SimpleLink Microcontroller LaunchPad Development Kit User's Guide," Revision F, 2018

[4]   B. Hur, "TI BH EDU Board Kit," DOI: 10.5281/zenodo.2538993, on-line: https://github.com/bh-projects/TI-BH-EDU-board-kit

[5]   Arm, "Cortex-M4 Devices Generic User Guide", Version 1.0, B.

[6]   Texas Instruments, "MSP432P4xx SimpleLink Microcontrollers Technical Reference Manual," Revision I, 2019

[7]   Texas Instruments, "Arm Assembly Language Tools," 2018

[8]   Arm, "Arm Cortex-M4 Processor, Technical Reference Manual," Revison r0p1, 2020

[9]   Arm, "Arm and Thumb-2 Instruction Set Quick Reference Card"

[10]   Velleman, "Keyboard 16 Keys - Matrix Output"

[11]   TDK Corporation, "Piezoelectric Buzzer," Model: PS1740P02E

[12]   Newhaven Display, "NHD-0216HZ-FSW-FBW-33V3C product specification"

[13]   Sitronix , "ST7066U datasheet," 2006

[14]   Analog Devices, "ADXL335 Datasheet," Rev. B,

[15]   Sparkfun, "SparkFun Triple Axis Accelerometer Breakout - ADXL335,"

[16]   D. E. Simon, "An embedded software primer," Vol. 1. Addison-Wesley Professional, 1999

[17]   Texas Instruments, "DRV8833 Dual H-Bridge Motor Driver Datasheet," Rev. E, 2015

[18]   Adafruit, "Adafruit DRV8833 DC/Stepper Motor Driver Breakout Board"

[19]   Maxim Integrated, "MAX220–MAX249 datasheet," Rev. 18, 2019

[20]   Maxim Integrated, "MAX3222/MAX3232/MAX3237/MAX3241 datasheet," Rev. 10, 2019

[21]   Maxim Integrated, "MAX485 datasheet," Rev. 10, 2014

[22]   Maxim Integrated, "MAX3485 datasheet," Rev. 1, 2019

[23]   Arduino, "Arduino," on-line: https://arduino.cc

[24]   Microchip Technology, "MCP3004/3008 datasheet," 2008.

[25]   Moelands et al., "Two-wire bus-system comprising a clock wire and a data wire for interconnecting a number of stations," US4689740A, Aug. 1987.

[26]   NXP Semiconductors, "PCF8574; PCF8574A datasheet," Rev. 5, 2013.

[27]   Sparkfun, "Sparkfun Logic Level Converter - Bi-Directional"

[28]   Vishay Semiconductors, "TSOP38238 datasheet," Rev. 1.7, 2018

[29]   Texas Instruments, "MSP432 Peripheral Driver Library User's Guide," 2016

[30]   Texas Instruments, "TI-RTOS Kernel (SYS/BIOS) User's Guide," 2018

[31]   Texas Instruments, "TI-RTOS 2.20 User's Guide," 2016

[32]   "Energia," on-line: https://energia.nu

[33]   "Raspberry Pi," on-line: https://www.raspberrypi.org

[34]   "BeagleBone," on-line: https://beagleboard.org

[35]   Texas Instruments, "Arm Optimizing C/C++ Compiler," 2018